Influencer Marketing

Influencer Marketing
Who Really Influences Your Customers?

By

Duncan Brown and Nick Hayes

AMSTERDAM • BOSTON • HEIDELBERG • LONDON • NEW YORK • OXFORD
PARIS • SAN DIEGO • SAN FRANCISCO • SINGAPORE • SYDNEY • TOKYO

Butterworth-Heinemann is an imprint of Elsevier

Butterworth-Heinemann is an imprint of Elsevier
Linacre House, Jordan Hill, Oxford OX2 8DP, UK
30 Corporate Drive, Suite 400, Burlington, MA 01803, USA

First edition 2008

British Library Cataloguing in Publication Data
A catalogue record for this book is available from the British Library

Library of Congress Cataloging-in-Publication Data
A catalog record for this book is available from the Library of Congress

ISBN: 978-0-7506-8600-6

For information on all Butterworth-Heinemann publications
visit our web site at books.elsevier.com

Printed and bound in Hungary

08 09 10   10 9 8 7 6 5 4 3 2 1

Contents

Foreword

If you're considering quitting, it's almost certainly because you're not being successful at your current attempts at influence. If you have called on a prospect a dozen times without success, you're frustrated and giving up. If you've a boss who just won't let up, you're considering quitting your job. And if you're a marketer with a product that doesn't seem to be catching on, you're wondering if you should abandon this product and try another.

If you're trying to influence just one person, persistence has its limits. It's easy to cross the line between demonstrating your commitment and being a pest. If you haven't influenced him yet, it may very well be time to quit.

One person or organization will behave differently than a market of people will. One person has a particular agenda and a single worldview. One person will make up his mind and if you're going to succeed, you'll have to change it. And changing someone's mind is difficult, if not impossible.

If you're trying to influence a market, though, the rules are different. Sure, some of the people in a market have considered you (and even rejected you). But most of the people in the market have never heard of you. The market doesn't have just one mind. Different people in the market are seeking different things.

Influencing one person is like scaling a wall. If you get over the wall the first few tries, you're in. If you don't often you'll find that the wall gets higher with each attempt.

Influencing a market, on the other hand, is more of a hill than a wall. You can make progress, one step at a time, and as you get higher, it actually gets easier. People in the market talk to each other. They are influenced by each other. So every step of progress you make actually gets amplified.

(From *The Dip*, by Seth Godin)
(Reproduced with permission. Thanks, Seth.)

Preface

Something had to break

When I first began investigating the role of influencers back in 2002, there were few signs that the role of the two most prominent influencer categories – journalists and industry analysts – was declining. There were no data at that stage to intimate that, nor had I read any articles to suggest as much. But having worked with journalists throughout the 1990s, I felt that the amount of money and resource being poured into securing press coverage, compared to the returns it often generated, was creating an unsustainable situation. Journalists in their twenties were routinely being flown all over the world, on business class flights, staying in five-star hotels in order to meet with top executives in the hope that positive news articles would result. Resentment was growing amongst vendors at the efforts they were having to go to entice journalists to meet them. And not all journalists were playing fair. Some were taking far more than they were giving, knowing they could do so because they alone held the keys to coverage in certain sought-after titles. I often wondered what would happen if those titles stopped being so sought-after?

The aftermath of the global downturn

In the early part of this decade, two events colluded to usher in this era of *influencer marketing*. One was the global economic downturn. The US and Japan were the first to suffer, seeing softening markets from mid-2000. Japan, having been held up as the economic poster child for much of the 1980s and 1990s, had quietly but surely become seriously unstuck. While Europe had been relatively inoculated to these early warning signs, it had no choice but to listen once 9/11 struck. In many industries, sales fell off the proverbial clifftop and wouldn't recover until 2004. On the basis that there was no point in marketing to people who weren't in a position to buy anyway, marketing budgets worldwide were cut, in some cases dramatically. Experience costs money so in-house marketing departments cut their most experienced staff. Marketing suppliers, especially advertising, PR and sales promotion agencies, saw income streams dry up almost overnight. Publishing houses which had been so lucrative throughout the 1990s saw advertising levels drop while production costs rose. The cosy and extremely profitable marketing sector faced its nuclear winter.

The second was an aftershock of the arrival of the web. By 2002 the almost universal adoption of broadband access enabled businesses to live on the web rather than merely visit it. The significantly lower distribution costs of online over physical, in tandem with the worsening economic climate, sped the move online. As companies searched for new income streams, as every cost was scrutinised, as our faith in our traditional high-cost advisors was waning, so all of our customers expected more for less. Accustomed to paying $250 for a magazine subscription? Cancel it and find something almost as good online for free. No longer afford that analyst firm subscription? Find a cheaper alternative. No longer have a purchasing support team in place to advise you on which solution to buy? Make up your own criteria. The old rulebook on B2B purchasing had been discarded. New people, new processes, new thinking had replaced it, and this time there were fewer kingmakers. Everything had fragmented.

Analyst firms had downsized, key staff had left and formed start-ups that now competed with their former employer. As had print publications whose former staff were now freelancers. So too with management consultancy firms, resellers, events organisers, forum hosts and others. Within the space of three years, instead of there being perhaps four main firms in a particular market sector, there were now ten, all much smaller but boasting similar client experience. As customers returned, they found they had greater buying power, greater leverage and could demand achingly high service levels from suppliers whose margins had shrunk out of existence. But the most important long-term effect of this fragmentation? Greater choice for the customer as a result of the greater dissipation of talent. There were now more influencers than ever before, and they were more evenly spread out.

So began the recent rise of the B2B influencer marketing concept. Purchasing decision-making had become a more drawn-out, more committee-based and more formalised process. For the suppliers, there were more people to reach, yet less money to reach them with. And they were people who didn't want to be marketed to. Research was beginning to show their importance to the buying process yet they weren't people that the salesperson could get to meet. Suppliers needed to appeal to them ... somehow. Because the traditional marketing mix just wasn't cutting it any longer.

The early enthusiasm of Europe

It was in this context that I began to research the early thought leaders in influencer marketing. I was living in London at the time, reading *The Tipping Point*, *The Cluetrain Manifesto* and *The Influentials*, all American. I saw how businesses needed to identify those people now influencing their prospects, and realign their marketing accordingly. I doubted anyone was doing this effectively. The first company I approached, a software company just got it. Straight away. They were salespeople, and smart. I'd rehearsed my responses to use when my would-be client questioned the existence of influencers, their importance or whether it was possible to successfully identify them. No one in the room asked anything of the sort. Their questions were all based around my ability to execute. We agreed a deal.

I talked to more and more companies in that summer of 2003. I read everything I could. It appeared that pretty much no one, except for Palm, the US hand-held device manufacturer, and Apple Inc., had devised any specific programmes for influencers. What they had in common was they were underdogs in their marketplace, ironically both competing with Microsoft and its vastly superior marketing budget. Both companies knew that they couldn't outpunch the Seattle giant, so they had to out-think it. They couldn't get to *more* people, so they had to get to the *right* people. This was exactly the message that I found resonated with those companies I was talking to. Our client base grew.

We established a methodology for evaluating and then ranking influencers according to their particular marketplace and we put in place activity programmes for what to do with influencers once we'd identified them. But one thing puzzled us. We'd continued to be surprised that so few others were talking about the same subjects as us. And how even the largest brand name clients that we met with had no such programmes underway in Europe, nor had they even heard of any from their US counterparts. Tentative budgets were beginning to return to the European subsidiaries of the US companies. I expected the full-service global marketing firms to stride into the influencer space in Europe with comprehensive service offerings. None did. Maybe they knew something we didn't. We attributed it to the still faltering European economy. That summer I left for the US, determined to find out how influencer marketing was really being done. What I found bemused me. If I'd thought that Europe was quiet on the subject of influencer marketing, American business was silent.

A strangely quiet America

I'd expected to find many of the West Coast brands busily integrating influencer programmes and hear of many marketing agencies aggressively launching themselves into the space. I found almost nothing. I met many agencies and found them concentrating on meeting the demand of their clients with 'vanilla' campaigns. By late 2005 the US economy was back on its feet and Silicon Valley was rediscovering its marketing budget. Marketing agencies were tentatively beginning to re-staff having culled their workforce to the bone over the previous few years. But the programmes they were now implementing were their traditional home-ground activities – direct mail, online promotions, PR and the like. That's what their clients were asking them for, and they didn't feel ready to push the envelope with ambitious thinking. I found it disappointing.

In 2005 WOMMA, the Word of Mouth Marketing Association, began gaining momentum. Its burgeoning membership proof that others shared the groundswell disenchantment with traditional marketing. By early 2006 a few agencies were working on real projects with real budgets and brand-name clients. Surprisingly, to me, most of these weren't in the tech sector, nor even in the B2B space, but companies like Proctor & Gamble, Pepsi, Budweiser, Virgin Mobile and Yahoo were all working with consumer-focused agencies to create genuinely new and interesting influencer campaigns. Agencies such as Ammo Marketing in San Francisco and beverage sector specialists Liquid Intelligence in Chicago. B2B companies were attending WOMMA events, not with their own examples, but there to listen and see how they could apply this consumer experience to their own sectors. It was clear that *influencer marketing*, a specific take on word-of-mouth marketing, had reached that part of the wave where there was no turning back.

Agencies … it's Show and Tell time

Today I look at Microsoft, Google, Intel and SAP and I see early stage programmes in place. Not in Europe but in the US. In Europe the major vendors are almost universally warm now to the concept of influencer marketing. When in doubt they contact their US counterparts and are getting supportive responses back. Often they're getting offers of funding from the US too. But no one is pushing influencer marketing onto the agenda of the European marketing heads. It almost feels, as seems to happen once each decade, that clients are leading their agencies. It's a situation that is rarely allowed to last long.

Nick Hayes
San Francisco, November 2007

Introduction

What this book is about

This book outlines a number of cultural changes since 1990 that have impacted how purchasing decisions are now being made, and how decision-makers are now getting their information. The fact is, marketing departments haven't kept up with those changes. They've been too busy moving to online tactics – web advertising, webinars, blogs and social media – to look deeper into who they're communicating with and what those people need to hear. Not surprisingly, they've primarily targeted the purchaser themselves.

What this book shows is that decision-makers act within communities of influencers. The stakes are too high for making decisions alone these days. Decisions are too complex for individuals to make in isolation, and personal risk is too high to chance a mistake. Instead, decision-makers are creating their own 'ecosystems' that frame their major purchase decisions. And marketers need to identify and engage with the individuals that populate these ecosystems. For these individuals are the real business influencers today.

Influencer marketing is a new approach to marketing, important because sales forces both understand and support it. It directly addresses the most common sales barriers within prospective customers and focuses attention on those individuals who advise decision-makers. We call these people influencers, and they are as crucial to the sales process as the prospects themselves.

What we don't cover here is how to exert influence, become more persuasive or win at negotiation. There are plenty of books on these subjects, and we suggest a few at the end of this chapter. We've focused in this book on understanding who has the influence, what they do with it, the dynamics that exist between influencers that operate in your market and how you can use influencers in your marketing activities.

Who this book is for

We're written this book with two audiences in mind. The first is the marketing profession, which is under so much pressure these days to deliver better results with reducing resources. Though we point out the deficiencies in marketing we are not anti-marketing. We support marketing as a discipline. We help others to do marketing. We do marketing ourselves. We think marketing is really important. Marketing is a major spend for firms. If marketing is not performing, then it undermines the whole business.

But we also admit that much of the criticism of marketing is justified, because marketing so often under-performs. More seriously, as the market changes and enabling technologies emerge, much of marketing remains static and decreases in its effectiveness, relevance and value.

Our second audience is the sales force. Salespeople get a rough ride, with their quarterly targets and relentless pressure. We couldn't do it. *Influencer marketing* is a new movement in marketing that directly and specifically enables sales forces. It directly addresses the most common sales process barriers within prospective customers and focuses on those who advise decision-makers. When we've shared our ideas with sales people they are among the quickest to 'get it'. We hope you do too.

Our background is predominantly the technology and telecoms industries, so we've leant heavily on these areas to provide examples of *influencer marketing*. But *influencer marketing* is equally applicable to every other B2B sector, and many B2C markets too.

Which businesses are doing *influencer marketing* already?

Of course, there are some companies who are already proving extremely effective in identifying and working with their major influencers, yet they prefer to keep their successes confidential. In researching this book, we have found this often to be the case. We wish we could have brought more examples to light, but the reticence of these 'early adopters' is understandable: they are gaining competitive advantage through their influencer programmes. In several of our chapters we have included mini case studies of companies that are leading the way in their targeting of influencers as a critical audience in their sales activities. Clearly more exist, and we would welcome their future inclusion on the website affiliated to this book (www.influencermarketingbook.com).

Who we've been influenced by

We make no claim to be the first to write about the power of influencers to affect decision-making. There are plenty of books that give the broad background to the subject, but a few individuals and texts stand out as particularly shaping our thinking.

Three seminal works cover the ways in which influence can work. In 2000 Malcolm Gladwell wrote *The Tipping Point*, a book that introduced to the mainstream the terms *mavens*, *connectors* and *salesmen* to describe the types of individuals that communicate ideas and views. His taxonomy of influencers is so powerful that his terms are now used in conversations everyday. Jon Berry and Ed Keller's 2002 book *The Influentials* brought to prominence the role of influencers in everyday life, both business and social, explaining how one in ten people affect what the other nine buy, think and do. It is considered the high water mark for sociological research into how influence works between consumer peers. And thirdly, Frederick Reichheld's 2003 paper published in the *Harvard Business Review* entitled *The One Number You Need to Grow*, set out the Net Promoter Score proposition that the single most important indicator of a business' future growth was how it fared when its customers were asked 'Would you recommend this company to others?' It has since had enormous effect on how companies seek to manage their reputation, promote their capabilities and create new customers.

To these three works we'd add Robert Cialdini's *Influence: Science and Practice*, which explains clearly and somewhat disconcertingly how we can all be influenced, and which provided the basis for the measure of influence we term the Cialdini test. And we must mention *Purple Cow*, by Seth Godin. It contains the idea that 'It is useless to advertise to anyone except *sneezers* (*connectors*) with influence'. That's a reasonable one-line summation of this book.

Case studies

In this book we set out to illustrate the concepts of *influencer marketing* with examples. But we hit three big problems: there are no widely referenced examples in the public domain; it's too early for many firms that have begun an *influencer marketing* programme to talk about their experiences; and those firms that have delivered tangible results are gaining competitive advantage, so have no inclination to divulge their strategy.

Some of the companies that were willing to share their stories requested anonymity to protect their commercial advantage. But we convinced others to identify themselves in the hope that their household name status will encourage others to adopt *Influencer Marketing* approaches.

To all of our case study participants we extend our thanks.

Marketing is broken

In this first chapter we look at the evidence for declaring that 'marketing is broken' and how marketing today rarely helps your sales force.

You know the scene

It's painfully familiar. You've just heard that a competitor has won a deal that you were banking on. You'd been marketing to that account for months. Your sales rep had a good relationship with the decision-maker, felt in control of the sales process and you'd submitted a strong proposal. Nothing left to chance. So what happened?

The rep calls the prospect to try and save the deal but it's too late. When you ask why you lost the sale, your prospect says that his team didn't believe your pitch, was unconvinced by your ability to deliver and was unimpressed by your service capability. But didn't they read the proposal? You don't know how or when, but your competitor managed to turn the prospect away from you and towards them. The decision was made before you wrote your proposal.

This is news that you didn't want to hear. You're finding it harder to get prospects' attention. You miss out on tenders because you just didn't hear about them in time. But somehow your competitor did. You're invited to tender on bids but you feel you're just making up the numbers. You find out about deals your competitor closed that you didn't even know about.

Your lead generation numbers are flagging, and your leads-to-sale conversion rate is down.

You want to apply more science to marketing, because you know much of your spend must be wasted. But you don't know what marketing works and what doesn't. You're doing this year what you've always done, but now it doesn't seem to work.

And the sales director is looking for you. A bad sign.

Look at the situation from the prospect's viewpoint. They are being bombarded by marketing messages from you and your competitors, pitching similar products with similar features at similar prices. Your attempts at differentiation are just adding to the noise. Your prospects are confused and they need someone to help filter the useful information from the background chatter. Who do they turn to? Who do they listen to? Who do they trust?

Marketing is broken. This shouldn't come as news to you. The fact that you're reading this book means that you're interested in marketing, you're curious to discover new marketing approaches and, we assume, you're aware that all is not well.

In the background research for this book, we examined the opinions of a range of experts in marketing, from academics to gurus and practitioners. It is depressingly easy to build a list of statements that confirm that marketing is failing. Here's our list, but you should try making your own:

- Chris Anderson cites in *The Long Tail* 'We're entering an era of radical change for marketers. Faith in advertising and the institutions that pay for it is waning, while faith in individuals is on the rise'.
- Jim Stengel, global marketing officer for Procter & Gamble (P&G), said, 'Today's marketing model is broken. We're applying antiquated thinking and work systems to a new world of possibilities'.
- Seth Godin, in *Purple Cow*, writes 'The traditional approaches (to marketing) are now obsolete. One hundred years of marketing thought are gone. Alternative approaches aren't a novelty – they are all we've got left'.
- McKinsey & Co. states that 'Today's chief marketing officers confront a painful reality: their traditional marketing model is being challenged, and they can foresee a day when it will no longer work'.
- Laura Ramos of Forrester Research writes, 'Marketers cling to marketing tactics that they admit fail to work . . . it's time to leave these outmoded methods behind'.
- Thomas Friedman of *The New York Times* states 'The new model in business is that you involve your community and customer in an ongoing conversation about every aspect of your business'.
- Richard Edelman, founder and head of Edelman PR, believes that 'traditional marketing is in its twilight years. (It is premised on) an old model of persuasion that worked from the '50s through the '80s'.

- Professor Philip Kotler, the marketing guru and author of the Harvard Business Review 'must read' text *Ending the War Between Sales and Marketing*, states that the average person 'is exposed to several hundred messages a day and is trying to tune out...marketers must consider other methods of getting customers' attention'.
- Robert Scoble and Shel Israel, in *Naked Conversations*, see 'a clear and present danger for practitioners of traditional, unidirectional advertising and marketing'.

Marketing no longer sells anything

Our starting point for this book is not to reveal that marketing doesn't work very well, but to try and articulate how we think it can be fixed. Our research has shown that, while everybody seems to be aware of the decline in marketing, few do anything about it. The lack of innovation in marketing is ironic, given its supposed creative core.

When we say 'marketing is broken' what do we mean? Simply, that it no longer does its job. Marketing is orientated around sales. If it doesn't initiate, assist or close a sale then it is failing. And failing it is. The largest single item on most firms' marketing spend is advertising, accounting for between a quarter and three-quarters of budgets. In some industries, marketing accounts for a third of revenues. Yet the link between marketing and consequential revenues is rarely demonstrable. Astonishing.

Marketing is based on notions that are 20 years out of date. The notion that if you put enough messages out there some of them will be heard. The notion that 'building the brand' is money well spent. The notion that people believe what they see and read. Recent initiatives to take advantage of Web 2.0 technologies are merely reactions that apply old techniques to new media. Marketing needs to rethink the messages it is communicating, to whom it's communicated and the methods being used. Many companies are disappointed at the lack of tangible return on their multi-million pounds marketing activities. Advertising remains the largest budget item on most firms' marketing plans. Advertising may be a fixture in a company's annual spend, but management boards are increasingly questioning why this is. The most recent Brandchannel survey in 2007 illustrates this point well. Four of the world's five largest brands have never conducted any advertising, and the same is true for seven out of the 10 fastest growing brands. There is no proven causal relationship between advertising and financial performance. And advertising is just the tip of the melting marketing iceberg.

There is no strong evidence to suggest that advertising has any effect on sales. The academic research on marketing and return on investment (ROI) is paltry in number and unconvincing in conclusion. There is an awful lot of assertion from the profession itself, and several claims to the link between brand and revenues or stock price. It is true that firms with big revenues and profits usually have well-known brands. Yet brand awareness could equally be an *outcome* of high sales, rather than a driver of it. Google has never advertised, yet it has become the world's most powerful brand.

There exists in most companies a disconnect between sales and marketing. This manifests itself at an operational level in departmental warfare where, according to marketing guru Philip Kotler, 'sales forces and marketers feud like Capulets and Montagues – with disastrous results'. If you haven't heard Philip's 30-min audio download of *Ending the War between Sales and Marketing* then we'd suggest you do.

Inside almost every company there lies a gulf between marketing and sales. Rarely is there harmony, at best just an agreement to silently walk past on opposite sides of the corridor. At worst, it can totally paralyse an organisation. Separate territories, with neither able to see the other's viewpoint.

Recent trends in marketing – the move online, campaign management systems, the creation of brand personalities – have done nothing to bring the two divisions closer.

Continuing disillusionment with traditional marketing and its dubious returns are leading many organisations to question how, or if, to continue with their current marketing levels. Marketing executives are under pressure to show results, ones that will impress the management team. There has never been so much interest and activity in marketing performance metrics and dashboards. While this focus on measurement is encouraging, most metrics concentrate on monitoring the effectiveness of the marketing operation, how well it does what it does, rather than the marketing execution. Does marketing result in more leads, more sales? The answer, across industries and geographies, is typically 'We have no idea'.

Is anybody there?

If the paucity of tangible and reliable ROI metrics from marketing, across all industries and geographies, suggests how marketing is broken, it begs the question: why is it broken? Why does marketing not deliver higher sales or better lead generation?

The answer is that nobody is listening anymore. By the time you go to bed tonight you'll have seen roughly 1000 commercial messages. There are just too many to remember, so they're all ignored. TV advertisers reckon they need to show an advert between 7 and 10 times before the audience can recall seeing it, and even then they don't necessarily remember what it was advertising – 'Yes I remember the house with the rubber floor but no, I can't remember which beer it was advertising'.

Besides the sheer volume of messages bombarding us everyday, have you noticed that they all sound the same? A consistent theme in marketing literature is the blandness of messages. Advertising is the price for being dull – you have to pay to get people to listen to you.

There is a chronic lack of marketing innovation in the technology industry. Compare your core message with that of your competitors'. Your product is easy-to-use, fast, leading-edge, proven, customisable, flexible, scalable and available in mauve. Welcome to the club. Part of the problem is the unsustainability of competitive advantage, due to the rapid transmission of ideas and technical capability. Your competitors can deliver a similar product 6 months after you innovate. If you work in a service-based industry your competitors can clone your offer by tomorrow.

There's also a problem in the way that marketers talk. Imagine you're at a party. A man comes up to you, but instead of introducing himself, he yanks your head back, pulls your jaw down and looks at your teeth. 'I'M A DENTIST!' he explains.

That how marketing sounds. It's one way. It's abrupt. It has no concept that the listener may not want to hear the message. It lacks social graces. It intrudes, by demanding your attention. There are no pleasantries. There's no engagement with the listener. It's what Seth Godin aptly calls interruption marketing.

In fact, it doesn't really matter if you're heard above the noise or if your message is innovative and relevant. Because your prospects don't believe you. You're selling something, which means you're biased. Prospects may like your message but they want to hear it from someone they trust.

We've decided to decide in a different way

A decade ago decision-makers used two types of sources to influence their opinions and agenda. The first was the printed media, either the general business press or industry-specific trade press. These covered current trends, macro-economic reports and experiences from the field. The second source was industry analysts, used heavily in the technology and telecoms sectors, but also appearing in retail, banking, manufacturing, pharmaceuticals and others. Together journalists and analysts made up the bulk of influencers on business decision-makers.

Our own research has tracked the continued decline in share of influence amongst journalists and analysts between 2003 and 2007 (Figure 1.1). The research begs a key question: if journalists and analysts are diminishing in their share of influence, who is replacing them?

The answer is that decision-makers use a wide variety of influencers to inform their judgments, from inception to implementation. We've

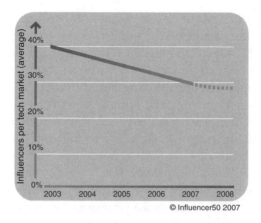

Figure 1.1   Journalist and analyst share of influence is declining

identified over 20 different categories of influencer and they may play a number of different roles throughout a decision process. For any one decision, there could be a dozen or more individual influencers involved at some level. In a market there are typically hundreds of people exerting their influence.

But marketing has not kept in line with this trend. The vast majority of marketing activity with influencers is still founded on PR (public relations) and AR (analyst relations). Our research suggests that, instead of devising programmes that target journalists and analysts and ignoring the remaining 15 per cent or so of miscellaneous influencers, as you could have done 10 years ago, you would now be missing out on at least half of the main influencers, an omission that can no longer be justified. Something has to change.

The most fundamental challenge for marketing is that it has no idea who these influencers are, nor their relative ranking of importance, and therefore has no formalised programme to contact them. If marketing was able to identify them, it could use them as a channel through which to reach prospects. And prospects would listen to influencers because they are, by definition, influential.

Why hasn't the power of influencers been realised until now?

It's a fair question. The answer is in three parts:

1. Those behind the scenes 'influencers' were being targeted as prospective purchasers in their own right and so it was believed didn't justify being treated separately as influencers.

2. The tools and research tactics weren't in place to economically identify who these influencers were.
3. The breadth of influencers used to be far narrower, such that journalists and resellers might have been responsible for upwards of 80 per cent of the influence. And these two categories have long been targeted separately. Today the influence circle is dramatically fragmented.

The rise of the decision-maker ecosystem

Most marketing directors plan their activities by reviewing their previous year's spend, then deciding how to tweak it for the upcoming year. It's astonishing that trade shows are booked, at a cost of tens or hundreds of thousands of pounds, without asking potential customers whether they're planning to attend those events. A more reliable approach would be to meet with, or interview, several prospective purchasers as to how they approach the buying process to start with. Where do they look for their information? What form does their research take? How do they involve others in their search? How do they decide which events to attend? At what stage would they let a vendor know of their interest? By asking such questions marketing departments would markedly change how and what they communicate, and to whom. For they'd identify many people they had not previously considered, yet who have a major voice in scoping, shaping, evaluating and approving the majority of deals. These people make up the *decision-maker ecosystem* (DME).

A good friend of ours, Nilofer Merchant, the head of California strategic marketing firm Rubicon Consulting, said recently that she sees such ecosystems as a direct result of the gradual decline in the role of 'trusted advisors' in all aspects of our lives, over several decades now. Hundreds of years ago there were religious leaders, coupled with senior, older members of the communities in which we lived. Earlier this century this small group of personal influencers would have included our school teachers, or elder relatives and our parents. For the past 50 years the rise of mass entertainment media meant that we deferred to radio presenters, news readers and TV show hosts, and in parallel, advertising that accompanied, and interrupted, their appearances. These shaped both our morality and our aspirations. We have seen the demise of the 'extended family', where several generations of a family lived together in the same house or community. We now don't expect a job for life, and most of us now work only a few years for the same employer. It is increasingly difficult to establish a stable set of trusted advisors either in our personal or professional lives. So, we now foster temporary advisors, perhaps running several in parallel, and often on very specific subjects. We feel free to recruit them when we need them and drop them as soon as we don't.

As a culture we are no nearer making our decisions in isolation than we have ever been. But our points of reference have changed. With our lessening respect for age and seniority, our immediate peer group has increased in importance, as have subject matter experts, those we need to help us navigate our way through increasingly complex issues. These people are likely to have been unknown to us yesterday, today we treat them as a close ally, tomorrow we will have moved on. All of these factors combine to mean that our circle of influencers are ever more transient, flexible, dynamic and therefore harder to predict. No sooner has an influencer circle been identified than it may be disbanded, or at least morphed into some other shape.

While DMEs in business are transient, and shift quickly depending on the decision focus and process, they are not impossible to map. One factor is that in business situations, such ecosystems are established primarily to help a linked, and time-bound, set of decisions. Though they may start off informally, they are stable and persistent for the duration of a particular project or activity. In fact, businesses try to keep such networks in place in a similar form over several years, both to benefit from previous experiences and to encourage cohesion from one decision to the next. There's little point zigzagging from one tactic to the next because the decision-making process relied on radically different criteria each time. So, if only for expediency, companies tend to try to keep their ecosystems intact for as long as they can. This means that longevity is an important attribute in influencers.

Now where there's money there's opportunity, and where there's opportunity there's someone looking to benefit from it. So inside every market sector there's an infrastructure of consultants, advisors, strategists, production houses, developers and others all with their own views on how companies should solve their business problems. Inevitably, those forming this infrastructure are, in themselves, fighting to become key influencers, some very successfully.

Think of Intel in the early 1990s. A company making computer chips that no user ever thought or cared about, suddenly faced lower cost competition to its traditional hegemony. Customers caring only for the brand name on their PC, and the fact that it would run Microsoft Windows, could have easily and unknowingly switched to lower cost PCs with non-Intel chips. Intel had to make their brand matter. In one of the most expensive and long-term single advertising campaigns in recent history, the chipmaker stamped the 'Intel Inside' logo into all of our minds. Customers decided that a formerly almost anonymous chip really did make a difference. We were well and truly influenced. But at a reputed cost to Intel of over $1 billion in marketing alone. Such expense was necessary because the chipmaker was forced to influence every individual decision-maker likely to buy a PC at the time. It would have been so much less costly had they influenced the decision-makers' influencers, rather than wait and so have to impact the decision-makers themselves. That should be a warning to all suppliers.

The implications for traditional marketing

There are two immediate implications of changes in influence. The first is that suppliers (or vendors as they are known in some industries) must identify and rank those influencers within their market(s). This is not a trivial exercise, since influencers are typically invisible to sales and marketing professionals. There is no off-the-shelf list of influencers. They don't have 'influencer' written on their business card and a person influential to your company may be irrelevant to another firm in a similar field. Importantly, influencers may never have bought, and may never buy, anything from you. You won't already have them in your customer database, because they'll never be customers.

The second implication for marketers is that they must focus attention on those individuals with most influence on their target market(s), and scale back relationships with those with less. This adjustment is necessary, because marketing is a finite resource, and the number of influencers to address cannot simply be added to forever. This reallocation of marketing budget, and activity, is not trivial since many influencers won't know that they are influential, won't appreciate your traditional marketing approaches, and couldn't care less about your market messages. A new approach is required.

When we discuss *influencer marketing* it is important early on to state that we are not talking about any form of illicit or underhand techniques. We are all aware of covert, guerrilla or stealth marketing, which misleads the consumer or intended audience. Remember the ill-conceived 'black-box placement' campaign throughout Boston in mid-2007. Designed to promote a games TV programme, an outsourced marketing agency placed flashing light boxes in public places overnight, causing the public to contact police in their hundreds fearing them to be explosive devices. Understandably, it led to the resignation of senior executives at the commissioning TV network.

Marketing agency staff loudly conduct conversations on street corners and in public places extolling the virtues of particular products, with the intention of weaving innocent members of the public into their conversation and making them believe this is natural word-of-mouth (WOM) recommendation. It's unethical at best, a con at worst and it drags marketing deeper into the mire than it is already. Our concept of *influencer marketing* could not be further away from stunts and scams such as this.

At all times it is to be open, honest and candid, made stronger by the fact that the vendor company wants to eschew its conventional marketing techniques in favour of a 1-to-1, near full-disclosure relationship. No money or material favours change hands. Influencers should, and hopefully could, never be 'bought'. Nor is there any form of coercion or pressure applied. The fact that only a relatively small number have been identified, certainly in comparison with the typical company's prospect database, means that each influencer is treated with more rather than less respect. *Influencer marketing* firms are to date at the forefront of ethical marketing, and the leading four or five companies are all members of WOMMA, the Word of Mouth Marketing Association, which takes a strong and very public stance on this issue.

We are proposing a marketing initiative with great promise, and which appeals to senior management, marketing professionals and sales force alike. *Influencer marketing* encourages greater selectivity in targeting segments, increases understanding of each sector, demands more thought when deciding how and what to communicate, and massively reduces the waste and white noise level of badly thought-out 'blanket' saturation onslaughts. Such an initiative must come well-proven, both as a concept and out in the field. This book is intended to convince you of both.

Key points in this chapter

1. Marketing is broken, because it no longer contributes directly and tangibly to sales. This situation pits marketers and sales forces against each other in animosity.
2. Marketing doesn't work because there are too many marketing messages bombarding prospects, all the messages sound the same, and even if your message is heard, prospects don't believe you. But they do believe influencers.
3. *Influencer marketing* is an approach that identifies and targets influencers in a market. Influencers make up communities called Decision-maker ecosystems, which revolve around a decision-maker.

2

What's wrong with traditional marketing today?

This chapter breaks down the traditional marketing spend and questions its usefulness.

By the numbers...

There is some interesting benchmark data regarding business-to-business (B2B) marketing budgets from Sirius Decisions, a US market research firm. The 2006 data show how B2B companies of various sizes and within various market sectors allocate their marketing programme budgets. This is a snapshot of spend breakdown for those with revenues of over $100 million.

- Field Marketing/Demand Generation: 64.7%
- Corporate Communications: 15.0%
- Product Marketing: 9.5%
- Branding/Advertising: 7.2%
- Channel Marketing: 2.5%
- Market Intelligence: 1.1%

A further breakdown of the largest category, Field Marketing and Demand Generation, shows the following:

- Tradeshows: 16%
- Tele-prospecting: 13%

- E-mail: 13%
- Live events/seminars: 10%
- Webinars: 9%
- PPC Search Marketing: 5%
- Search engine optimisation (SEO): 4%
- Other (direct mail, associations, online, etc.): 30%

IDC Corp., the tech industry-focused analyst firm, has published the following 2007 technology vendor spend breakdown on marketing:

- IT vendors spend an average of 3.0 per cent of revenue on marketing. Software vendors spend the most (5.1%), hardware makers spending 3.2 per cent and IT service firms spend only 1.0 per cent.
- IT vendors spend 63.5 per cent of their marketing budget on programmes and 37.5 per cent on headcount.
- IT vendors spend the largest portion of their budget on advertising (21.7%). Other significant budget items are events (19.5% of the marketing budget); sales tools such as case studies, white papers and interactive online tools (15.8%); direct marketing (14.6%); PR (7.1%) and AR (1.9%); and collateral (5.6%).

Dividing up the budget

Using the above guidelines, marketing directors in a mature company with a turnover of say, $100 million probably control a marketing budget in excess of $5 million. And they spend every penny of it, because they know that if they don't they'll get less the following year. It's part of the job requirement that marketing directors must act as if it's never enough. So once the budget's been confirmed they sit down to divide up the spend. Of course there's no definitive way to do this, but few stray far away from the following. They sit down with the management team and agree the company's key goals for the year, including target market sectors. Then they look at last year's plan and see how much of that can be repeated. Then they add up how much budget has already been committed (to trade shows, partnerships, etc. that work to long lead times). Over the previous few months they'll have taken pitches from any number of competing marketing agencies, some already on the company's roster and some prospective, helping them decide which ideas best fit in with their plans.

Almost without exception these will be limited to operational silos – PR, AR, events (including trade shows), direct mail, online (intranets, web promotions, etc.), sponsorship and marcomms collateral. Rarely will the spend ratios differ significantly from the previous year. But that's not the most surprising aspect. For the truth is every marketing director knows that much of this spend will be totally wasted. Now it's one thing to admit that before the activities have begun, but even when it becomes clear what's not working, most will continue to spend on those areas of zero return. Can you imagine that in any other company department? This behaviour is allowed to continue because none of the above marketing activities are mapped onto sales activity. If you don't measure them against sales achieved, then they can't disappoint. Simple. They all have different woolly metrics – and the agencies like it that way.

Trying to measure PR through sales

PR companies don't measure the media coverage they've generated against sales figures, and so they shouldn't. It's too much of a leap to equate one with the other, even though there's constant pressure to do this. So they're measured on the volume of media coverage and perhaps its quality, whether judged on which titles the coverage is in, how favourable it is to the client, and somehow still, its EAV (equivalent advertising value, a now seriously outmoded and laughable scale popular in the early 1990s).

Now PR companies know who butters their bread. Clients are rarely if ever aware of which magazines or websites are read by their customers, so they want coverage in the most impressive 'looking' titles. Favourable headlines, photos, box-out quotes, those are what impress clients. Not unnaturally CEOs are even further from understanding the local customers. They're probably only in the country for a day or two, so they want coverage in daily newspapers that have published their interview by the time they're sitting at Heathrow Airport on their plane out of Europe. Achieve this and the CEO considers their trip well spent, the country manager is congratulated and the agency praised. Job done. But it doesn't bring a single sale any closer.

Yet because CEOs don't appreciate the broad influencer community, and DMEs, they don't take the time to create relationships with those less impressive looking titles, often with minimal production budgets, perhaps on slower publishing lead times and certainly those less interested in meeting the CEO just because the opportunity arises. If the CEO hasn't heard of the title (which usually requires it to have a well-established US readership), then it likely won't even be allowed to stay on their provisional travel schedule. There's little discussion involved, for only appointments with the 'top-tier' media are allowed. It's a game, and good PR people know it's one they can't change, so it's allowed to continue. As a result, PR companies continue to work towards generating press coverage in the most impressive 'looking' media, which is rarely if ever the most effective for sales. The in-house managers responsible for managing the agencies understand and accept this, but they're part of the game too.

The anomaly of the 'business' press

Today it's all about 'business' coverage, away from the emphasis on the company's particular vertical market. There's an assumption that suppliers should already naturally feature in the vertical sector press, so it's no longer considered an achievement. Ask any publisher, they all want to be perceived as a 'management' or 'business' title, yet the advertising department is equally adamant that they can only sell ad space on the back of very specific product or market-specific features. There are few examples of 'management' publications in Europe – they're economically hard to sustain for publishers – yet they're the only titles which many marketing directors are interested in appearing in!

Analyst relations is not a volume activity

Now AR is another strange one. Analysts tend not to like dealing with dedicated AR people (those people, whether in-house or agency based, specifically employed to liaise between the company and interested analysts). They prefer to deal directly with a company's senior management, not a filter. Especially not a PR representative. But the senior management in vendors neither have the time nor inclination to be the first port of call for analysts, so they put intermediaries in place. Whatever people think of it, that's not going to change.

But if you look at how AR departments are measured it's clear where the problem lies. Just as PR is largely measured in column inches, so AR is most commonly measured on the number of 'analyst impacts' – whether face-to-face meetings, phone conversations, webinars or whatever. So it's a quantity-oriented metric. Quality-based metrics are far more difficult to achieve. How can you tell what the end-result will be when you've only conducted a first meeting? The end-result that you want, one where the analyst immediately makes a crucial referral to a prospective buyer, landing your company with the deal rather than your competitor, is altogether too difficult to measure in any but the most isolated of cases.

And as for which analysts to engage with, companies tend to do little research into this one too. The main priority is to meet with whoever is writing on a relevant subject to you, which means you focus on the most prolific, not the most important.

Finally you have the little understood issue of buy-side and sell-side analysts. Most PR companies, and certainly the majority of in-house marketing heads, are unaware of the important distinction between the analyst firms that make their money by selling their time and advice to end-user companies, advising them on their strategy, on new technologies, on vendor directions, etc.; and those firms that make their money by selling their market understanding to the vendors within that market. To analysts this is a critical difference, yet the majority of people trying to meet with them aren't even aware of this. It's irrelevant to the way they're being measured. So once more, meetings are arranged, budgets are spent, time is wasted.

The question behind advertising

If you're reading this then you're already well aware of how advertising budgets are wasted. But by example, Jeffrey Citron, the CEO of Vonage, announced he was reducing his firm's ad budget by over $100 million because 'we continue to be extremely disappointed by the returns we've seen from it'.

John Stratton, Verizon's Chief Marketing Officer, adds, 'Last year I spent well over a billion dollars buying space, time, air, hits and clicks across a multitude of mediums . . . I'm not perfectly happy. And I'm not alone . . . (Marketers) need more than an audience. They need an audience that cares about what they have to say. They need their message to be relevant to the audience they are saying it to'.

In a BBC Radio 4 'Today' programme interview recently, the marketing boss of Unilever, a company that spends more money on evaluating its marketing than almost any other company spends on the marketing itself, admitted that they still struggled to demonstrate any measurable impact from their advertising. Fiona Dawson, Managing Director of Masterfoods UK, stated on BBC's PM programme that, 'There is very little evidence to show that advertising has any effect, despite the amount of money that we spend on it, in term of driving purchasing behaviour'. Even the interviewer was taken aback by the admission. Andy Sernovitz, the founder of WOMMA, said 'Advertising is the price you pay for being boring'. Enough said.

Yet advertising is frequently the largest line item on any marketing budget. Why do we persist with it?

The guesswork of trade shows

Trade shows are also notoriously difficult to rationalise. There an emotive subject within many marketing departments. Where a company's attendance is based more on the show's sales executive striking up a cosy phone relationship with the vendor's marketing manager than with any tangible business reason. Or at least it is in the first year or two of the event. And after that? Well a constantly evolving show means that whatever the vendor's qualms over the previous year's attendance – light on numbers at the door, light on floor traffic, light on decision-makers – next year's show can claim to have addressed every one of them. Too often it seems to be a case of 'well, we have to attend a few shows, and these seemed the best hopes', rather than anything more scientific.

Sponsorship ... our favourite

And we haven't even come on to sponsorship. Many companies make this their single greatest marketing expenditure – their flagship activity. We've seen a marketing director present to his management team on his decision to sign a £3m agreement to place his firm's logo on the wing mirrors of a Formula 1 racing car. His rationale, which we assume he believed himself, involved the numbers of global TV viewers, multiplied by the total length in minutes of regular TV coverage and somehow weaved in the potential revenue opportunity to his sales force. This is, of course, complete non-sense and we shouldn't need to point out the gaping holes in such an argument. The deal was done for one reason and one reason only. Ego. There is an absurd assertion that by namedropping and rubbing shoulders with TV names, some of the glamour can be attributed to closing sales. We think not. But it looks great on the marketing director's résumé, which was, we suspect, surely its purpose in the first place.

Marketing fuelled only by inertia

What each of the above activities have in common is that they all take their place on the budget sheet as a result of the marketing director sitting at their desk looking out. Looking out at an inanimate group called 'prospects' and thinking, 'What new twists on last year's marketing might get their attention, given the money I have?' It would be far better, and we think more obvious, to put themselves in the shoes of a prospect and to think 'if I were looking for a solution to Problem A, how would I go about finding it?' The two questions generate very different answers. But the second would demand a number of new skills in the marketing department.

And this raises an additional issue. People stick with what they know. A marketing director can also easily rattle off a list of things that he or she believes the journalist or analyst would want from a vendor. They've been brought up through the ranks dealing with these categories and so, to some extent at least, understand their needs. They would not be able to say the same for an integrator or consultant, two categories of influencer that have comparable and often greater influence in B2B sectors. Among the new skills needed within a typical department are those knowledgeable in how integrators and consultants operate. And there's not too many of those kind of people around.

Marketing's vicious cycle

The lack of broad skillsets within most company's marketing departments has meant that if a market sector has a traditionally strong reliance on three or four trade shows each year, then most vendor's marketing departments are staffed to fit that profile. Since that is where their skills and interests then lie, those people don't look to exploit other potentially influential channels, which continue to suffer as a result. It becomes an ongoing cycle when a more balanced approach would have been more effective. As a result, too much money over the years has been spent on marketing directors' favourite activities, and subsequently too little attention paid to others. The marketing activity/budget split in some industry sectors, that is industrial goods, petrochemicals or warehousing and distribution, will be massively and unexplainably different than other apparently comparable sectors. P&G spends 3 per cent of revenues on marketing. Automotive firms spend nearer 20 per cent of revenues, once promotions and discounts are factored in. The champagne industry spends over 30 per cent of its sales on marketing. The sales process for each may share many similarities, but historical legacies and marketing conditions mean that the preferred channels for marketing are unrecognisable to each other. *Influencer Marketing* would dramatically update marketing attitudes in these sectors.

The traditional mix only targets prospects

Whoever laid down the guidebook used when dividing up a firm's marketing budget into the various activities? At one stage such thinking must have made sense but today it makes little at all. It exists because too few people have questioned it and because of what John Jantsch in *Duct Tape Marketing* calls 'copycat marketing'. In the past decade the optimum marketing mix for most companies has changed irrevocably, mostly as a result of the new outbound channels now available (predominantly online) and the vehicles through which purchasers now want to view their information (increasingly online too).

The marketing mix has traditionally focused on preparing prospective customers (through awareness, familiarity, comfort and knowledge) for their walk down Sales Avenue. And there's the issue. Marketing has always aimed directly at prospective purchasers, and not their influencers.

Though it often seems otherwise, business prospects are relatively easy to identify. They may have a job title that identifies them as such, they may have a history of buying related products or services, they may have already made an enquiry to your company. At least they'll probably be employed within the same company that will eventually use that product or service. And that's a very helpful start when tracking them down.

None of those features may be the case for influencers. Influencers will most likely not be employed within the user company, they'll have every variation of job title you can think of, except one helpfully called 'Influencer', and they likely won't ever buy anything from you, so they won't be on your customer database. What's more, while some influencers love to be thought of as such, many do not, some even believing that such recognition will negatively affect their ability to do their job. Because 'influencer' is such a subjective term, candidates have to be treated particularly sensitively until their views are known.

Key points in this chapter

1. Most firms decide their marketing budget by looking at what they did last year and making minor modifications, or following what other firms are doing. Yet there is precious little measurement on marketing effectiveness carried out by marketers, on which to base investment decisions.

2. Activities such as advertising, trade shows and sponsorships demonstrate almost no tangible benefit, if they are measured at all. What metrics do exist, in PR and AR in particular, are typically based on quantity rather than quality. Little research is done to determine which analysts and journalists are influential to the target audience.

3. Almost all marketing is aimed at prospects, virtually none at influencers. Which means that when marketing messages are thrown at prospects they usually bounce off. Influencers, though, are harder to target than prospects because they are difficult to identify.

Case Study A – Nortel

A different kind of thinking

In 2006 Nortel faced a problem. Its UK operation wanted to penetrate the financial services market, particularly for its home and mobile working solutions. The sales force approached the marketing department for ideas. 'The initiative driven by our sales force who were saying that they needed to get into the financial sector', explains marketing manager Robin Sansom. The sales team had access into Nortel's traditional market, the IT and communications departments, but they quickly realised that the purse holders were the business owners and the operational managers. 'But we had no traction in this space', says Sansom.

Sansom was tasked with engaging business executives in the financial services sector. He also had to shift the perception of the firm as a 'box shifter' and create the impression of the firm as a thought leader and trusted advisor. Importantly, the marketing manager also faced opposition from inside the firm. 'We lacked a belief that a different approach would work. It was cutting against everything we had done before'.

The approach that Sansom took was to organise a debate, with a motion that read '*This house believes that homeworking is inevitably doomed*'. 'It was a risky subject', says Sansom, 'had the vote gone against us, we would have been shooting ourselves in the foot (in talking down the market for our mobile working solutions)'. But the benefits in engaging the audience in discussion were deemed to outweigh the potential downside.

The debate was structured formally, with the invitation to prospects serving a dual purpose, both as a voting card to encourage engagement in the debate, and ultimately to facilitate a ballot. Influential speakers and a chair were invited. To propose the motion Nortel invited Dr Carsten Sorenson, a distinguished and controversial lecturer at the London School of Economics and Political Science (LSE). 'Academics always come up very high on the lists of getting people's attention whether they are on the business or marketing side', believes Sansom. To speak against the motion, and to fight its corner, Nortel invited Emma Spencer, the employee relations director at Citigroup EMEA, an advocate of homeworking.

The debate format was innovative and allowed the views of two influential speakers to be heard equally, with the audience able to ask questions. As Sansom says, 'We stepped away from the usual approach of murdering people with PowerPoint, talking at them about our technology and features and functions and our kit. Instead we took a back seat and let the audience and the panel discuss a topical subject matter'.

The event was a success. As one customer commented, 'I enjoyed it and found it very useful – lively debate, intelligent presentations, and an open forum for exploring the issues'.

And the sponsoring (and initially sceptical) sales team also saw the value. Nortel' sales director agreed that the debate 'was a success in that it was exactly what (the prospects) *didn't* expect to see. We didn't do any product pitches, just allowed the customers to discuss what their business issues were. And on the back of this we got some great results'.

Sansom reflects on the debate by observing that taking a risk 'does work if you're willing to stick your neck out and take the opportunity'. He also notes that 'The customer now chooses when they hear and what they listen to and by what means. Unless they take that on board (marketers) will just continue to make the same mistakes as they've done before'.

3

How buyers buy

Here we look at how decisions are made within businesses today, and the various stages open to influence.

Buying has become a serious business

In the economic boom of the late-1990s, corporate purchases were designed to give 'competitive advantage'. It led to a huge surge in spending as companies trawled all those in their supplier chain for something, anything that would differentiate them from their competitors. The money was available to do this, from venture capital and from high share valuations. The dotcom boom as it became known was not restricted to Internet start-ups but impacted the entire technology and telecoms sectors, and those that either bought into the emergent innovations or funded them. With the beginning of this decade times changed, both politically and economically. The boom stopped, abruptly, in March 2000 and the IT industry didn't see positive growth again until 2004. For four years every company was forced to make sense of what it already owned, rather than buy anew. It's been a slow road back for the tech firms.

There are several long-term impacts of the dotcom boom and bust, that still persist today. The 'Year 2000 bug', which had cost businesses billions of dollars globally, proved to many that money spent on IT had been wasted. Those companies that spent fortunes on rewriting or replacing systems seems no better off than those that had ignored the problem.

CIOs (Chief Information Officers) that had campaigned hard for massive additional funding, often using scare tactics to achieve this, had had their bluff called. Never again would IT be allowed to wield such influence over business. The CFO would see to that.

In 2003, still in the midst of the recession, Nicholas Carr suggested, in the Harvard Business Review, that IT cannot provide competitive advantage but is a commodity, a utility to be switched on and off as required. While IT remains necessary it no longer matters as a strategic and differentiating component to businesses. The long term impact of Carr's '*IT Doesn't Matter*' paper is that end-user organisations now ask difficult questions of suppliers: 'Prove to me that your product gives me competitive advantage'.

Throughout the late 1990s, the largest organisations had embarked on a relentless upgrade cycle for their core business systems. In the new decade upgrades were deferred. When the finance directors refused funding for IT upgrades, they initially intended the action to tighten purse strings in the short term. 'Let's wait three months and see what happens'. Remarkably, the sky did not fall in. So they waited another three months. And another. It dawned on organisations that they had been paying for upgrades they didn't really need. And they still don't. Many major software vendors of the time saw their revenues dry up, resulting in a massive consolidation. There are now just three major business application vendors in the world.

Across the board, not just on tech purchasing, the outcome has been the rise of the purchasing committee. The recriminations over Enron, WorldCom and Parmalat caused a rise in regulations, and with it a heavy compliance burden. As a consequence, senior managers have less autonomy than ever before. Every major purchase now has to be justified and accounted for, and allocated to the right financial quarter, not offset over the longer-term. Shareholders now have greater rights of access and veto. This has created a climate where individuals find it harder to go 'out on a limb' in any one purchasing decision. The purchasing process has therefore become formalised, documented and inevitably longer.

How decisions are made in firms

It's worth considering the decision-making process in firms. In our personal lives we typically make decisions by ourselves or with the input of a significant other (spouse, partner, parent, close friend, etc.). Rarely do we make personal decisions that involve more than ourselves and one other person. In cases where we are forced to involve more than one person, such as who to invite to a wedding or whether to move grandma into a nursing home, they typically become fraught affairs. Differences of opinion can create rifts between family members, long arguments and even legal battles. Painful stuff.

On the other hand, in business, decisions are rarely made in isolation. Trivial purchases such as stationery can be delegated quickly, but most decisions above a certain value or importance involve some form of discussion. Why is this? Simply, the stakes in business decision-making are high, involving large sums of money and impacting on business success. Choosing the right commercial partner might be the difference between growth and demise. Few people are comfortable in making such a decision on their own.

This is not to say that one person isn't ultimately responsible for a decision. Clearly a nominated person must take final responsibility – the buck must stop somewhere. But in the decision *process* several people will be involved, so that the risk of making a bad decision is minimised. This is just good business sense and there are important drivers to encourage this type of behaviour in companies:

- In making decisions, data points are often asked for in justification of the proposal. These often come from third party sources, but they should be credible (= influential).
- Involving other parties, including outside influencers, means that the ultimate decision-maker has some protection (or someone to blame!) if the decision works out badly.

It's like being on trial. You call witnesses (influencers) to give supporting evidence. The more credible the witness the greater their credibility, and the more likely the verdict will be in your favour.

There is also another driving reason for involving several people – decisions usually affect more than one part of the business. A new sales strategy affects product distribution. A new telephony system affects customer service. A new accounting regime affects pricing and billing schedules. And so on.

IDC, the technology analyst firm, has detected this trend as far as IT spending is concerned. It says that 'managers from outside the traditional IT department are exerting an increasing influence, direct and indirect, on the IT decision-making process'.[1] We think the same is true in all major decisions.

When to influence a decision

The truth is that in order to influence a decision you must do it at the beginning of the process – when the firm decides to do something – or at

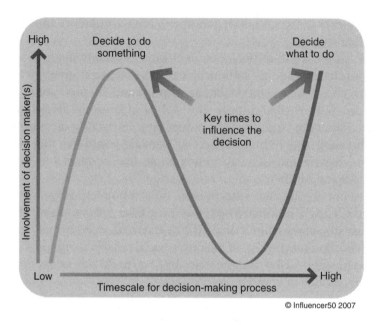

© Influencer50 2007

Figure 3.1   The key times to influence a decision

the end (Figure 3.1). The phase in between is just detail – someone else's job. This should tell you two things:

- If I'm talking to the decision-maker the decision process is either just beginning or just ending. Find out which. Then find out which influencers are relevant to this part of the process.
- If I'm talking to someone else, for example a junior information gatherer or technical specialist, then either there's no decision to be made (I'm too early) or the decision process has already started (I'm probably too late).

It's a common misconception that a decision process is a linear activity with a discrete and evenly spaced set of hurdles to clear. This is a very seller-orientated view of the world. Decision-makers make only two types of decision:

- Decide to do something
- Decide what to do

Decision 1 – decide to do something

Let's examine these decisions in turn. A company has an uneasy feeling that something is not quite right. This feeling could be driven by negative forces such as a poor sales quarter or bad customer service reports.

Or perhaps just driven by the desire to do even better, to maintain market leadership, to sustain competitive advantage. Or maybe that the industry is changing due to new regulations.

Where is the first point that influencers can influence? It is in creating this uneasy feeling in the first place. Influencers can make decision-makers aware of some latent pain that they were previously unaware of. Influencers can uncover operational inefficiencies, or spot an opportunity to create competitive advantage, or some other imbalance. Whatever, the uneasy feeling needs corroboration, and so more opinions are solicited, data are crunched and the problem (or opportunity) is scoped. The firm reaches a decision that it needs to do something.

There are two important elements in this first decision that relate to influencers. Firstly, in the corroboration of the uneasy feeling influencers have an impact. In some cases the problem and action is clear. (Problem: we missed our first quarter sales. Action: sell more stuff next quarter.) But usually the problem is softer. It may not even be clear whether there really is a problem or, if there is, whether they need to do something about it. So the firm seeks out people it trusts to inform and confirm the decision to do something.

The other important aspect of the decision to do something is that once a firm decides to do something it also commits itself to deciding what to do. To make this a manageable task, it sets out a number of options, decides on a decision-making process and allocates responsibilities. Influencers typically help firms in the first two of these, by using their knowledge and expertise in mapping out the choices available and the process to follow. It is no surprise that professional procurement experts have risen in their individual influence over the past decade, as complex decisions require expertise to guide firms through the process. The decision to do something is absolutely the most important part in any decision-making process. Influence that and you influence the whole deal.

Management consultants have perfected this pattern of influence. They are called in to validate and qualify the uneasy feeling – 'Yes, there is a problem and you need to do something about it'. The consultants then help to define the process, perhaps drafting a set of requirements to be sent to potential suppliers. They then have two options: to oversee the assessment and selection of the supplier, or to extract themselves from the decision-making process so that they can bid for the supply. In this latter case they are bidding for a contract that they have already influenced, and thus stand a better than even chance of winning it.

Is this unethical? Not as long as the consultants extract themselves early enough in order to avoid conflicts of interest. That in itself is a skill. But their inside knowledge of the client firm and the requirement gives the consultants a huge advantage. In fact, if they are good at their job there may be no competitive selection process and they get the follow-on work automatically.

Decision 2 – decide what to do

Most suppliers hear about a deal at this stage. They are sent a tender document to which they respond. They then get shortlisted, give a final presentation and, if they are lucky, they get the work. Lucky? Of course, since they've had no input to, or impact on, the people that are influencing the decision. There is a huge amount of luck involved in winning tendered work without help from influencers. It is near-impossible to affect the decision process once it is set in motion. The only option you have is to influence the outcome.

Critically, a key element in deciding what to do is also deciding what not to do. Decisions are as much about prioritisation as taking action, and influencers are just as capable of giving negative advice as they are giving positive recommendations. For example, whittling a high number of suppliers into a shortlist of three can be done in the most rudimentary and ruthless manner.

You need to identify the influencers that impact the final decision. Sometimes there is an influencer that runs throughout the process – like consultants. But often there are different influencers that appear and disappear, injecting their expertise and opinion at appropriate moments. Find out who the influencers are and when they apply their influence. If you do your homework well, and you know the influencers that are impacting on the deal, then luck starts to transform into certainty. You need to be able to fulfil the spirit of the project brief. But if you can influence the decision-makers you change the *details* of the brief and win the work.

Every supplier tendering for work wants to position themselves as innovative and competent. Those that win offer something else of value. By identifying the influencers you will know what that something else is, the influencers will know that you know, and they will communicate to the client your ability to fulfil it. Let's be in no doubt – there is an order of magnitude in difference of difficulty between influencing a decision at the start of the process and influencing it at the end. If you can, influence early.

How to detect deals at the start of the process

All of this begs the question: how do I know when a decision process is about to start? Because you can't influence a deal at the start if you don't know when it starts. The problem is that decision processes can start at any time in multiple organisations. How can you keep your finger on the pulse of all your prospects and their likelihood of deciding to do something?

We are often asked if it's possible to identify the influencers on a specific deal, such as a big outsourcing contract. The truth is that it's extraordinarily hard to identify the specific influencers on any one deal. Even if you could identify them, it's likely that the key influencing has already been done.

That fact that you know there's an outsourcing contract being tendered means that the client firm is well down the decision process road.

One approach might be to identify the influencers inside a client organisation, and watch to see if they are about to decide to do something. Either you have an insider source of information, or you place someone close to the organisation. Some salespeople can perform this role, or perhaps consultants that are working on-site inside the client firm. If you have a retainer with a client then you stand a better chance of uncovering a new deal. This is why the top consulting firms are successful – once inside a client organisation they constantly scout around for the next project, and the next and so on. Consultants often talk about *seams* of consulting within a client that need to be mined. They just keep digging until the opportunities are exhausted.

Even if you know the influencers inside one client prospect, this approach is not scalable to all of your prospects. The scalable approach is to identify the external influencers and use them to detect decision processes that are starting up. You can't guarantee you'll find all deals but you will gain a good coverage.

Importantly, if you are influencing the relevant influencers in a constant and consistent manner, then your messages should be being carried to prospects possibly without you knowing it. The first you may hear of it is being invited to submit a tender. It's vital that you then understand why you've been invited, who recommended you, and what their role is in the decision process going forward.

Key points in this chapter

1. Decision-making is a complex and strategic process. This means nowadays that although there is an ultimate decision-maker there are numerous other parties involved, to inform, support and validate the decision.
2. There are two critical points to influence a decision: at the beginning of the process and at the end. In order to affect a decision you need to know where in the process the decision-maker is.
3. Those people that influence a decision early on have a greater impact on the outcome. Some influencers initiate the decision process by pointing out a latent pain in the firm. These influencers are in the best position to define the problem scope and thus to provide the solution.

Note and reference

1 Stephen Minton (2007). Evolution of the IT buyer. IDC, May.

4

Decision-maker ecosystems

Decision-makers today rarely act alone. They create ecosystems to frame and arrive at their decisions. Here we describe their formation.

Many parts of the world exhibit their own micro-climates, which are driven by local geographic features and weather conditions. These localised ecosystems can be unpredictable, and are often radically different from the surrounding broader climatic conditions.

In the same way, decision-makers construct (often subconsciously) their own ecosystems of individuals which they consult when forming their thoughts on a given subject, person or action. We all do this intuitively – we look for people off whom to bounce our thoughts, our opinions and our intentions. It's a sanity check of our intended decision-making process. Business decision-makers act in the same way.

The term 'DME' is new. We chose it because it reflects the dynamic and transitory nature of decision-making units, which form for a specific purpose then dissipate once their natural course has run. Just like weather systems. And at the risk of stretching the weather analogy too far, the only way to really understand what's happening in an ecosystem is to be in it. We have radar and satellite imaging to predict rain, but there's no substitute for getting wet. Similarly, we can make predictions about a DME but unless you're in one it's hard to know exactly what's going on.

Figure 4.1 Influencers protect buyers from the pressure of competing firms' marketing

Ecosystems of influencers form around decision-makers, and they are rarely based on any formal structure (Figure 4.1). They are more loosely tethered webs of connections, and are certainly not hierarchical. Its members are of varying business levels, of mixed experience, and typically from more than one organisation. Rarely will they have ever met in the same room before, nor is this required for them to influence any one particular decision. Some influencers emerge as more important than others, but the nature of this depends on a large number of variables specific to each decision. External influencers will give, or be asked, their opinion on a particular subject, with perhaps no knowledge or inclination as to what that advice will be used for. And when the core founders of the DME are asked why they have the view they have on a subject, they quite likely wont be able to recall who shaped their argument. The source of the influence may never be tracked.

There are two broad constituents of people in a DME: those internal to the decision-maker's organisation and those external to it. This is important in the context of *influencer marketing*, because it is far easier to identify external individuals that are likely to form part of such an ecosystem. Determining internal influencers on a specific decision is very hard, if not impossible.

The invisible influencers

Imagine a taskforce being created within a business as it readies a new product introduction. Your firm is hoping to be a chosen preferred retailer for it. The project leader invites a number of company colleagues with relevant job roles and experience to join the team. More senior executives, who will need to sign-off any high-value order, are copied on update mails but do not attend the regular progress meetings. Everyone is capable of exhibiting influence on the project, through suggestions, reminders of company protocol, particular subject matter expertise, sales expectations, budget implications and so on. Various questions during these meetings need to be taken offline and brought up with employees from other departments within the company. Their views may affect eventual decisions so they too carry influence. Sound familiar?

External suppliers upstream in the supply chain need to be involved throughout the process, though they may never attend the progress meetings. They're responsible for much of the production process so they will have vital opinions on time to market, delivery capability, build quality and so on. They too tangibly influence the eventual product, which in turn affects the product's market positioning, and this is a major factor in the company's eventual choice of retailer.

The core team will authorise certain representatives of the company to meet with industry analysts, market intelligence authorities, heads of sales channels, management consultants, perhaps even a journalist or two, to gather feedback on the expected impact of such a product. This is where the internal influencers interface with external opinion leaders. This may be done throughout the development process, and will be started early enough to incorporate the fundamental feedback into improving the eventual product. These external influencers – 'trusted advisors' – will help shape all aspects of the product's development, including whether your company offers the best reseller channel or not. In these 'closed door' meetings, you simply cannot afford the mention of your company name to be met with a 'Never heard of them' or 'Don't know much about them, but I've heard good things about this other company . . .'.

You can see how a DME may be formed, how it increasingly adds members, however temporarily, and may well lose them with equal regularity. No one person ever keeps the names of all members on a sheet of paper and many wont even know of the existence of the other members. Nor will they care to ask. They see themselves having a 'point-in-time' role rather than a strategic one. And it can get a lot more complex than that.

There will always be the random contributor to such an ecosystem – the conversation over the fence with a neighbour, the phone call with the brother-in-law that works in a similar field, or the 'friend of a friend who can get a good deal' from a particular supplier. While these tend to operate around the periphery of the network, they still form part of the influencer community.

The above example relates to a company- and activity-specific require- ment, in this case a new product launch. But the core founders of the decision-making team will have been influenced, however subtly, long before they were ever appointed to lead the team. Most likely over a period of years. In that time they will already have been pre-disposed to certain suppliers and partners, particular technologies and methodologies. Your chances of winning the resulting deal have already been affected one way or the other, though you wont be aware of that.

And you'll never meet the majority of the decision-makers. They are invisible to you, embedded deep within the prospect's organisational struc- ture and third party suppliers. Your only chance to influence them is via the external influencers, those that directly impact the decision-making team. These influencers *are* visible, if you know where to look. Finding them, and influencing them, is what *influencer marketing* is all about.

The golden rules of DMEs

DMEs are dynamic in nature, and it's impossible to predict the constituents at any one time. Importantly, a DME is specific to the decision being made and also dependent on the choices of the decision-maker themselves. So, for example, the DME for a CEO is different to that for the head of retail banking or to that for a network manager. Once the target market segment is defined only then does it make sense to identify a DME's influencers. And this is why many people guess their influencers wrongly.

However, within a market segment there are sufficient similarities between the external influencers in an ecosystem for one prospect and that of another. It is this consistency amongst external influencers that facilitates *influencer marketing*.

To understand the nature and structure of DMEs, there are a few golden rules:

1. Decision-makers never pack their ecosystems with just one form of influencer (such as journalists or regulators or work colleagues). Buyers hate risk, and they spread it around as much as they can. There is safety in numbers, but also in diversity within the ecosystem.
2. Influence does not work in real-time. Decision-makers have long memories and are more likely to have registered an influencer's actions from a year ago than an updated one a month ago. It is wrong to assume that anything you issue is received and digested immediately.

3. Decision-makers ignore or push back on some influencers within their circle (say, journalists) more than others (say, management consultants).
4. Decision-makers do not adhere to the same 'credibility ranking' understood by those inside the industry (including the vendors). In IT buying, Gartner and Forrester are the two most credible analyst authorities, yet a significant minority of in-house decision-makers will be unaware of that and listen closest to other firms many places 'down' the credibility list.
5. When questioned by internal management as to why particular choices have been made, decision-makers have been known to abandon all notion of this 'credibility list' and justify their decisions by quoting selectively from the full array of influencers. They retro-fit particular influencer views to fit their own.
6. Some influencers are influential because of their personal standing, others because they are the representative for a particularly influential company. This is an important distinction. When some influencers move companies, their influence moves with them; with others, it stays with their former employer.
7. The emotional pull is almost always the strongest influence. Unless regulatory or budgetary issues prevail, decision-makers are swayed in their choice for emotional reasons, then persuade themselves they were anything but. Salespeople have always known this.
8. Influencers rise up and fall down in importance to decision-makers as they progress through their decision-making process. Some are more influential at the beginning, others at the end. So influence and influencers aren't smoothly distributed.

Fragmentation and convergence in DMEs

Influencer marketing is about influencing the decision-making process so that traditional sales barriers are minimised and your path to closing sales is smoothed. You'll see that influencers are a complex mix of individuals beyond the current scope and attention of your current marketing activities.

The traditional influencers – journalists and industry analysts – are declining in their share of influence. Why is that? There are two core reasons. One is because of the influencer fragmentation that has naturally occurred over the past two decades. As markets mature so their infrastructure broadens and deepens. Where once there may only have been a cottage industry of magazines, specialist advisors and networking groups, most maturing sectors are now home to a complex web of loosely connected advisory firms, tactical suppliers, vendors, channels, reporters and the like.

While researching on behalf of our clients into specific marketplaces, it is not unusual for the number of 'Players', those we uncover in our initial stages as potential influencers, to number over 400 in a single country. Wherever there is a high number of influencers, their concentration within just a few categories is unlikely. It is only to be expected that the 'influence' is shared out more equally.

We particularly notice that in the very early months of a new market emerging, there is a higher prevalence of suppliers appearing as influencers. This is because many new markets are created by suppliers, those new markets are first given a name by those same suppliers, and it is they who first create the noise about it. This is before analysts or journalists are tracking it and before user groups, regulators, consultants and others have organised themselves. It is part of the vendor 'marketing 101' book to 'create' new marketplaces. In that way you're sure to be the number one supplier to it!

Take, for example, Steve Jobs' NeXT company as they launched themselves in the early 1990s. NeXT was competing with industry leader Sun Microsystems in the workstation (high-end PCs) marketplace. Its sales were dwarfed 50-to-1 by Sun, with NeXT only selling successfully into high-margin professional services firms willing to pay extra for the machine's striking looks. So Steve Jobs briefed each of the major analyst firms about a nascent (and at the time, imaginary) market emerging for 'professional workstations', ones being adopted by lawyers, doctors, accountants and so on. In this new market, NeXT could truthfully claim to be outselling Sun 10-to-1. No actual sales figures were released. In reality they were low. But the analysts accepted his words and legitimised a new, albeit tiny, market. Neither for the first nor last time, the now-Apple CEO was sufficiently influential to move the industry goalposts.

As a market matures the make-up and balance of the broader influencer community, and DMEs, changes. Vendors become much less of a feature, and implementers (consultants, systems integrators, equipment installers) become more so. Lower value products also attract the attention of magazines, blogs and web comparison sites. High-value items attract analysts, events, regulators and so on. We arrive eventually at a relative degree of equilibrium, where the spread of influence stays more or less the same. But the spread is much wider than it used to be.

Figure 4.2 shows what a typical fragmentation might look like today versus a decade ago.

As many formerly separate and diverse market sectors converge, especially in retailing, telecoms and entertainment, so they are uniting already entrenched influencer infrastructures, with the outcome that no single influencer category stands out as the undisputed most influential. In this context it is only natural that journalist and analyst influence is diminishing, and is the fault of neither.

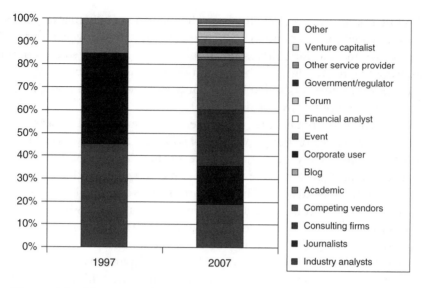

Figure 4.2 Change in influencer distribution, 1997–2007

Declining trust

But there's an additional explanation. Journalist and analyst influence is diminishing because our trust in those advisors that we have traditionally held in such respect is declining. We no longer believe every word just because it comes from their mouths. There's a saying that some business executives use industry analyst data in the same way as a drunk uses a lamp post – not as it was intended, as a considered source of illumination, but instead as a last-ditch source of support. This analogy perpetuates the view that executives only refer to analyst data or advice when it suits their ends, and they feel entirely justified in ignoring it when it doesn't. There is also the cynics' view that you can always find an analyst to support the view that you want. In fact, many analyst companies turn a good profit on commissioned White Papers that say, in essence, what the sponsoring clients want them to say.

The much respected Texas-based Knowledge Capital Group (KCG) does a great job of clarifying to its clients the differences between various analyst firms. A few firms, the top echelon, are classified as DMBs (Deal-Makers and Breakers), others as PPs (Point Providers) and still others as AFHs (Analysts for Hire). This latter category can often be commissioned with a pre-determined result in mind. Few vendor companies seem aware (or seem to care) of such analyst differentiation, to the detriment of the best quality analyst firms.

Whatever the case, the reputation of analysts isn't what it once was. They remain *an* influencer, but not *the* influencer. Only a few die-hards seem to even doubt this view these days. And those die-hards aren't the analysts themselves.

Key points in this chapter

1. DMEs are loosely tethered webs of connections, and are not hierarchical. They are informal in structure, and a decision-maker may not even be aware of many of the influencers that form their ecosystem.
2. There is no way to determine an ecosystem for a specific decision, because of internal influencers. But it is possible to map the external influencers likely to impact on similar decisions between firms. These external influencers make *influencer marketing* feasible.
3. The individuals that make up a DME may come from a wide variety of organisations and backgrounds. The sources of influence are fragmented, due partly to an organic dispersion of influence across the various parties that play in a market, and partly to the decline in trust in traditional influencer types.

Case Study B – Wipro

Working the CXO ecosystem

Indian IT vendors like Wipro are increasingly setting their sights on are moving up the value chain to emerge as strategic partners for their customers, working with them to enable business transformation as opposed to just being tactical vendors. This shift implicitly means that the target audience for Indian vendors is no longer just the IT director or the IT organisation, but the business leadership that includes the CIO, the CTO and the CEO.

Wipro extensively researched its customers and their buying processes. It realised that there exists an influencer ecosystem, consisting of both formal and informal channels, and that customers rely on this community to make strategic business decisions. It also discovered that this ecosystem is complex and multi-tiered. At the core layer Wipro puts the influencers who impact buying decisions directly – these primarily comprise of the leading sourcing advisory firms that play a recommendatory role in choosing vendors. At the next layer sit the business consulting firms that advise customers on business strategy, which increasingly includes sourcing strategy, and technology analyst firms that provide detailed vendor coverage and analysis: both these influencer types rarely recommend vendors directly. They have a softer role to play in the ecosystem. The final layer comprises academics, who sometimes consult with these organisations, and thought leaders and peers who are a part of professional networking groups. They often play an indirect, but highly valuable, 'WOM' recommendatory role in the ecosystem.

The influencer programme at Wipro was rolled out in early 2006 to distinctly reach out to the ecosystem with focused programmes targeted at each of these influencer groups. The objective of this programme was twofold:

- The first was to provide the influencers with detailed information on its services and solutions that would put the firm in the consideration set for requests for information (RFIs) and requests for proposal (RFPs) for deals that it would not have featured in earlier simply because the influencers did not know it offered the specific service or did not enough about its capabilities to recommend the firm.
- The second objective was to use the interactions with influencers to understand specific client problems and requirements and match our service offerings to these requirements.

In the 18 months that Wipro has been running this programme, it has come a long way from playing a reactive role in the process by responding to RFPs and catering to specific briefing requests. The influencer relations team at Wipro now covers over 15 influencer organisations in US and Europe that include sourcing advisories, technology analysts, business consulting firms and even cost management consultants. The team proactively maps key influencers across industries and technology areas and sets up briefings, roundtables and webinars involving the business leaders as well as the technology and delivery leaders at Wipro, ensuring that a holistic view of its capability is provided to the market. It has engaged with key influencers at industry events as well as Wipro custom events and hosting guided campus tours for visiting influencers to ensure that they have a first-hand experience about the company. Wipro is also working on joint thought leadership papers, technology points of view, CXO-level research and case studies with the influencers.

With a success measured by the significant increase in RFI/RFPs and deals it has received through these influencers after the commencement of this programme, it is now building the outreach strategy for the third layer of the ecosystem that comprises academics, thought leaders and peer networking organisations.

5

How influence works

You should by now agree that marketing isn't the aid to sales that it was designed to be. You can see how buyers are buying and your company's marketing isn't mapping on to this. You know that buying decisions are being shaped, scoped and framed by influencers. The next four chapters look at these influencers in greater depth and how you can identify them.

Individuals play a myriad of roles in influencing business decisions. This chapter clarifies these roles and explains their importance.

The first modern DME

The early proponents of *influencer marketing*, though they never termed it as such, were the American political parties, who from the 1950s onwards spent millions of dollars segmenting America geographically, demographically and ideologically so that they could identify precisely which messages would, and would not, 'win over' particular groups of voters. Today, as a new election campaign gets underway, there are a few key states, just three or four out of 50, whose views and trends are seen to influence the other 47. The Democrat or Republican candidates know they do not have to win over the 220 million American voters. They must win over the one to two million most influential, for those people will look after the rest.

As a marketer, the smaller the number you need to focus on, the more likely you'll find a message that resonates.

Gladwell's influencers

Malcolm Gladwell's The Tipping Point remains a seminal book since its publication in 2000. There are several useful and relevant concepts in the book, but the one that we encounter most is the notion of three types of influencer: *connectors*, *mavens* and *salesmen*.

Connectors talk to people. Lots of people. They are networkers in the extreme, and love making introductions. They typically know people across an array of social, cultural, professional and economic circles. *Connectors* are essential for word of mouth (WOM) communication of a message.

Mavens are knowledgeable people. But more than just consuming information, they also share it with others. Because they hoard knowledge they can detect patterns and trends, and are often insightful.

Salesmen are the charismatic persuaders, people with powerful negotiation skills. They exert 'soft' influence rather than forceful power. Their source of influence may be the tendency of others, subconsciously, to imitate them rather than anything more deliberate.

Connectors, *mavens* and *salespeople*, in combination, are responsible for the generation, communication and adoption of messages. Gladwell's model is useful in considering the social aspects of how messages spread, but it has some limitations. For example, it doesn't account for a business context of a message, in which there may be influencers that don't fit comfortably into the taxonomy, such as regulators or executives in customer organisations. Influencers are also hard to identify, and Gladwell offers no methodology to find them.

The main trouble we have with using Gladwell's taxonomy in a practical B2B sense is that the influence of connectors is overstated. There are two reasons for this:

■ There are only a few genuine social connectors. True *connectors* collect people like other collectors collect stamps. It is their social *modus operanda*. It's just in their nature, and they do it the real world as well as online. We estimate that there are only about 3 per cent in any population that are true *connectors*.[1] The rest are what we'd call false connectors.

■ Connections do not equate to influence. False connectors are connection gatherers. They have a fascination with connections. We know people that have more than 500 connections on LinkedIn. Some MySpace accounts have thousands or even tens of thousands of connections. While some of these people will be genuine *connectors*, the majority are collecting names as badges of popularity.

There are even ways to fake the number of connections – fakeyourspace.com was notorious before it was shut down in early 2007. Why would someone fake hundreds of connections?

False connectors are equating connections with popularity, and popularity with influence. All you need are email addresses and some persistence to increase your connections on social media. Faking the number of connections fakes neither popularity nor influence.

Of three types of influencers described in the *The Tipping Point*, everyone (it seems) wants to be a *connector*. There is an assumption that *connectors* are the most influential type. In fact the most powerful type of influencer happens to be a *salesman*, in Gladwell's terminology. A *persuader* in ours.

The terms *connectors*, *mavens* and *salesmen* describe how individuals pass messages along. But they don't describe what types of messages are being passed. The messages are different, depending on where in the decision process the decision-maker is. There is also no reflection of the sequence or order of the messages.

A taxonomy of influencer roles

We've looked at how influencers impact on the decision process, and we've mapped a series of specific messages that are carried, based on various key points in the process. This allows us to identify a number of roles that can be played by influencers (Figure 5.1).

We should make it clear that these influencer roles are not necessarily played in each decision. Their impact is specific to the decision being made. There is a logical sequence of progression from role to role, but it's not mandatory to fill every influencer role, and the decision process may skip several steps. Decision processes are not linear and don't follow a predictable path, other than they start somewhere and end somewhere else.

In addition, the locuses of influence roles overlap, so that there may be more than one influencer role relevant at any one time.

Finally, our influencer roles do not describe types of influencer, but rather the roles that they may play. A single influencer may play a number of roles throughout one decision process, or have a single impact at one particular point.

Idea planters

Idea planters are the thinkers in your industry. These people ask *what if?* They are the innovators, and may be drawn from outside the normal

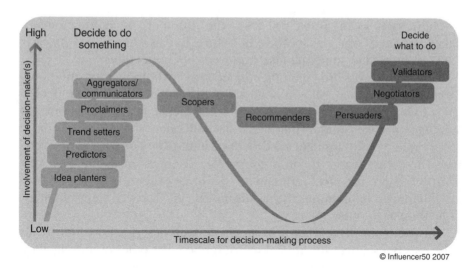

Figure 5.1 Influencer roles in the decision process

industry boundaries. Typically, they provoke and challenge opinions and conventional wisdom, and raise questions that begin to break inertia. They are disruptive forces, but may be ignored or sidelined if their ideas are too wacky or controversial. Still, they sow the seeds that grow into future agenda items, point out deficiencies and inefficiencies in current practice. They are the sources of uncertainty.

Authors and thinkers like Seth Godin, Tom Peters, Trevor Bayliss (inventor of the clockwork radio) and Nicholas Negroponte are all *idea planters*.

Predictors

Predictors tell us what (they believe) will be adopted soon. They ask *what next?* Much of the origination of this kind of influence comes from the supplier community, which is essentially telling us what's next in their product pipeline. But this market priming is held in check by third parties such as analysts (who sanity check the plans), financiers (who fund new product development) and other commentators such as bloggers and management gurus.

Predictors come from analyst firms like Gartner and Forrester, but venture capitalists like Jon Moulton at Alchemy and Akhil Gupta at Blackstone are also known predictors.

Trendsetters

Trendsetters are the early adopters. They set themselves as reference points and create the direction for the rest of the market. They are important because they not only validate the market but also communicate success to the market. They are influential due to their early adoption, and the fact that they spread the news of their success.

Trendsetter status is specific to a specific market and doesn't translate from one product type to another. So for instance a *trendsetter* in implementing financial management outsourcing could easily be a laggard in adopting lean manufacturing principles. This is because the influential individuals within these organisations tend to be executives responsible for specific operations.

Citigroup has become a *trendsetter* in homeworking policy, and Dell was a long time trendsetter in supply chain management.

Proclaimers

Some influencers just stand up and proclaim that the world will be how they want it to be. They mandate (as far as they can) the *what and how*. They are therefore in a position to be listened to and acted upon. Sometimes this is due to their position (such as regulators), sometimes just down to the weight they carry in their market. Some financial analysts, for example, proclaim the top of a bull market, which then fulfils the prophecy.

Proclaimers most often work for government agencies and departments, regulators and legislators, or standards bodies, but may also include buyer groups or co-operatives, and industry commentators.

Aggregators/communicators

One of the most important roles an influencer can play is that of information gatherer and disseminators. It's where the media and analysts get the majority of their influence: their knowledge of the detail of the market allows them power as to who has access to that knowledge. The market, of course, for information aggregation and communication has changed radically in the past 5 years, due to the emergence of web-based media such as blogs and social networks. This has both reduced the influence of traditional information sources and boosted that of newer players.

Non-media *aggregators/communicators* might include events, industry commentators, buyer groups, government agencies, industry bodies and industry analysts.

Scopers

At some point a definition of the decision to be taken has to be made. That's the role of *scopers*, to map out the limitations, parameters and dimensions of the problem and its likely solutions. *Scopers* tell us *what now*.

Scoping a decision is critical because it defines the likely set of solutions and, by implication, the likely set of suppliers. For example, a firm may have a problem with its customer service operation, but the *scopers* will determine whether the decision to be made is to outsource the operation, invest in training or implement a new customer relationship management (CRM) system.

Scopers usually work for suppliers/vendors, consulting firms, other customer organisations (via forums and networking) and events.

Recommenders

Recommenders suggest *what you should do*. They are sometimes, but not often, able to dictate a decision. Most often they will make their professional judgment known, and then leave the final decision up to the ultimate decision-maker. They are therefore usually somewhat passive in their influence, which is advisory in nature.

Players in the supply chain are typical *recommenders*, as they're in the best position to recommend. Independent they are not, as they're trying to sell something, but they still wield considerable influence as part of the DME.

Persuaders

Persuaders tell you *what you must do*. They are not passive at all, conveying precise direction rather than advice. These are your closers, salesmen in Gladwell's terms, the people who are able to make or break a decision.

The balance and interaction between recommenders and persuaders is always an interesting one, especially if they happen to meet. *Recommenders* tend to gain influence by weighing up the options and making a judgment on balance and analysis. *Persuaders* may not have the evidence to back up their opinions, but they convey them with passion and conviction.

The most effective *persuaders* work for supplier firms: you and your competitors. It's their job to swing the decision in their favour. To balance this bias, some firms employ independent influencers from (typically) external consulting firms.

Negotiators

Once the supplier is picked the fun begins. How are you going to implement the decision, and how much do you, or should you, pay? Cue the *negotiators*, who decide *how and how much*, advising on the financial elements of the deal, as well as the mechanics of how to construct a deal. This may mean procurement procedures, adherence to environmental and ethical codes of practice, clawback clauses and so on. Some of these elements may be non-negotiable, but others are tradable, so be aware of the differences that apply.

Validators

Validators say *it's okay*, and are the safety net for a decision-maker. Not the oft-perceived rubber stamp, they give any decision the health check, to make sure the decision-maker has covered all options. They can halt a deal, or send it circling back for additional scoping or negotiating.

The best examples of *validators* are reference site visits. In the majority of cases these exercises occur after the decision is made, but before it is communicated to the supplier. The decision-maker is using the *validator* to prove to his superiors that the decision is low risk.

Super-influencers

There are in some markets *super-influencers*, key individuals that command the highest respect and attention. *Super-influencers* are rare, and it is even rarer for one to appear in a DME. These people typically influence macro industry directions, rather than purchase decisions within a market.

Think Steve Jobs at Apple. His keynote speeches at US conventions have massive repercussions on the global entertainment sector these days. Many thousands of companies worldwide quote things he did or didn't say as backing for decisions they then make in their own businesses. And his words arguably have indirectly altered or shaped decisions within tens of thousands of additional companies. His influence is immense at an industry level (though we wouldn't advise including him in your top-tier of influencers to target).

How influencers gain influence

If we understand the roles that influencers play, how do influencers obtain their influence in the first place, and sustain it long term?

The answer is that influencers get their influence from each other. It's impossible to influence in isolation. Influence is always being tested by decision-makers, and they sometimes play influencers off against each other. They'll quote an academic research paper to a consultant, cite a user group resolution to a regulator and arrange a meeting with an analyst at an influential event. Decision-makers want to see that they are, in fact, influential. So influencers depend on being known by other influencers.

Academics gain influence by their research work being reviewed by peers (influencers) in their field. Consultants gain influence through the firm they join: McKinsey is a firm of influencers, which recruits and trains 'wannabee' influencers. Journalists gain influence, partly from the publication they write for (which employs other influential writers) and partly from the influential people they connect with. And so on.

So how do you tell who has influence to start with? There is an intuitive credibility test that determines the validity of the message and the messenger. The test is this:

■ Does the person have authority to speak on the subject, and
■ How trustworthy are they likely to be? Do they have a vested interest?

We call it the Cialdini test, after the eponymous professor who described the criteria for true authority in *Science: Influence and Practice*.

The Cialdini test is useful because it allows us to determine, not whether an individual has influence (since influence isn't all or nothing), but the extent to which someone has influence. If you use the two parts of the test as axes on a chart you can map out who is likely to be influential, and the extent of the influence (Figure 5.2).

So vendors may be experts but they always have a vested interest in the decision. Independent consultants and analysts normally do not (but they may be commissioned by vendors, so independence is not given). A reseller has a vested interest in making a sale, but may not care which product they sell, so they have a qualified vested interest. You get the idea.

Expertise is usually easier to determine, but there are occasions where credentials should be sought. In particular, seniority is rarely an indicator of expertise, especially where technical knowledge is concerned. Expertise is relative to the subject in question.

No influencer hierarchies

If influencers need to connect with other influencers, then there are two consequences of this connectedness of influencers. Firstly, there's no pyramid of cascading influence that emanates from one influencer, or

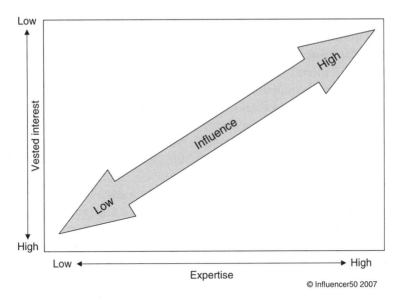

Figure 5.2 Determining the extent of influence

influencer type. Influencers gain influence from two-way communications with each other. Influence does not ripple out in one direction from a small set of individuals. Rather than a hierarchy, influence works across a network of individuals, with some having more connections than others. Influence flows in multiple directions, as industry professionals discuss and debate ideas and opinions. The emergence of DMEs demonstrates this important dimension.

Industry analysts are sometimes touted as '*super-influencers*', whose influence 'ripples' across other lesser influencers (media, consultants, system integrators, financial analysts). Nonsense. Analysts depend for their influence on a network of fellow influencers working at vendor firms, customer organisations and within their own companies too. The success to which they interact with other influencers drives the subsequent influence they hold. That's why not all analysts at Gartner are as influential as others.

Influencer clusters

The second consequence of the influencer 'support group' is that influencers cluster together. One way of identifying an influencer is that they hang out with other influencers. They reinforce their own influence and that of their peers, by exchanging views, stories or gossip. This can in some cases lead to an inner circle, what bloggers and celebrity watchers would call an A-list. There are perhaps five or six influencers in such a circle for a market, of differing categories, and they hold the balance of power. These clusters are never formally identified and rarely discussed.

But other clusters of influencers also exist, often in the 'second-tier' players. It's an effective way of boosting one's own influence, and ego, by sharing time with others in the same field. It also fuels influence if they can drop a name or two into their conversations with others. Influencers love to influence, and they love appearing to do so in the process. So they'll happily drop the fact that they had lunch with a *Wall Street Journal* journalist, or met with the Head of Mortgages at HSBC Bank earlier in the day.

Clusters are important because they enable a groundswell of opinions within influencers to form. They then carry this to their networks, and influenced WOM messages spread. There is no better way to create buzz in a market than to tap into the influencer community, seed and promote ideas to influencers, and watch them influence their own communities.

Key points in this chapter

1. Connectors, mavens and salesmen are three well-known types of influencers. But they are insufficient to describe the complexity of a business decision and the roles that influencers play within it. In particular, the importance of connectors is often overstated.
2. We've detected 10 different roles that an influencer can play in a decision process. But remember that not all roles may be played, a single influencer can play many roles, and that roles can overlap.
3. Influencers gain their influence from other influencers. Influence is transmitted between influencers, and there is no rigid hierarchy. But often there are small cliques of influencers that cluster together, which can create a groundswell of influential opinion.

Case Study C – a top 10 infrastructure management software vendor

Knocking on the CIO's door

The firm, a leader in service management software, has traditionally played in the IT management and support services market. But through an aggressive acquisition programme, and organic market share growth, it now has a substantial portfolio of integrated products, which demand a higher ticket sale. Its traditional mid-managerial level market often compares individual products with other 'best of breed' competitors. The firm needed to highlight the importance of an integrated solution, and also raise awareness of the increased value the integrated portfolio would deliver. These demand the attention of the CIO.

The firm embarked on a 24-month programme focused entirely on gaining access to the CIO. But traction was slow: its reputation as a technology-led company led it back to the mid-managers it was trying to move away from. The CIO's door remained firmly closed.

The European marketing manager knew she had a problem, but the US corporate HQ had already mandated a specific approach, prescribed the agencies and media that were to be used and set the budgets accordingly. The marketing manager went out on a limb and asked, not for new budget, but to spend her allocated budget in a different way. A UK pilot project was approved.

The scope of the pilot was defined as the top 300 firms, across all sectors, in the UK. The results proved to be critical in forming a revised go-to-market strategy for the firm. It identified that CIOs are influenced by a completely separate ecosystem to that for mid-managers and technical specialists. The modern CIO has little time to care about technology specifics – they care instead about service to the business. So they read business newspapers, not technical journals. They talk to top-tier consulting firms, not lower level resellers and niche consultancies. Blogs were unimportant as few CIOs have the time to filter the few useful insights from the vast quantity of rubbish.

There were major differences in *how* CIOs were influenced too: CIOs don't have the time to go to events, so the few conferences and trade shows that made it into the top 50 influencers proved to be low down the ranks. But they are attracted by exclusive CIO clubs and forums that deal specifically with CIO-level issues.

Importantly, the firm discovered that several of its target market's key influencers were senior executives at competitor organisations. Worse, the top systems integrators were also partnering with competitors. So the project, even at its most basic, focused attention on a serious competitive threat.

While the projects results were sinking in, the firm, led by the marketing manager, reached an important conclusion. The results confirmed their fear that they didn't know who was influencing their core audience. But the research had identified a way to rectify this by using influencers as a route to market. Projects were then commissioned for Germany and France.

Although they expected some local players to emerge, the firm expected a reasonable overlap between influencers in the UK and those in France and Germany. Most of the analysts covering their space have a European brief, though most are based in the UK. And the top-tier consultants – they would be the same, wouldn't they?

But the French like to speak in French, and Germans in German. Influence, it turns out, is a local game and if you can't speak the local language it's hard to influence, especially time-poor CIOs of large organisations. Although the influential companies were similar, the individual partners or analysts or practice leaders were all different.

The marketing manager now feels vindicated in her approach, and the risk is paying off in terms of credibility and visibility within corporate HQ. More importantly, the CIO audience is listening. They're listening to influencers, but the influencers are talking about the firm.

Note and reference

1 Based on our own observations, *The Tipping Point* and *The Influentials*.

6

Who are your influencers?

Here we analyse what we mean by influence, how an influencer influences and we outline the most common influencer categories within an organisation.

What is influence?

Influence can be broadly defined as the power to affect a person, thing or course of events. Influence manifests itself in many ways, from direct purchase advice to subtle shifts in perception of a vendor's credibility. Influence can be the action of creating an environment conducive to affecting another person's opinion on a particular issue. And in business that's very important. The ability of one person to 'win over' another is not only one of the most valuable skills possible in a salesperson, but also in any position of leadership, whether in business, politics, sport or entertainment.

In this book we're looking at how to identify, interpret and benefit from influencers on business decision-making. Those are the people who, often from behind the scenes, pull the strings of the eventual cheque signer in order to sway their opinion, and therefore their decision.

When it comes to business purchase decisions, power rests with many different types of individuals including consultants, management gurus, partners, distributors, trade association executives, financiers, industry authorities and numerous others.

So what makes an influencer?

We define an influencer as follows:

> A third-party who significantly shapes the customer's purchasing decision, but may ever be accountable for it.

Is it how well connected they are in social or business networks? Is it their status or job responsibility? Is it their force of personality, their deep subject knowledge or maybe just a case of right time right place? It can be one or a combination of these. There is no formula to follow.

How influencers influence your prospects

Influencers influence in many different ways, sometimes at the emotional level ('You want to overspec this project five-fold – you can't afford this one to fail!'), sometimes at the regulatory level ('You need the auditors' sign-off at every stage of this project – get their name on every decision'), sometimes at the strategic level ('Now that we're a public company we need to be seen to be partnering with the right kind of people – get Accenture to oversee this'). There can clearly be many other pressures – those that are tactical, résumé-minded, fuelled by internal politics, cost-based, etc.

For some, influence occurs mainly in 1-to-1 situations, which are barely visible to the outside world. For others, such as high profile CEOs and conference speakers, their influence is predominantly in front of large groups. Journalists, industry analysts and financial analysts don't even need to leave their desks to wield their influence. There is no set pattern to how influencers influence: what we do believe is that those with greatest influence are individuals enjoying an independent, direct, and usually face-to-face, relationship with the end-user purchasing company.

Our focus for this book is not how influence happens, but who
has it and what they do with it. And our research indicates that
when asked "Who are your influencers?" most marketers have no
idea.

Can you guess your influencers?

There are two ways to identify influencers. The first is to guess. So here's
our challenge. Choose a target market segment that you use today, and
write down the top 50 people that are currently impacting buying decisions in your favour. The top 50! Okay, let's make it easier – write down
just the top 10 influencers on your market.

So that you understand the complexity of the task, here are a few
pointers:

- You need to be certain that the name you choose has influence over
  buying decisions, and not simply high level commentary on market
  conditions. So picking Bill Gates, Warren Buffet or Sir Terry Leahy
  doesn't count.
- It's too easy to pick the CEO at a firm whom you believe to be influential.
  It's more likely that a feet-on-the-street consultant has more influencer
  over buyers.
- You'll need to assess whether blogs are very important, background noise or in between. And you'll have to pick the bloggers
  that have most influence with decision-makers, not just with other
  bloggers.

Oh, and you must be specific about which product or service line you
are considering, and the segment of prospects you're targeting. There's no
point in identifying influencers on selling tractors to farmers if you want to
sell bulldozers to builders (even though your company may make both
products).

The next step is to get a colleague to repeat the exercise, in secret, and
then compare the results. Are your lists close, or miles apart? How do you
know which list is more accurate?

The alternative method, and the only reliable way (as far as we know)
of identifying your influencers, is to conduct an in-depth market research
exercise. In other words, in order to establish who influences a community of decision-makers, you've got to ask those decision-makers. It is

therefore critical to understand exactly what community you're looking at. This is all to do with market segmentation. For example, the set of influencers for the retail banking segment is different to that for the local government segment. There may be overlaps, but unless you do the research you'll never know whether the overlap is 10 per cent or 90 per cent.

Ideally, you should narrow the segment even further. If you're selling insurance you'll have different influencers to those if you're selling mortgages. If you are a multi-product firm, you'll have a different set of influencers for each product, in each industry sector, each country and so on. Segmentation is a dark art, and you'll intuitively know what makes sense for your market.

Why is identifying influencers difficult?

Asked to write down the names of the top influencers in their market most marketers are hard pressed. So try this instead: think of the people you would write to, not including prospective customers, to promote your company if you only had 50 letterheads left. Most people might name politicians, journalists and industry associations. The smartest suggest writing to their existing customers, for these people can be truly influential in generating new business.

We've tried this exercise with over 100 business executives. What is striking is that the top three influencers suggested by the managing director typically have no overlap with those from the head of sales or from the head of marketing. Only recently we met with an extremely senior, very experienced manager in a world-famous company and asked who he imagined his customers' influencers were. He's an honest man. He didn't even guess. He admitted he had no idea.

What is also obvious is that most people have never even thought about the question before. The experienced manager had spent many years as a very successful salesperson, which no doubt involved countless evenings poring over wall maps of his major prospects' organisation charts and hierarchies. In these, he was identifying the product champions, the human barriers and the inter-departmental politics that affected his chances of a successful sale. And within them, he was identifying some influencers, though perhaps only in a linear hierarchical way. But developing a marketing programme aimed specifically at these influencers had never occurred to him.

It rarely occurs to anyone.

Recent changes in influencers

Though the web has unquestionably changed almost every facet of business, it's what's known as Web 2.0 that has radically changed the influencer landscape. Web 2.0 involves social networking tools such as MySpace and Facebook, along with user-generated content sites such as YouTube. Just as Web 1.0 announced the arrival of online shopfronts and e-commerce sites such as Amazon, LastMinute and eBay, so Web 2.0 has brought the new wave of interactive sites, wikis and blogs that have torn down the former distinctions between who was the publisher and who was the consumer. And it's affected the influencer landscape because it's further dismantled the notion that the influence of a person is directly related to the title on their business card. Time Magazine's 'Person of the Year' in 2006 was 'You, the User', emphasising how the understanding of who has power and who does not has been irrevocably changed. Not withstanding the continuing global 'digital divide', the ability for individuals to express their opinions and to be heard by anyone interested in listening has now undoubtedly arrived. And corporations, much as some have tried, have been powerless to stop it.

The result is that feedback on the success or otherwise of an expensive product launch, a strategic IT installation or a new consumer service is no longer guaranteed to be through an approved company publicist towing the company line, but as likely from an anonymous mid-ranking individual intent on telling the warts'n'all truth. Suddenly that mid-ranking manager has become extremely influential to decisions being made at rival firms. It's a radical departure from the traditional understanding of 'top-down' influence.

The 'top-down' effect is now indistinguishable from the 'bottom-up' approach

It used to be the case that you could either communicate to a few really senior people, and they had the power to communicate to the wider community, or you could go mainstream and communicate to the mass public, predominantly through national advertising. The former could be phenomenally effective, but it depended largely on whether you had a message worthy of such select attention. Let's be honest. Few have such a message. The latter could be effective, and the quality of the message was less critical, but it required phenomenal budgets. In recent times a third option has emerged, the 'bottom-up' approach, as delivered by YouTube,

MySpace and others – individual, user-driven content – negligible cost, the quality of the message all important, and through the web, capable of almost instant, global attention.

We all now have a voice

We've become a race of far more independent thinkers than we previously were. Hundreds of years ago it was commonly accepted that there were 'advanced thinkers' who simply had greater, almost divine, rights to knowledge and opinions than everyday folk – think church leaders, royalty, heads of wealthy families, etc. Fifty years ago individuals, while privately querying the official views, would willingly go along with the verdicts of those more socially powerful than them.

This was the case even 20 and 30 years ago for consumers across the world. Whether it was in the entertainment field where we were fed a regular stream of untouchable cinema stars, or calendar-based TV programming, or government-approved radio stations, we accepted that others in power could decide when and what we could relate to. In industry, small businesses used to accept that they were treated as second-class customers to the big corporate names, and as such could not enjoy the same favourable buying terms. That has changed too. In short, we agreed to accept certain conditions, certain terms, certain expectations, without complaint. If a critic of a company wasn't an employee of a major company, or a journalist wasn't from a major publication, their voice carried little weight. They had no ability to amplify. Today they do. Two decades of increasing autonomy and individuals can now negotiate more persuasively with industry giants than ever before. We all now have a voice. We all now expect to be special.

Today, the background, location and age of individual influencers is less predictable, meaning that companies looking to work with them cannot expect to apply a 'one size fits all' approach. Just as Peppers' and Rogers' 1994 book *1-to-1 Marketing* was intended to show companies how they could individually target sales prospects, so now the same principles can be held for forging relationships with influencing purchasing decision-makers. 1-to-1 is the only approach that influencers will now accept. We need to get used to that.

This means that scale has become an issue. How can we scale to reach all of the influencers in a market? In fact, in anyone B2B market segment there are relatively few influencers, perhaps 150. Of those, perhaps 50 are particularly influential and worth targeting. Importantly, identify influencers is just one step: for ranking them into 'tiers' is also critical.

Who are the 'new' influencers?

In our research experience there are over 20 types of influencer that now impact corporate purchasing. Of course, these categories have always existed in their own right. However it's the recognition of their influence, and the need to address them directly as part of any company's marketing outreach, that is new. These include:

- Competing suppliers
- Business and trade journalists
- Top-tier management consultancies
- Second tier consultancies

- Individual and niche consultants
- Systems integrators

- VARs (value-added resellers), distributors and other channel partners
- Online forums and blogs
- Consumers and consumer groups
- Commentators and other individuals
- Buyers groups, purchasing lists and procurement authorities
- Financial analysts

- Customer firms
- Conferences and events
- Authors and management thinkers
- Government agencies and regulators
- Standards bodies
- Venture capitalists and financiers
- Industry bodies, forums and federations

- Retailers
- Academia

- Complementary partner brands

- Industry analysts

- Internal influencers

The make-up of influencer communities differs in each market sector. Sub-$100 consumer products exhibit a very different influencer model than that for a professional services firm for instance. Here are 15 of the most common influencer categories.

Suppliers

Suppliers are often the loudest voices in a market, after all they have the largest vested interest. It is rare however for a representative of a supplier firm to be the most influential person in a market. A rule of thumb says that unless a supplier commands a greater than 40 per cent share of a market, they won't be the prime influencer on that sector. And few suppliers or vendors enjoy that kind of dominance. Suppliers typically exert their influence through constant bombardment of direct mail, frequent public speaking roles, proactive sales calls and omnipresence in the relevant trade articles and analyst reports.

But vendors are inherently (and understandably) biased in their messaging and decision-makers look for ways to neutralise this. Alternative vendors will be asked to bid for work, if only to create a sense of balance, and a variety of third party opinions will be sought. Decision-makers therefore have a tendency to balance any vendor influence by involving other influencers as a counter-measure.

Industry analysts

In the business and technology markets, Gartner is simply the most influential organisation on the planet. It's not just the largest analyst firm, it's four times larger than the second player, Forrester Research. But that doesn't tell the whole story. According to Knowledge Capital Group there are three types of analyst firms – Deal makers and breakers (DMBs) like Gartner and Forrester, with reputations that truly influence major corporate decisions. Then there are Point Players, like AMR and Tower Group, who specialise in specific markets, and finally AFHs. No firm likes to consider itself in this category, but historically it has included those firms that have made themselves available to be commissioned to write 'objective' papers on behalf of vendor clients.

Geographically, the analyst picture differs markedly, with only Gartner strong in every territory.

We discuss industry analysts more fully in Chapter 10.

Business and trade journalists

The publishing world has fragmented over the past decade, with a trend away from a few dominant print-only titles to a broader spread of highly focused vertically integrated brands encompassing online title, interactive site, associated user group and exhibition/conference.

For strategic and/or high-value decisions, the top-tier business press, primarily the *Financial Times* and *The Wall Street Journal*, dominate. At the other end of the scale, the most influential print titles are where product reviews are prominent. For instance, the camera, consumer PC and gaming titles exert enormous influence in both short-listing models for consideration.

Top-tier management consultancies

While every business vendor aims for a close relationship with Accenture, few achieve it. The consultancy is notoriously difficult to partner with, frequently moves its management staff around and puts little effort into opening itself up to third parties. Although perhaps the best-known name, Accenture doesn't dominate its market in the way that Gartner does, and the other top-tier horizontal players (in professional services – Ernst & Young, KPMG, PwC and Deloitte, and in integration – IBM and EDS) receive far less attention and often prove easier to approach. Each firm has differently rated specialist groups, such that one may well be the most influential in one field, whereas another will be the clear leader in a neighbouring specialty. Vendors rarely allocate a single executive to forge relationships with these top-tier consultancies, with the result that relationships are sporadic and tactical. A mistake in our opinion.

Second-tier consultancies

These people are criminally underrated. The top players each have their specialist areas of expertise, such as Telecoms or Public Sector, and within these often have greater influence than the top-tier firms. Yet they're structured with a partnering attitude, their client relationships are second to none and the value of their contracts is increasing dramatically. Five years ago a prime annual contract value for a second-tier firm was $6–10 million. Today it's $30–50 million. Their secret is to bring in people with extensive knowledge of, and senior contacts in, a few key vertical sectors, and then go deep rather than wide within these. We see the second-tier only getting stronger.

Aside from these vertically oriented firms, there remain a few horizontal consulting firms, such as PA Consulting, who are rarely covered in the media, don't have the breadth of the top-tier players, but year after year walk off with more industry awards for their client commissions than every other firm.

Systems integrators

Once more, most vendors think only of IBM Business Services and EDS when it comes to Integrators, and while IBM is ubiquitous in most enterprises, EDS's European coverage is much more patchy, especially on a vertical basis. Time and again our research has shown that the next tier of firms – CSC, Fujitsu and others – hold significant influence within many of the largest corporations. And it's the executives from these firms who best network at corporate user forums, speak at industry events, show strategic thought leadership and assemble the most creative solutions for their clients.

Online forums and blogs

Everybody wants to know about the significance of blogs. While it's clear their role is increasing, they're still nowhere near as influential in board-room decision-making as the blogosphere would have you believe. In fact, only in our recent US research, in the sales and marketing space, have blogs been at all influential on decisions. They're currently mostly used as mouthpieces for individuals who would like to be influential but aren't, or by those who are influential primarily through other vehicles.

Blogs can be influential, but their influence tends to be specific and short-reaching. The more technical the subject, and the younger the audience demographic, the greater the influence.

See Chapters 15 and 16 for a deeper discussion of blogs and other social media.

Online forums are a completely separate issue, and categorically are influential already. In some sectors it's the online forums that have taken the place of the traditional annual conference as a place to chat with peers, search through industry resources, catch up with industry news and see demos of the latest products. Forums such as Church of the Customer and John Jantsch's excellent Duct Tape Marketing have become indispensable sites for US marketers, and their popularity has in turn further built the personal influence of their founders.

Speaker platforms – conferences and seminars

Ten years ago speaker platforms were largely the domain of vendor salespeople pitching their latest product to anyone who would listen. Declining delegate attendance led to conference organisers reconsider-ing the structure and content of their events and led to the rise of user-led content. Moving away from paid-for speaker slots to subsidise free attendance, and towards highly targeted high-paying user delegates, speakers are now increasingly vetted for end-user appeal and so those that do qualify speak to prospects very willing to believe. End-users routinely acknowledge that their opinions on particular vendors and technologies have been shaped through speeches they attended.

In fact, the majority of conferences are still funded largely by vendor sponsorship, which is a major factor in why they lack influence. It is where they are delegate financed that they gain credibility. The Gartner Symposium is a rare example of an event exhibiting high influence, to a senior audience, while accepting a level of vendor sponsorship.

Exhibitions and shows

Every industry fondly remembers the days when one or two large-scale exhibitions in its calendar year-after-year would bring together all of the individuals and personalities within that sector. Yet as more and more industry sectors become vertically integrated, so there are fewer events relevant to the entire supply chain. The level of attendee has also declined and today, exhibitions are less about networking and more about enticing the business cards out of the attendees' pockets. Attending these events as an exhibitor is expensive, time-consuming and unlikely to generate short-term sales. Companies often attend only because their competitors do. Once in a while an exhibitor gets lucky and is in the right place at the right time to meet a serious prospect. But exhibitions remain an expensive, high-risk activity for most suppliers in an industry. There is little evidence to show that influencers regularly attend.

Individual consultants

Individual consultants fall into two categories for us – those with high influence and those with none. Often there is no obvious way of telling one from the other. Most individual consultants operate on a local basis, often specifying one particular vendor's services or products simply because they enjoy a closer relationship there. They exert little influence beyond their immediate small- to mid-sized clients. But we often uncover individuals whose influence is anything but small, and their client-base is often a number of Times1000 companies.

Authors and management thinkers

You wouldn't imagine that book writers yield much personal influence, but time and again our research shows they do. In some cases this is through the impact of the book alone but more commonly because of the platform their book provides for their other activities, whether as a consultant, a management thinker, a journalist or whatever. Sometimes even a vendor. We have plenty of examples of online forums, newsletter publishers and event organisers leaping in popularity once their associated book becomes the de facto industry bible.

Examples include Geoffrey Moore, whose 1991 bestseller *Crossing the Chasm* has become the tech sector's marketing bible for almost 20 years. Tom Peters' *Searching for Excellence* book is even older and has paved the way for a lucrative career as an inspirational speaker ever since.

Buyers groups, purchasing lists and procurement authorities

Perhaps the least understood and acknowledged of any influencer category, a significant number of major organisations now outsource their business services purchasing to external purchasing groups. These evaluate the client's requirements, shortlist the beauty parade, conduct each round of negotiation and 'appoint' the winner. All too often vendor salespeople fruitlessly knock at the door of the end-user organisation, never knowing that the decision process is being made externally. And some of these purchasing groups are responsible for one purchase after another, vendors every time unaware of their involvement. Offen, the procurement professional works in its client' offices, making it even more difficult to differentiate between special experts and the firm's own staff. Such groups are particularly prominent in the public sector, in heavy industry and in construction.

We once asked a client's sales force what percentage of their client and prospect-base operated a formally approved purchasing list of suppliers. The response amongst the twenty salespeople averaged 22 per cent. Over a 3-month period we surveyed almost 300 of their clients and prospects, and found the figure was actually 47 per cent. So for one in every four prospect calls made by that company over the past year there was no chance of ever securing a sale, because their company wasn't part of an official, but unknown, approved supplier list. Think of how much time and resource had been wasted.

Industry bodies and federations

In some sectors these are all but irrelevant, an amateur talking shop for a few industry stragglers. In others they are central to the entire marketplace, with every major player a member, every senior executive on its steering committee and the organiser of the industry's annual networking event. It's important not to blindly disregard them.

Channel players

Channel players is an umbrella title for a vast range of influencers, dependent on the particular routes to market employed. These can range from the traditional VARs through to distribution wholesalers through to high street retailers. And there are several levels of influencer within the retailer itself – for instance, the buying directors at Best Buy and Currys yield enormous influence on what consumers will be able to buy in a store, and those who head its online promotions impact which suppliers are most heavily promoted. While consumers may undertake many weeks of online and print research into which brand or product to buy, all of that research can be thrown away in a minute if the 17-year-old shopworker persuades the customer that an alternative manufacturer offers a better value solution. Very often it's among the lowest paid employees in any retail organisation, the part-time Saturday staff, who collectively hold enormous influence on consumer buying behaviour.

In the B2B sector there are a number of hugely important VARs and OEMs (original equipment manufacturers). These are fundamental to the supply chain in many sectors, and top influencers frequently lie within each.

See Chapter 10, and supply chain influencers in Chapter 18, for further discussion on channel players.

Complementary partner brands

A firm's sales can multiply overnight if their product is included in a successful complementary brand promotion. 'Buy an Orange phone and receive free local cinema tickets for the next month' allegedly multiplied sales of Vue cinema merchandise (mostly refreshments) by 300 per cent for the 6 months of the promotion. So the most influential individual on Vue sales during that period was probably the marketing director of Orange! That could hardly have been predicted.

Some consider the influence of complementary brands to be little more than through discount promotion offers. But if they have the power to influence, however they do that, they're worth considering.

Academics

Particularly in the tech, biochem, pharmaceutical and medical professions, the role of specific academics can be extremely influential. Not only do some academic institutions play a prominent part in the day-to-day fabric of some sectors, but the major vendors lean heavily on their academic links in order to leverage the kudos of perceived thought leaders. Yet academics are rarely even considered by sales or marketing staff as having any effect on a company's prospects. They're often wrong. Academics have been proven at times to be heavily influential.

Rounding up

There are many other influencer categories worth considering, too many for us to detail here. In many industry sectors, the roles of regulators are essential influencers, especially in highly regulated industries such as finance, pharmaceuticals and telecoms, and they are becoming more so in other sectors because of increasing 'green' concerns (automotive, retail and logistics).

Less so in Europe, but particularly highly in the US, venture capitalists (VCs), whether individuals or whole firms, can be significantly influential to a company's prospects. They too need to be considered. Marketing departments typically have next to zero involvement with VC firms. The VCs like it that way.

Once any company acknowledges the breadth and importance of its influencers, and determines to engage with them in a professional manner, they break the habit of the traditional marketing mix and begin to allocate their marketing spend in line with those that make purchase decisions. It's a seismic change to the way that marketing is actioned right now.

Mapping influencer roles onto influencer categories

In the table below we map each influencer category onto the roles that we introduced in Chapter 5. Note, however, that there are no absolutes, and potentially any influencer could play any role. We've illustrated the mapping to show how different influencers are *likely to* influence a decision process, but you should check this out with your own influencers.

Don't be tempted just to add up the ticks and conclude that analysts are the most influential type or that academics can be disregarded. The table shows where types of influencer may be influential, so it identifies the places where analysts might have an impact. In fact, decision-makers are smart people, and they spread their risk. So if an analyst is used early in the decision-making process, they are less likely to appear at the end.

	Idea planters	Predictors	Trend setters	Proclaimers	Aggregators/communicators	Scopers	Recommenders	Persuaders	Negotiators	Validators
Academia	✓									
Authors and management thinkers	✓	✓								
Business and trade journalists					✓					
Buyers groups, purchasing lists and procurement authorities				✓	✓		✓		✓	
Commentators and other individuals				✓	✓					
Competing vendors	✓					✓		✓		
Complementary partner brands										
Conferences and events					✓	✓				
Consumers and consumer groups			✓		✓	✓	✓			
Customer organisations			✓			✓				✓
Financial analysts				✓						
Government agencies and regulators				✓	✓				✓	
Individual consultants						✓	✓	✓		✓
Industry analysts		✓		✓	✓	✓	✓		✓	✓
Industry bodies, forums and federations				✓	✓					
Internal influencers										
Niche consultancies						✓	✓	✓		✓
Online forums and blogs	✓	✓	✓		✓					
Retailers										
Standards bodies				✓			✓		✓	
Systems integrators						✓	✓	✓		
Top-tier management consultancies						✓	✓	✓		✓
VARs, distributors and other channel partners							✓	✓		
Venture capitalists and financiers	✓	✓	✓							

Key points in this chapter

1. There are multiple categories of influencer, which makes it extremely difficult to guess who might be influential, and to what extent, in a specific market. The difference in perspectives between sales, marketing, product development and other operational functions increases the danger in assuming the set of influencers.
2. A further degree of fragmentation has emerged due to Web 2.0 technologies. This means that influence is no longer the preserve of an elite, but can also bubble from the bottom up. The background, location and age of individual influencers is unpredictable, meaning that companies looking to work with them cannot expect to apply a 'one size fits all' approach.
3. The influencer categories we identify can map onto various influencer roles. But the mapping is indicative, not absolute. There are always exceptions, so understand your influencers well.

Case Study D – PalmSource

Tapping into the influence of enthusiasts

PalmSource develops and licenses the operating system (OS) software used in Palm smartphones and numerous other mobile devices. PalmSource is primarily an engineering services and licensing company, with very little budget available for marketing initiatives; however it needed to increase the awareness of its product benefits.

More than 20 000 third party software products are available for Palm devices, but most people were unaware of those applications or assumed they were just games. The company had a rich supply of vertical-market applications tailored to the needs of customers in a wide array of professions and interest groups. PalmSource knew that when customers were educated about the software they were much more likely to buy, and device manufacturers were much more likely to license the OS.

But PalmSource didn't have the resources to document all the verticals and applications, let alone mount marketing campaigns in each of them.

To solve this problem, PalmSource partnered with enthusiastic users in the Palm OS community to document and publicise the applications base. Volunteers wrote extensive guides to the software available in their vertical industries, including descriptions of the software, recommendations on which applications to use, links to online resources for more information and user stories.

These 'Expert Guides' were published on the PalmSource website, and were promoted heavily through press releases, speeches, weblogs, user groups and other websites. The total cost of the programme was approximately $2500 per quarter, plus approximately one person-day a week of staff time.

There were four stages in the project:

1. Setup. PalmSource created a document template for the development of an Expert Guide, and also created an instruction manual for contributors. These guide authors were allowed to identify themselves online, and the status of being a recognised 'expert' was a primary motivation for the authors. They were also paid a $50 amazon.com gift certificate every quarter for writing and updating their guides.
2. Recruitment. PalmSource spread the word that it was seeking authors, by sending announcements to user groups and Palm-related websites. Potential authors were directed to an online form asking them to describe their desired topic, their qualifications and to give samples of their writing. There were several hundred volunteers.
3. Creation of guides. Authors completed the templates, and content was reviewed by a PalmSource employee for grammar and clarity of language. PalmSource also created a legal disclaimer making clear that the guide authors were solely responsible for their opinions. Some of the guides were very extensive, with close to 100 applications listed, and numerous user stories. When printed, the largest guides totalled more than 20 pages each.
4. Rollout. PalmSource launched the Expert Guide website through a press release and announcements to Palm OS websites. The guides were also printed and used as education tools for reporters. PalmSource used the guides in discussions with potential licensees – a printout of all the guides filled a large binder. The volume of information was very impressive to partners.

The Expert Guides programme demonstrates that it is possible to work with volunteers to create very large pieces of collateral, tackle vertical markets that could not be reached affordably in other ways and spread marketing information online at very low cost.

Providing public recognition to expert users is a very powerful motivator for volunteer work. When supplemented by a small cash payment, it was very effective at getting volunteers to not only create information, but also keep it up to date over time.

The Expert Guides are still available online at: http://www.access-company.com/support/expertguides/index.html (© Rubicon Consulting 2007)

7

Identifying and ranking influencers

How can influencers be ranked against each other? What metrics exist? How can the importance of one influencer be compared with another in a very different job role?

Measuring influence

There are a great many papers on how influence can and should be measured. Suffice to say that because humans are involved, it's destined to be subjective rather than objective measurement. But so long as it's consistently applied, we don't see that that's such a problem. Keller and Berry's great text *The Influentials* addresses measurement at length, though in a social context.

One thing is clear, 'loudness' is no indicator of 'influence'. Many is the time that marketers have assumed that the most prominent voice in their sector is therefore the most influential. Far from it. The real decision-makers know that power is less 'share of voice' and more 'force of persuasion', that the most influential people are often behind the scenes, pulling the strings, the 'kingmakers'. They are not the ones usually singing their own praises. Because a journalist writes frequently on a subject, because a reseller specialises in just one product line, because an advisory firm has a narrow area of expertise, doesn't necessarily make any of them the most influential. Knowledge helps, but even that is not the key factor. Influence is too complex to be based on any single attribute.

Comparing influencers from different categories

How can an influencer from one category such as journalists, be compared with another, say, formal purchasing groups? It's a good question. In many ways of course they can't. They conduct their business in such different ways, with such different intentions, interacting with such different people, that it can seem pointless to try and compare. Until you consider that we're not suggesting that you compare their activities at all. We're comparing their likely *effect* on the decision-maker. How far we believe their views have the power to move a decision along the scale, away from selecting one supplier and towards the selection of another. In no way are we judging their validity in the process. Some categories will naturally score much higher on certain criteria than others, regardless of the individual merits of each person. We trust that using multiple criteria to measure influence will balance out such anomalies.

An early attempt at measurement criteria

Our own company currently operates a four-dimension metric for this purpose, though we're investigating a more sophisticated six-dimension one. All those individuals, companies and events initially considered as potential influencers are termed Players. Our original four-dimension metric comprised:

- Market Reach
- Frequency of Impact
- Quality of Impact
- Closeness to Decision

Let's review the central four dimensions in turn.

Market Reach

Market Reach, the 'clout' that that Player enjoys in their particular marketplace. Remember the old Zen quote about 'If a tree falls in a forest but no-one hears it, does it really fall?'. There's no point in having a credible opinion on a subject if no one hears you. So Market Reach is an important factor, a measure of awareness. How well-known, well thought of, how prominent is that firm or individual? How 'out there' in the market, ensuring its views are heard? Sometimes the Market Reach relates primarily to the employing organisation – Microsoft, Accenture, Starbucks or whoever, and sometimes the Reach is of the individual themselves. Having the support of a major brand certainly helps, but many times our client-commissioned research has highlighted individuals not employed by a major organisation to be in the very highest tier of market influencers.

We reviewed whether to separate the level of Market Reach due to the organisation, and make this distinct from that of the individual themselves, but complications soon arise with that approach. It also becomes a particularly subjective decision, and we prefer to stay clear of those as far as possible. We intend our research methodologies to be scaleable, allowing them to work globally across many varied clients, and subjective decisions are rarely scaleable. The constituents that contribute towards Market Reach include market leadership, brand strength, longevity or dynamism as a leader, organisation size and strength of outreach activities.

Frequency of Impact

How often is Player's voice is likely to be heard by prospective decision-makers. As mentioned earlier, this can be very different from how frequently they open their mouth on the subject. For example, journalists can write often about a particular subject, but if their copy is rarely seen at the influencer level, their frequency of impact is low. Similarly, some of the most oft-quoted industry analysts appear in publications that are not read by those influencing at the decision-maker level. Others may be rarely referenced, but whenever they are, it is at the most influential levels. It is the frequency of impact, not frequency of effort, that we are measuring. That's why blogging is taking time to appear in Decision-maker Ecosystems.

Some influencers influence on an even year-round basis while others are seasonal or event-based. A conference or trade show is a perfect example here. It impacts just once a year, but when it does, its influence may be significant. In the UK, whole industry sales cycles are based around the National Boat Show, the Car Show or the Chelsea Flower Show. Sales of products in these categories may jump 200 per cent in the one month immediately afterwards. Their significance is immense. These would rate lowly on our 'frequency' metric (but may score highly on other dimensions).

Quality of Impact

How independent and authoritative is that Player's opinion? The opinion or verdict of a regulator may be final, such that the 'quality' of their impact is peerless. In real terms their decisions cannot be questioned. With the rise of end-user feedback, the quality of impact of online user reviews on Amazon.com for example is high, especially because there tends to be multiple consecutive reviews on which to consult, rather than isolated opinions. This allows the viewer to 'weed out' the most extreme rants and trust the median. As readers we believe the reviewer has no political or sales agenda in publicising their views and we feel kinship with them as both 'innocent purchasers'. A strange thought considering we have never met them!

Conversely, our trust in the views of the manufacturer has never been lower. Not unnaturally, we presume they will focus only on the product or service strengths, and not the actual end-user experience. It is also in their interests for them to persuade us of what features, specifications or capabilities should be most important to us, and therefore, should affect our eventual buying choice. How often have we all bought products largely on its stated performance on a particular criteria, only then to never use that aspect of it. The sales or advertising talk has successfully moved the purchasing goalposts. It's a short-term win for sales, but an ongoing loss for manufacturer credibility.

Rarely do we rate manufacturers, or those directly in the sales channel, any higher than mid-range in Quality of Impact. Occasionally, a market sector has been so over-sold to, so over-commoditised, that it is hard for any manufacturers to rise above poor on this scale. In contrast to this, those with the most independence on the eventual purchasing choice tend to receive higher ratings here. Industry forums (whether real-world or online), educational institutions and those from academia, and in some sectors the role of Quangos are all considered to yield high-quality impact.

Closeness to Decision

How close in terms of both timing and physical presence is that Player to the eventual cheque authoriser? As we mentioned earlier, this can be comprised of two distinct metrics, and so we have sought recently to separate them. But as it stands, 'closeness' refers to how close in proximity terms is the Player in question to the decision-maker, or how close in their *timing* is the influencer's opinion heard relative to the final decision being made. If the influencer is heard in the early stages of the evaluation process then they may be able to shape the eventual shortlist and selection criteria. If their opinion is heard in the final stages, then their view may be a deciding one and may merit a higher rating. A further complication arises with certain influencers when their actions and opinions are aired either sporadically in an ad hoc fashion throughout the decision-making process, or uniformly, perhaps as part of a formally documented process.

Combining the criteria

It is a simple formula but a complex set of criteria. Typically, we weight all four criteria equally, though this is a subjective decision. You may decide that in your particular market sector, 'Closeness to Decision' is significantly more important than say 'Frequency of Impact' and so opt to weight accordingly. We've discussed weighting many many times with clients and to date not one has been adamant enough on the subject to require differentiated weighting. In fact, we think the exact ordering of the Players is a side issue compared to the significance of understanding for the first time just how disparate their roles are.

By taking into account the four influencer dimensions we can see how categories of influencer might rise up the rankings.

For example:

- Top-tier management consultancies, authors and management thinkers, and conferences will typically have high Market Reach
- Regulators, standards bodies and academics will enjoy high Quality of Impact
- Journalists and analysts, and some blogs, will exhibit a high Frequency of Impact
- Individual consultants, procurement authorities and systems integrators will often score highly on Closeness to Decision.

The influencer dimensions also explain how competing vendors can influence their own markets, by virtue of their relative market awareness (Market Reach, Frequency of Impact), thought leadership (Quality of Impact) and sales processes (Closeness to Decision). The dimensions also demonstrate the importance of customer referral programmes. The Quality of Impact of an organisation that has implemented a new process or technology will surpass the influence of an analyst who lacks the hands-on experience that CxOs crave.

Expanding the dimensions

We constantly feel the need to develop our thinking on influence metrics because several criteria have become blurred – 'Closeness to Decision' could be considered a chronological rather than physical proximity measurement, and 'Quality of Impact' is partly a measure of independence and partly a measure of 'thoroughness' or 'completeness' of impact. As our clients became more and more granular on such matters we have reviewed this measurement. We have recently added, and are now testing, 'thoroughness' as measured by 'continuity of Player involvement' and 'Stage of Impact' – whether a Player impacts during the earliest stages, as the project in question may be being scoped or evaluated; during the middle stages, as the review process gets underway through specification setting and supplier shortlisting, through to late stage, where a Player can influence the eventual choice at the 11th hour. It's an important evolution when understanding the purchasing process and we believe a significant development when evaluating the degree of influence enjoyed by each Player.

Our most recent thinking on improving the objectivity of our measurement contains two elements. We'll split two dimensions – 'Closeness to Decision' and 'Quality of Impact' – into four, thereby removing the degree of duality and ambiguity that they contain. And we'll provide our research teams with more structured grids for each of the criteria, once more further improving our scaleability. In a bid to boost our accuracy still further, we have even thought about opening up our criteria online using a wiki, encouraging those far outside our own company, but within the relevant industry sectors, to contribute their opinions and ratings. The model adopted by the founders of Wikipedia, one largely of public editing and self-policing but with an appointed overarching 'standards' committee, has we think huge ramifications for a great many fields, not least our own. But we are at the earliest stages of where this thinking will lead us.

One criteria we continually look at is 'Level of Expertise'. To many this should be a fundamental in our scoring, but there are also many counter arguments. In a logical society, decision-makers, whether in business or in their social lives, would seek out the opinions of those with maximum expertise in the subject matter. So long as these people made their expertise aware to people, then they would naturally become the most sought-after advisors. We obviously don't live in an entirely logical society, because time and time again in our work for clients we see examples where this hasn't happened.

The most common reason seems to be company politics and infrastructure issues – where say Bob with 35 years experience of dealing with customer support issues isn't part of the DME because he no longer works in that department, because there isn't time to bring him up to speed and keep him involved, because 'he won't understand the business issues involved', because his knowledge may not be up-to-date, because it's too difficult to get his boss to release him, or whatever. Companies sometimes seem to erect as many barriers as possible to stop in-house expertise from benefiting others throughout the organisation. The result is that there are often duplicated learning paths within DMEs.

This occurs less often with external organisations – consultancies, marketing agencies, etc., where there is a greater skills matrix outlook. Those with the best experience in a particular field are more easily made available, even if they work within different business units. It appears to be a philosophy at the very heart of many leading consultancy firms. The flipside from a career progression aspect may be that within a large organisation, Bob, with his 35 years customer support experience, gets to migrate to a broader portfolio, whereas within a consultancy set-up, he is used time and time again within his narrow experience area. Whatever the merits, the end result is that we see 'Level of Expertise' as a clearer indicator of influence within professional services firms than in most end-user organisations.

It's easier to say No to some than others

As we mentioned earlier, we are also looking to analyse the degree to which opinions from certain influencer categories can be rejected or sidelined. We have high hopes we can integrate this into our methodology soon. Receive a press release informing you that a new car is being launched and it is easy to ignore. Especially if it doesn't fit with the current direction of your decision-making. See an advert on TV for it and once more it's easy to ignore. Receive a letter from your accountant informing you that this new car will save you considerable tax and it becomes more persuasive. The accountant's view is harder to ignore – at all sorts of levels.

Take this into a business setting. Imagine evaluating an office refit incorporating new desks and workstations. Colleagues from another department tell you that they've just installed the new desks and they're popular with the office workers. Reassuring advice but easy to ignore. Your building facilities manager recommends three other styles that they would approve of. More difficult to ignore because they have partial access to the budget. The CEO's PA tells you that undoubtedly one option is her favourite. She's a forthright lady. She has no official role in your decision-making, she doesn't have any access to the budget, but seeking her view, and then choosing something else, will not do you any favours with her. And she can heavily influence the CEO's view of you. She brings to your DME considerable political weight. You wish you'd never involved her.

When making strategic business decisions, the views of an industry analyst, however expensively acquired, can always be ignored. The views of your appointed management consultant less easily sidelined (because of the internal politics that are inevitably involved), but the opinions of the appointed systems integration firm, brought in to advise on a new IT business infrastructure, can rarely if ever be declined. In bringing in such a firm, the end-user company is effectively outsourcing the eventual decision, even though they retain the 'rubber-stamping' duty. Objecting to the SI firm's recommendations can be a 'make or break' for the relationship, and relationships at this level can be worth tens of millions of pounds to both sides. Some advisors, once appointed by a client, do not then take lightly to their views being questioned.

The difficulty of incorporating this 'persuasiveness' factor into our core criteria is largely because such firms advise at two very different stages: (1) at the open proposal stage where they have been invited in to competitive tender, where their views can easily be ignored, and (2) after they have been appointed where their views are given with the expectation of being accepted. Depending on which stage we would be measuring affects the criteria rating significantly. Until we have resolved this we cannot accurately measure it.

You can clearly add more criteria of your own. But we have to balance the thoroughness and credibility of our measurement with the reality of our task. Ours is an imprecise science, and our eventual rankings affect no one's life or death. At the time of writing we think that six objective criteria is an optimum number and we are expanding our research to this. If a Player would rank at number 32 using one set of criteria, and move to 39 using another then so be it. Far more important is the question of how to subsequently handle each Player, regardless of their exact position.

Some of you may decide to identify an influencer and then devise a way to measure their influence, rather than agree how to measure and then see who rates on that scale. If you choose the former, there's a real danger that you'll select people who you naturally assume are influencers, and then back-fit your measurement criteria to justify their inclusion. But we've also found that simply applying our criteria in a blanket fashion to a small group of people and then seeing who rates highest doesn't seem to reflect reality. The fact is that charisma, or at least 'personal magnetism', is an extremely strong influencer characteristic within small groups, yet one that's impossible to measure from afar.

Be realistic

So when evaluating influencers within your business prospects, we'd suggest you start with the four tried and tested criteria mentioned earlier. You should also be realistic. Many companies might suggest that George Bush, Gordon Brown or Bill Gates are the greatest influence on their customers, because of policies they do or don't support. This may well be true at a macro-economic level, but however innovative your marketing plan, you're unlikely to be able to measure its effect on the US President. Your influencers should not be so elevated that they are beyond the reach of your company. You'll simply be left disappointed, and you'll have established a business objective that you're destined to fail on. Rather than the UK Prime Minister, establishing a relationship with say a Minister within the National Health Service, or a backbench MP, is likely to yield far better and more measurable returns for your business.

Similarly, we've battled many times with the concept of 'actual' versus 'possible' influencers. Take *The Economist* magazine. Were *The Economist* to write an article let's say on 'The Rise of the Shopping Mall Beauty Clinic' then it would undoubtedly prove highly influential to anyone in that sector looking for investment, business partners, employees, well-to-do clients, etc. But to the best of our knowledge it hasn't. So the title has probably had zero effect on that marketplace to date. Should it still be considered influential? For the sake of practicality, we've come to the conclusion that if we think persuading *The Economist* to cover the subject within a year is a realistically achievable goal, then it's influential. This rule of thumb can be expanded to cover every influencer category. It's easy to set your horizons too low and discard any individual, company or event because to date they haven't impacted your sector. They could, and if they do, it's probably because a competitor encouraged them to. You would hate to be the one to realize this.

There is always the possibility of a wildcard entry into your market from left field. In 1998 the smart card industry was dominated by the card manufacturers like Gemplus (now Gemalto) and Schlumberger. Microsoft entered the market by offering an operating system and developers' kit, and became – overnight – one of the most influential firms in the market. Bill Gates himself launched the product and the market's great and good were flown to Seattle for an audience. In fact, the influence Microsoft wielded was generally negative on the market, as it caused many end-user organisations to stop any decision-making until Microsoft proved its ability (or rather inability) to deliver.

But there are many examples where the effect of a new entrant is positive, from a competition viewpoint. The entry of supermarkets into financial services is an example, where Tesco and others bring their efficient and detailed customer services approaches to the banking world, with great impact.

Influencers are individuals, not categories

We should add here a reminder that the influencers that we are identifying, and that we are encouraging you to work with, are individuals, not categories. It's an important point to remember. It is misleading to say, in whatever market you work, that 'analysts' are the top influencers, or 'resellers' or whomever. There are some individual analysts who are extremely influential and some who aren't. Some resellers who will be influential and probably a great many who won't be. It's not enough to identify a top-tier consultancy as an influencer – you have to identify the partner or practice leader that carries that influence to the market. You cannot look at a marketplace, decide that industry events are the most influential and so pour your marketing budget into them all – our research indicates that very few events are influential. Granularity and detail is vital.

Key points in this chapter

1. Measuring influence is inherently subjective. Our four suggested criteria are stable and proven, and balance any differences that exist in how influencers exert their impact. So we can compare apples and oranges.
2. Avoid selecting industry leaders and CEOs as influencers. Reaching such people with marketing is extremely difficult. It may also be plainly wrong: most decision-makers are influenced by individuals much closer to their business.
3. Influencers are individuals, not categories or firms of people. You need to identify not only the influential businesses but also the key staff within them. Again, avoid picking the CEO, as the influencer may be lower down the organisation structure.

Case Study E – an innovative data management provider

Forging new routes to market

A specialist provider of data management tools discovered that its core market was shrinking. It was under severe pressure from the three giants in the industry, and from several emerging niche players too. As its traditional market slowed, it moved into the emerging opportunity for data compliance solutions – a hot sector as a result of Sarbanes Oxley, Basel II and other regulatory and legislative initiatives. Influencer50 was commissioned to identify the most influential individuals in this new sector, and redirect the company's marketing spend accordingly.

The research showed that buyers were confused by the variously named technologies within the market. They were therefore looking to those people who could make sense of the market for them either abstractly (analysts), practically (systems integrators) or historically (early adopters). With no clear market leader it was understandable that analysts were being swamped by vendor seeking help with strategy and marketing support. While Gartner dominated amongst the analyst placings, the top management consultancies failed to make any significant impact, and it was a number of prominent corporate end-users who were steering public opinion most.

As a result of the research, the firm took several direct steps to engage influencers. It commissioned previously unidentified influencers to keynote at its five-city European seminar tour. It invested in two further reseller managers to tap into unsatisfied channel capacity, and it tasked its senior management team to formally network with the top 50. It also reallocated its marketing spend to emphasise corporate speaker opportunities, vertical seminars and public sector specialist consultants.

It has also successfully built an influencer networking schedule, based around a dinner table. It invites a group of 15–20 influencers to dinner and facilitates conversation on a given relevant subject. Importantly, the firm doesn't sell, nor try to dominate the discussion. It listens and learns from the influencers, taking their inputs and advice on board. In return, the influencers are talking to their contacts and clients about the firm's approachability, credibility and market engagement.

Though it's too early to claim quantifiable ROI, the company is confident this will emerge through more streamlined, and less costly, channel management, PR campaigns that are now heavily risk–reward based, greater attendance at its seminar series through using its keynote speakers as the 'pull' and improved targeting of direct mail, the company's highest single marketing expense.

The VP of sales believes that, 'It's easy to follow the traditional marketing mix. It's harder to disrupt that conventional thinking, with new insight and market knowledge. Influencer marketing is definitely disruptive thinking and genuinely exciting because of it'.

8

Who should evaluate the influencers in your market?

Identifying your company's key influencers is critical, the cornerstone of every other activity. But who should be responsible for identifying them in the first place?

While we're on the subject of identifying and evaluating your influencers, now would seem a good time to discuss *who* we believe should be carrying out the influencer identification process. A critical process for your new initiative to succeed. Let's begin with the obvious candidates.

Analyst relations firms

There are some terrific quality AR professionals in the UK, some that have really impressed us with their understanding of what industry analysts need (and don't need) to do their job, and the pressures on their time. The AR capability within IBM Europe for instance is second to none. But we've become exasperated by some of those in the AR profession who are attempting to blur the distinction between AR and Influencer Relations. No one's arguing that there's overlap – in almost every research commission that we've undertaken industry analysts have proved to some degree to be influential – but we're seeing an attempt by some to deliberately confuse marketers into thinking that the words analyst and influencer are in some way interchangeable. That AR somehow means Influencer Relations.

Analysts are one category, and only one category, of influencer. Any attempt to hide that fact smacks of people trying to jump aboard a new ship because it appears newer and shinier than the one they're on.

The very obvious danger of AR representatives being charged with identifying the wider field of influencers is that it would only be human nature to overemphasise the importance of analysts within their findings. They'd be stupid not to. They are unlikely to oversee research highlighting the fact that in their particular market space, analysts are of surprisingly little relevance. Not unless they were planning to leave anyway.

PR companies

The same goes for PR companies, though we think their claims are destined to be taken less seriously. PR companies, at least those that specialise in consumer media relations, simply can't afford to objectively tackle influencer relations – because in some markets the media are way less important than PR companies like to think. And you can't build a business model around targeting a group of people, in this case the media, who you've already admitted to your client aren't influential! So while PR companies will increasingly tack the moniker 'Influencer Relations' onto their strapline, we don't think many will give it more than cursory attention. They are too entrenched in the media marketplace.

Now it's one thing if PR companies are chosen to identify the broader sweep of influencers, but quite another if they're then tasked with handling the influencer/client relations role. The fear here is that PR companies will naturally migrate to a press relations model – issuing mass communications with the aim of maximum quantifiable 'coverage'. Now that would be a sure way to disrespect those you most need! We're not saying it can't be done, but it would need to be closely monitored.

Channel representatives

At least we can see a little logic in this choice. Channel reps understand the focus on sales, and how the twists and turns of the sales process involve many disparate people's views. Their natural inclination will surely be to up-rate those nearer the closure of a sale rather than at the earlier, scoping stages, but we guess everyone has some kind of bias. Our main qualm here, as with almost any choice, is that identifying the key influencers is not easy, there's no blueprint or replicable formula, and few peers to learn from. No one gets it right first time, or second, and channel managers have no experience in this.

Market intelligence specialists

We could almost see some sense here too. Except that comparatively few companies employ in-house market intelligence staff, those that do are already overstretched and most have absolutely no experience of the sales process. Three good reasons why not.

An external *influencer marketing* firm

Yes. For the immediate future only specialist firms are likely to have the knowledge, experience and methodology to deliver the identification stage. That will change, but not in the short-term. These firms would have no bias in favouring certain influencer categories, and would not be learning, at the commissioning company's expense, 'on the job'. A downside is that few of these specialist firms currently exist.

A newly created in-house 'VIP engagement manager'

Yes. To us, aside from outsourcing to one of the very few proven *influencer marketing* firms, this is a strong opinion, so long as your company has the headcount to allow it. What better way to bring your new VIP (very influential people) engagement manager up-to-speed on those he or she is to work with than for that person to lead the influencer identification process.

Key points in this chapter

1. At this early stage in the market the best type of organisation to identify influencers is a specialist *influencer marketing* firm. Few companies have the experience, methodology and understanding of how influence works in its widest context.
2. Some organisations are talking about influencer relations, but what they really mean is traditional influencers such as journalists and analysts. So while PR and AR firms will attempt to identify influencers they are doing so from an inherent position of bias.
3. You should consider hiring a 'VIP engagement manager' to manage you firm's internal relationships with influencers, and to promote the concept of *influencer marketing* throughout your firm.

9

Marketing to influencers

Once you've identified those influencers you want to talk to, how should you approach them?, and what will they want to hear?

We've now covered why marketing is broken and what needs to be done to fix it. We've talked about the changing nature of decision-making and how your company can best identify those shaping the decisions. Now comes the detail. Engaging with influencers, and it's too important to get wrong.

So you've got your shiny new list of influencers. What now? Let's recap on what you have in your hands. You have a list of the most important people in your target market, important not because they buy from you (they don't) but because they influence those that might buy. Treat this list with care and respect.

It's typical to find that, of the 50 or more influencers you identify that have real influence over your prospects, you don't know more than 20. Which means that at least 60% of your influencers likely don't know you either. And let's distinguish between awareness and knowledge. You may even be aware of your influencers, and they may even be aware of you, but awareness is just above consciousness in mental capacity. Awareness does not infer interest or knowledge, or a desire to acquire such. Spending time and money on market awareness alone is pointless. Plenty of firms have high awareness without it necessarily translating into success. But it's a good starting point.

If you were in this situation with your prospects, where you had no knowledge of them, you'd define a programme of go-to-market activities. You'd research your audience to identify its needs and wants. You'd determine its motivations, issues and constraints. You might create a file on a specific customer account, detailing its revenues and profit history, key personnel and business agenda.

So, take the same approach to *influencer marketing*, and define a Go-to-Influencer programme.

Marketing to influencers should be straightforward, as long as you remember the golden rule:

Influencers don't buy anything from you.

Influencers are not customers. There is no point in pitching your usual marketing collateral to influencers – they don't care about your products or your firm's success. While the activities may be similar to those in marketing to prospects, the inputs are not the same and the end result is quite different. You must instead treat influencers in the same way as you would any other segment. You find out what they want, what their interests and motivations are, and what their interest is (professional or otherwise) in you. To draw on *The Long Tail* theory, your top influencers are at the head of the influential sources market, and you can ignore the tail.

The influencer identification process should have yielded who your influencers are, and some relative ranking of them. You'll also have picked up some insight on how they derived their influence, and how they use it. That said, many questions will remain unanswered, such as

- Who specifically do they influence? Do they have generic market influence, or a subset of customer firms? Or do they only influence influencers from a distance (such as a regulator)?
- What decisions do they influence? (e.g. purchases, market adoption, awareness, credibility)
- When do they influence in the sales cycle? Are they *idea planters*, or *recommenders*, or *validators*? Or all three?
- How do you use each of these influencers to best effect?

Segmentation is the place to start

As the saying goes, you don't eat a whole elephant in one go. You eat it in small bites. So break your influencer list into segments, to make it manageable. Most firms take one of two approaches to segmentation:

- Splitting influencers by category, making separate lists of analysts, journalists, consultants, regulators, etc. Depending on your categories, and the numbers in each you may want to segment further, for instance, breaking down consultants into top-tier, second-tier, niche and so on.
- Splitting influencers by importance. You may discover that, of your 50 or so top influencers, a dozen are substantially more important than the rest, in which case it makes sense to focus on this select group. Again, influencers are a scarce resource so spend your time with the ones that will return most value.

Once you have a segmentation you're happy with, you need to prioritise your efforts. Clearly, if you have a segment of 'VIPs' – very influential people – then start here. Look for groups of influencers that have relatively greater influence *where you need it*. You may find, for example, that you have as many journalists as channel partners in your list. So which group has the greatest total influence? Which group will serve your firm's greatest need? Are you constrained by channel bottlenecks or are you being ignored (or misrepresented) by the media?

Another aspect of segment prioritisation is the prior existence of any relationship you have with influencers or influencer groups. Some firms embarking on *influencer marketing* find that they get early and easy returns just by focusing existing activity on newly-identified influencers. So by determining the most influential journalists you can focus your PR programme only on these selected few (and de-emphasising the rest). You can focus your AR programme on the most influential firms for your target market, rather than continuing the annual road show of 20 different analyst firms.

The existence of relationships with certain influencers may focus your attention on these individuals for quick returns. Or you may decide to leave your activities with these known influencers to current plans, and invest primarily in those influencers that are new. It's your choice, driven by your firm's greatest needs and opportunities.

Knowing more about your influencers

Just as salespeople compile profiles of their key accounts, so you should create a profile of individual influencers. There are varying degrees of information that you can generate on people, from simple textual descriptions to deep analytical profiles. Some firms compile profiles on their influential prospects, including 'personal and lifestyle' details (wife's name and birthdate, cat's name, favourite football team, that kind of thing). This information is then used to design specific marketing tactics individualised to each influencer. There is no point in offering tickets to see Chelsea to an ardent Arsenal supporter. But send two tickets to the opera to a CEO whose wife's birthday is next month, and you may get their attention.

Our experience is that personal information of any kind, personal or professional, is extraordinarily difficult to find, and even more onerous to confirm. The best, and most ethical, way is to engage with the influencer themselves through a direct conversation. You should also network with other influencers in the community, and we'll discuss how to approach influencers in a moment.

There are a number of Internet-based services that claim to assist in the profiling of people. LinkedIn works well because it is self-verified – the information available has been created and is maintained by the individuals themselves. On the other hand, don't bother with people searches such as Zoominfo: while these services may improve over time, today they are based on trawling through web pages. They are therefore liable to be out-of-date, incomplete and in other ways inaccurate or unreliable. There are 225 Duncan Browns in Zoominfo, and 146 entries for Nick Hayes. Which ones are us? You can't ever know if they are all us, or some of them, or just one. Even we don't!

What are influencers doing?

One thing that is very effective in understanding influencers is activity tracking. It's one of the more popular activities that we carry out for clients, because it is targeted specifically at influencers. Think of the press coverage clipping service that most PR agencies provide. Invariably these are a hotchpotch of articles referring in some way to your firm or market, and are a mechanism for measuring the effectiveness of PR in getting your name 'out there'. But there's little relationship between column inches and influence, or follow-on business.

Influencer activity tracking watches what specific influencers are doing (from a distance, no stalking!). For example, as well as noting when an influencer is quoted in the press, you can focus on what they are saying about you and your competitors. You can identify which conferences they are speaking at, which research papers they've produced, and which by-lined articles they've written.

You can also determine, if you know where to look, specific deals influenced or won by a particular influencer. Some of this you may pick up on the grapevine, or from press releases, and more still from specific services that track deals of a kind. NelsonHall, for example, tracks business process outsourcing contract activity (meaning deals) on a global basis. The trick is to know where to look (and you do know because you know who your influencers are) and keep your eyes and ears open.

Another aspect of influencers' activity is their movements between employers. Influencers are the most sought-after hires, for what we hope are obvious reasons, and they tend to move around a lot. It is not uncommon for influencer churn to hit 20 per cent per annum. That is, of your top 50 influencers today, 10 will not be in their current roles in 12 months' time. Some will retain their influence in their new role, while others won't.

Activity tracking is the mechanism for keeping your list of influencers up-to-date. It will tell you which influencers are active, what they are saying, who they are working with, and how and when they are influencing decisions. What it won't tell you is what your influencers think of you.

What do influencers think?

There's only one way to find out what an influencer thinks of you and that is to ask them. Before you embark on a market research project to do just this, there are two things you need to know about influencers:

- They are busy. Really busy. Sixty hours a week busy. So the chances of you calling them up and getting an hour to chat about you are slim.
- When you do get their time and attention, they will tell you what they think. Influencers love to influence. So if and when they do talk to you, listen.

You can, of course, wait until you have approached the influencers as part of your marketing programme, then drop into conversation your desire to know what they think of you. Or you can commission a third party to conduct an analysis.

BT does this kind of thing on an annual basis, and has done for 12 years. It therefore has some of the most detailed longitudinal survey data on influencers in its market. The sorts of things that it tracks are influencers' perception of BT and its closest competitors, plus the degree of favourability (or lack thereof). BT can track the relationship between its favourability scores and those of its peer competitors, thus tracking the effectiveness of its influencer marketing programmes, outreach activities, corporate marketing and so on.

We suggest running a poll of influencers on a regular basis. If you are just beginning an *influencer marketing* programme you might want to do this every quarter for the first three iterations, in case things are not working as planned, before setting on a six- or nine-monthly cycle.

Influencer message development

If you were developing a set of messages for your prospects, you'd want to understand their needs first. Then you'd develop a set of propositions that mapped onto those needs, demonstrating how your offering delivered value on those propositions. Marketing to influencers is no different. They do, however, have different needs. Remember that influencers don't buy from you, so they don't care what you're selling. What is a very important detail for a prospect, who's comparing one competitor with another, is irrelevant to an influencer. But they do care about their own agendas.

For example, journalists care about creating copy. They have deadlines and column inches to fill. Their primary goal is to fill those inches. In a Maslow-like hierarchy of needs, journalists can think about higher orders of fulfilment, such as imparting insight or opinion, only if the quantity is present. So give them content, not spoon-fed (most journalists are too savvy for that) but through 1-to-1 contacts with your senior executives. Journalists love a scoop, or insider information. Because you know your journalist influencers you can target them specifically, and build a relationship between them and your spokespeople. Your message to journalists is: "We have some great insight on *xyz* product category, and we're only going to brief you and two other influential journalists on this."

Note that we said that you should build a relationship between journalists and your spokespeople, not with your PR operation. A key measurement of success is the degree to which influencers external to your firm interact with influential people inside it. You will have, or will need to create, influential individuals working for you. Get them connected with the wider influencer community. We'd hope that it goes without saying, but we often hear of bad examples. So, for the record, don't send your most influential journalists standard press releases. Why would they read them? They don't care about you, any more than they care about the 200 other firms that also send them releases.

You do need to ensure that you are speaking in the appropriate language to influencers. Each influencer category has its own vocabulary, and you need to articulate your messages using the right dictionary. Just as vertical industries have their own jargon, influencer categories have their preferred terms. So when you're talking to channel partners for example, make sure you are talking bundles, ASPs and attach rates.[1] Again, you need to develop a specific set of messages for channel partners. The message might be something like: "You're one of the most influential partners we have and we're going to give you special treatment. We want to be a preferred supplier for you."

Other messages you might use include:

- To analyst influencers: 'We'd like to get your thoughts on our new vision'.
- To regulatory influencers: 'You're important and we're listening'.
- To standards body influencers: 'We want to contribute'.
- To venture capitalists and financier influencers: 'We can direct you to the next big thing'.

- To academia influencers: 'We want to commission a research project'.
- To competitor influencers: 'If you join us we can further your career'.

And so on. Ideally, you'll create not one but a series of messages, a curriculum that educates (or re-educates) each influencer or influencer type. As the term curriculum infers, *influencer marketing* requires a long-term commitment from you, because that's what you want from your influencers.

There are two special cases to be treated even more carefully than 'normal' influencers. These are the influencers within customers and groups or clubs of customers. We've said this before, but the most significant type of influencer is a customer, preferably though not necessarily one of your own customers. A variant on this type of influencer is the collective, such as buyers groups, purchasing lists and procurement authorities. It's tempting to create messages for these types of influencer that are based on, or are copies of, your standard sales pitches. This is a bad idea: influential customers will respond even less favourably to your pitches than most prospects. This is because they are influential for a reason, because they are early adopters or market leaders, or whatever. The best message to a customer influencer is "We want to learn from you". Humility is a rare thing in sales and marketing, and if your approach is genuine you will get their attention.

Approaching influencers

Once you have created your specific and tailored messages for influencers you then have to deliver that message. This is where the rubber hits the road, the moment of truth. Tread carefully. In fact, if you've done your homework this should be straightforward. The approach we suggest is twofold: get the influencers together, then engage them on a 1-to-1 basis. Firstly you need to know that influencers gain and sustain their influence largely by networking with other influencers. So if you can identify your influential spokespeople and get them networking, then you stand a good chance of engaging influencers in conversation, which is where you should start. Influencers are real people, so you need to use those of your own people that are of sufficient gravitas to carry a conversation with them.

Given that influencers like to talk to other influencers, we suggest you manufacture a reason for them to get together. We have found that influencers cluster together in small groups, with only one or two super-connectors that seem to know most people. They rarely get a chance to meet in a group larger than four people, and they don't necessarily know the other influencers in your market (though they may well be aware of them).

A successful model to use is an influencer event, a dinner or breakfast that is exclusively for influencers. Why would they come? Two reasons: to hear something interesting and relevant, and to network with other influencers. Just like decision-makers. So you'll need to develop some insightful content, possibly engaging (on a commercial basis) one or two specific influencers that have pulling power on the other influencers. For example, if you wanted to invite the top 50 influencers in marketing to an event, who is the one person that you'd make sure was there, to draw the rest of the influencer community? Seth Godin? Steve Rubel? Charlene Li? The idea is to get the number one and two influencers on your list to the table. Our experience is that the rest will follow.

It is imperative that you communicate the exclusivity of the event ('No, you can't bring a friend or send a substitute'.) and that you tell people why: that the event is only for influencers in your market. Influencers like to influence, but they also like to know that they are influential. This may be the first time they've heard this, which will endear you to them no end.

If holding an event in real space and time, you could try to develop an online community. This can work extremely well, especially if it is tied to a specific, time-boxed issue (such as a product launch or regulatory deadline). A mobile device maker launched its innovative handset in Germany using this approach. It identified the top 120 influencers in the business community, and then sent out a handset to each influencer. It directed the influencers to an online forum, where it facilitated discussion and debate on the handset's features and usability. (See Case Study H for more information.) The product launched into a pre-influenced market, and the people that were asked for their opinion on the new device were unsurprisingly the influencers that had already seen, touched and influenced the handset.

What you are trying to do is to create a community of influencers. There is one huge advantage to doing this – there will only ever be one community of influencers, and influencers will have neither the time nor the inclination to join another. You want to be the firm remembered for creating, and sustaining, that community. It's one case where first mover advantage really does exist.

Be aware that there may already be a forum or focus for influencer activity. There may be an annual event where the great and the good gather. There may be a blog that attracts the top influencers. Or there may be an informal gathering format for some influencers, a Wednesday night wine club or similar. Whatever, wherever influencers meet, you go.

If you miss the opportunity, and a competitor colonises the influencer community first, then move onto step two: engaging in 1-to-1 discussions. Marketing to influencers is a necessary means to an end – that of turning the key influencers towards your firm or products. But it has its own benefit in increasing your awareness amongst the most important people in the market. If you've done your work well, your influencers will be eager not only to talk *to* you, but also *about* you. The next step is to give them something to say.

There is little specific to say about this stage, other than that your conversations should be aimed at engaging the influencer in more than just conversations. That is, there is a greater motive for engaging influencers than simply good relations. This is a point critical in understanding the difference between PR, AR and so-called influencer relations, and what we call *influencer marketing*. The difference is hinted at in the names: we want influencers to be a tacit part of the marketing strategy.

So all conversations with influencers should be orientated around enlisting them into your marketing programme. The ways in which you do this, without corrupting the ethical sensitivities or commercial mindsets of the various personalities involved, is dependent on a variety of factors. Each influencer will have their own agenda and preferred method of engagement. There are two broad approaches, which we'll cover in the next chapters: marketing *through* influencers, and marketing *with* influencers.

Key points in this chapter

1. Influencers don't buy from you, so you can't market to them like you would a prospect. You need to find out what their needs and wants are, to create messages that are relevant and interesting to them.
2. Prioritise your influencers. There will be some that are more important than others, so you need to focus on those. Understanding more about your influencers, and knowing their perceptions of your firm, is useful input to prioritisation.
3. Approach influencers in their networking groups, or create a group for them to meet. Then move this to a 1-to-1 basis. The objective of influencers talking *to* you is to get them to talk *about* you.

Case Study F – a tier 1 network equipment supplier

Reaching out to influencers

This firm is a $400 million NASDAQ-listed company. It is one of the pioneers of 'next generation networks' – selling a range of telecommunications applications including residential and business voice services, wireless voice and multimedia network switches. It sells to global telecoms service providers who are building global Voice over Internet Protocol (VoIP) infrastructures. Influencer50 was commissioned to identify the most influential individuals within the US-based infrastructure space, and work with the company to then build ongoing relationships with these individuals.

The majority of the firm's sales are derived from being part of huge multi-vendor tenders with long lead times, frequently in excess of a year. The firm itself is rarely a lead in such tenders, often finding itself part of competing bids too. It not only needs to influence prospective end-commissioning companies, but also a myriad of bid partners, yet it often finds itself in competition with vendors on one bid and in partnership with them on the next.

The research uncovered many names previously unknown to the firm's executives, notably within individual partner companies, as well as the proliferation of influential middle-ranking executives inside a number of niche consultancies and integrators. The print media were found to provide useful 'air-cover', generating press coverage that actively built company name awareness but could rarely be tied directly to initiating sales tenders, whereas coverage from a small number of industry analysts could be.

As a result of the research, the firm went on to:

- Formalise its outreach programme to over 60 individual influencers.
- Emphasise to its direct and indirect sales force the importance of influencers and how to get them onside.
- Tasked its senior management team to formally network with the top-rated 25 names.
- Brief its PR, AR and IR teams on those influencers relevant to each.

The firm's director of Global Business Development commented that, 'Our next generation telecoms business is based on a growing number of strategically important long-term deals with the major global carriers and infrastructure players. Gaining insight into the factors affecting those buying decisions is therefore critical to us, and the role of key influencers something we are extremely keen to better understand'.

Note and reference

1 If you're interested, bundles are collections of related products and services, ASPs are average selling prices, the prices at which goods are actually sold (usually different to list prices), and attach rates are the rates at which support programmes are sold with, or 'attached' to, products.

10

Good, bad and ugly influencers

Your sales channel and your competitors are two extremely important influencers on your prospects. How should you go about influencing them?

The channel and its importance

The sales channel is arguably the most important category of influencers after peer customers. After all, your sales channel partners are the ones that are talking to your customers and (you hope) selling your products.

The reality is that sales channel management is done badly. Although there are several exemplary instances, typically our experience tell us that most firms have a hard time in optimising their channel partners. Even firms like Microsoft, which derives nearly all of its sales through its indirect channel, have a remarkably patchy delivery record.

A leading European telecoms company was recently complaining to us about the poor execution it experienced within its channel partners. Across 13 European countries it numbered 700 separate partner firms, ranging from top-tier consulting firms to one-man-band reseller agents. What struck us most was not the ridiculously high number of partners but that the telco seemed surprised that its approach wasn't working. The assumption had been that the more partners it had the more services it would sell.

Partnerships are a clear case where 'less is more' applies. You cannot reasonably manage this number of partner organisations and expect them all to deliver high returns, without serious investment in management. For one thing, the chance that one partner's territory conflicts with another's was not only likely, it was all but guaranteed. While some overlap is inevitable, even desirable, this degree of clash proved counterproductive.

We know firms that don't know how many partner organisations they have, because the structure of the channel is too complex, with distributors selling to intermediaries, who then sell on to smaller firms. They lose track of who is selling to whom, even though they have licence agreements in place that should stop the practice of selling on. The channel operates within a law unto itself. In this respect, the sales channel is not unlike peer consumers, in that suppliers can often lose control of the market messages, and thus lose visibility of the sales process.

There are some endemic issues with selling through channel partners:

1. Sales channel partnerships are typically non-exclusive. This means that you are fighting with other suppliers to gain attention from the partner. You are in competition with your partner's other suppliers even before you get to market.
2. Suppliers and partners are rarely evenly matched in size or importance. You may think it's great to have Accenture as a partner, but if you are regarded as a small-time player with a niche offering, they will bring you into a deal at their convenience only. Conversely, if you are a major player you can largely dictate the terms of your partnerships, because you know the partners' customers want to buy your products or services. Understanding who holds the dominant status is critical in making partnerships work.
3. Partners often see you as a tactical solution. Because you are non-exclusive, and especially if you are the subservient party, you'll often be regarded as a nice-to-have. It often makes sense to focus on partnerships where size and importance (to the market) are close together.
4. When partnerships are unbalanced you'll find that your target markets may be out of kilter. We've had clients whose solution is aimed at mid-tier firms yet proudly proclaim partnerships with top-tier consultants. They sold very little. The reverse is also true: high-end goods sold through commodity channels undermines the value perception of the product. That's why Calvin Klein doesn't want its jeans sold in Tesco.

The best partnerships are those where the parties are more-or-less equal in stature, and that there is a strategic benefit in the relationship for both players. Neither party wants to be a nice-to-have player.

How to influence the channel

Margin isn't it! If you have to discount you haven't demonstrated the value, or your product isn't appropriate to be sold via those channels.

Good ways to influence partner organisations are:

- Make sure your partner is aiming at the same market as you are. The most common mistake we see is the mismatch between suppliers' core markets and that of their partners.
- Require your partners to make an investment in you. If partners put skin in the game they're more likely to execute on the partnership. Training is the obvious investment to promote, but it also includes co-marketing material and joint proposition development.
- Position your partners as influencers – promote their solutions, competencies and customers in your own marketing collateral.
- Market your partners into your existing clients. This is you putting skin in the game. If you're willing to share your customers then the partner is more likely to reciprocate. Note that if you can't easily sell your partner in to your customers then maybe your offerings don't fit together so well.
- Get your partners networked with other influencers in your market. You'll have to identify the appropriate person within the partner organisation, someone that has the gravitas to network successfully in the influencer community.
- Make sure your success is aligned with your partner's. If they are successful it should mean that you are. And the converse is also true.

Competitors as influencers

One of the biggest sources of influence on your prospects are your competitors. Many people react to this news with apathy. They think it's pointless to know this information, because they can't see a way to influence their competitors. We say, think again. There are at least three ways you can influence your competitors, and probably more, but keep things ethical. There's no excuse for underhand tactics.

Talk to your competitors

The first thing you should do to influence competitors is talk to them. This may seem a strange approach but it makes perfect sense. Talking to competitors gives you a chance to discuss general market trends, find out what the competitor culture is like and to network in the industry. You may find that you are not competitors at all, or at least not on all fronts. There may be partnership or referral arrangements that are possible.

One subject always on the agenda when talking to competitors is that of your mutual competitors. My enemy's enemy is my friend, and all that. You can share insight and stories, and swap tips on how to deal with others' strengths and capabilities.

Most of the top CEOs in an industry meet each other at least once a year, either privately or at an industry event. What we're suggesting is that this practice cascades down the organisational structure. There are plenty of opportunities to make contact with competitors, at trade shows, media events, or wherever. It's hopefully unnecessary to say, but just in case, we would never encourage gloating or bad-mouthing competitors, or any such nonsense. Always be professional – and legal – no price fixing or such things.

Be talked about by your competitors

The second thing you can do to influence competitors is to talk about them, and to get them to talk about you. As Oscar Wilde said, the only thing worse than being talked about is *not* being talked about.

How do you ensure that your competitors talk about you? The answer is that you get them to worry about you. Remember the rule of influence: influencers don't care about you or your products. They care about their own agenda. This is just as true for competitors as for any other type of influencer. When you carry messages to prospect customers you'll talk about what your product can do for them. But when talking to, or about, competitors you must change the message. Don't talk about features and functions of your product, or pricing or subjects that you'd discuss with prospects.

The things that will worry competitors include (but are in no way limited to):

- Your percentage growth year-on-year
- Your expanding client list
- The fact you've been commissioned to write a book
- Invitations to speaking engagements
- Awards and prizes
- Quotes in influential journals and media

Pick three, but only three, things that you think would worry a competitor. In fact, anything that gets them talking about you in a positive sense (and we mean positive for you, negative for the competitor). Stuck for things to talk about? What would worry you if you heard them about your competitors? Use these things as a starting point.

Now, how do you measure how worried your competitors are? A powerful indicator of your influence in the market is what your competitors say about you. You can find this information out by asking your prospects, or by asking influencers. A key question that influencers like to ask is, who are your primary competitors? Do your competitors mention you? What do they say about you?

You want your competitors to talk about you, to acknowledge you as a competitor. Why? Simply, it acknowledges you as a credible player. Don't worry that a competitor will rubbish you in front of a prospect or influencer. It is generally accepted as poor form and reflects badly on the detractor.

We've also noticed that competitors that are worried about one particular player start to mirror the language that they use. You'll see this in marketing literature, where one company introduces a new concept or terminology. They may even start blogging on the subject that you introduce. This is a sign that you've got them worried.

Recruit your competitors

There are two valid ways of recruiting you competitor: acquire the company or hire key staff. Acquisition is a bit of a cheat, since you have to buy the whole company, not just the bits that are influential. It's also open only to those with sufficient financial clout.

It's much easier and cheaper to hire key staff: that is, the market influencers that work for your competitors. You will have done your homework and you will know which person to approach. It's much more straightforward, direct and lower risk than any other recruitment strategy, including headhunting. (In fact, it has been suggested to us that a list of influencers is the ideal headhunter shortlist.)

Recruiting competitor influencers happens all the time. There are often restrictions in place to prevent this – that is non-compete clauses in contracts. If this applies, check the terms carefully, as you don't want to incur long delays between the influencer leaving the competitor and joining you. You also want to avoid legal issues.

Remember too that the individual's influence may be related to the position they currently hold. Hiring them may stop them being an influencer for your competitors, but it may also stop them being an influencer altogether.

The influence of analysts

What is an analyst?

There is one category of influencer that is often cited as the most important, especially in highly technical, complex or high value sales: that of the analyst. But what value does an analyst offer, why are they influential, and is their influence as great as many claim?

Analysts come in two broad types: financial analysts and industry analysts. If you are buying *into* a company you'll use a financial analyst. If you are buying *from* a company you'll use an industry analyst.

Financial analysts typically (though not exclusively) work in large investment banks and they analyse financial data on (mostly) publicly quoted companies. They create and collate information on broad financial markets, specific company financial performance, and likely future performance (and risks attached). Banks with financial analysis expertise include Goldman Sachs, Cazenove, Deutsche Bank, Dresdner Kleinwort Wasserstein, Lehman Brothers and Merrill Lynch. Non-bank financial analysts include Bloomberg, Thomson Financial, Interactive Data Corporation, Standard & Poor's, Moody's and Reuters.

Financial analysts help businesses decide how to invest their money. They are powerful influencers of investment decisions with their buy/hold/sell recommendations and credit ratings. If investment is the decision that you need to influence then financial analysts are the primary targets for you. Both types have considerable influence, and both types use data and opinion from each other (though they don't always acknowledge this).

Industry analysts typically have a sound working knowledge of the finances of the firms they follow, but they are specifically interested in the market dynamics in which the firms play. They provide comment, opinion and insight on players in a market. They advise suppliers on what to sell, and buyers on what to buy. Importantly, industry analyst firms are independent of the suppliers they follow. This means they should have no vested interest in the advice they give to buyers. It is this independence and trust that conveys considerable influence to industry analysts.

Industry analysts are particularly powerful in the technology and telecoms[1] sectors. But they are also important in scientific, technical and medical markets, manufacturing, food and beverages, retailing, automotive and others. Analysts exist where decisions are complex and high value.

This begs the question: what do analysts do? There are three components to most analyst firms' offering:

- Syndicated Research: conducting self-funded research into markets and players, which is published to customers. Research can be survey- or interview-based, depending on the type of deliverable being researched.
- Advisory and Enquiry services: an extension to syndicated research, this allows clients to probe deeper into research findings, making use of 1-to-1 calls and meetings with individual analysts.
- Consulting: conducting custom research to specific requirements of a client. Sometimes, analysts will conduct a multi-client study, which is a cross between syndicated research and single-client consulting.

Knowledge and expertise comes from the combination of these three activities. Market research provides a good grounding in the subject matter, enquiries help to inform analysts of the current uncertainties and concerns in the market, and consulting allows a deeper insight into individual clients' needs and issues. Based on this information analysts distil opinions and predictions, which form the basis of the value to, and influence on, the market.

What do analysts do?

So how do analysts influence the market? The closer an analyst gets to a decision-maker the greater the influence. In terms of the standard analyst offerings, influence increases from Syndicated Research, to Advisory and Enquiry services, and again to Consulting (Figure 10.1).

This may surprise: most people assume that analysts get their influence from publishing research papers and being quoted in the press. But remember that influence is orientated around the decision-maker, and specific advice from an analyst firm will always be more influential than generic comments in a research paper. The higher the level of engagement with a client, the greater the influence.

Analyst firms may have dedicated consulting arms, or entrust research analysts to conduct consulting (often called client engagements), or a combination. For our own direct experiences it is clear that influence is highest when an analyst has done the research and applies this knowledge directly onto a client's specific situation.

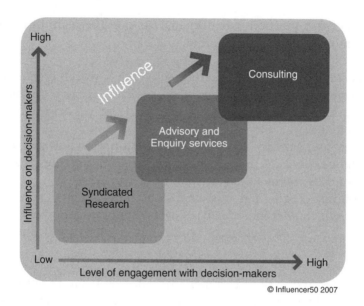

Figure 10.1 Analyst influence increases with engagement with decision-makers

How do analysts influence a decision?

Analysts provide a variety of influential inputs to decision-makers, including the following (in increasing order of influence):

- General trends and directions: providing scene-setting information on the market, the key players and new innovations. Typically delivered in research notes and conference presentations.
- Market definition and classification: taxonomies of market elements, useful in segmentation and market forecasting. Delivered in chunky reference-type works as part of a larger research programme.
- Identification of good practice: often based on client case studies, anonymised where appropriate. This type of information is valuable but often made available through individual enquiries and not to general subscribers.
- Insight into specific vendors and their products: specific research notes and reports on named vendors and their offerings. Some analysts include competitive positioning and market share data.
- Shortlisting: compiling shortlists of potential suppliers can rapidly cut down the time to select a winner. Best done in consulting, after requirements are understood.

- Assessment and selection: pure consulting, and a project may take several months to complete. Usually offered by dedicated consulting arms of analyst firms.
- Decision validation: may be conducted over days, rather than months, leveraging the knowledge of a single analyst.
- Price comparison/negotiation. The hardest advice to give, but arguably the most valuable. Suppliers rarely provide pricing information (unless required to by regulation), but commodity prices are available. Analysts are able to aggregate prices from multiple sources and calculate averages, which can help in negotiation.

Why analyst influence can be overstated

There is, frankly, a lot of nonsense talked about the influence of analysts. In some markets they hold near god-like status, with the ability to make or break deals. This may have been widely true a decade ago. But today information, expertise and influence is dissipated across a much wider array of individuals.

We have read that analysts are influential in between 60 per cent and 80 per cent of large sales, especially in the tech sector. The inference is that analysts are the most important influencers, and/or hold some position of exclusive influence on decisions. But this high degree of *involvement* doesn't translate into analysts then enjoying 60 per cent to 80 per cent of the *available* influence. We can't think of a major sale where the winning supplier didn't influence the decision. Or where a reference client wasn't used. Indeed it's arguable that the greatest influencers on a decision are the preferred suppliers and the reference customer.

It's meaningless to quote percentages of involvement. The range of involvement in decisions might range from zero to 100 per cent depending on the market. We know that a big four consulting and integration firm estimates that 0.5 per cent of its sales are influenced by analysts. No, that's not a typo. It's one half of one per cent. It even uses the figure in its calculations for ROI on AR. And it's a figure that's accepted by the firm's senior sales management team.

The important factor is not involvement but *share* of influence. Our own data, drawn from more than a dozen studies of influencers, shows that the average share of influence for analysts is 16 per cent. But it is highly variable, ranging from 4 per cent to 22 per cent, depending on the market segment and maturity.

Few analysts have real influence

There are, by all admissions, very few analyst firms that have the deal maker/breaker power. In the tech sector there are three, worldwide. In telecoms there are four. In every industry there are more deal making/breaking consulting firms than industry analyst firms.

This point is made well by Michael Speyer at Forrester in his 2007 report on Hidden Influencers. Speyer writes that 'While (analysts, bloggers and the media) are easily identified and reached, the impact of their advice and perceived value is highly variable. Analysts in particular are used early on in the procurement process for due diligence where the impact of their advice is low; their highest impact is in providing vendor shortlists. It's rare that they are involved in later steps in the procurement process, like site visits or contract negotiations. Because analyst reputations and influence vary, vendors need to identify the few that IT buyers listen to most'.

This is because most analysts, and analyst firms, do not go beyond providing insight into specific vendors and their products. That is, they don't conduct consulting engagements for decision-makers in shortlisting, assessment and selection, decision validation or price comparison/negotiation. Most stop at producing research outputs, or conducting consulting engagements for vendors. These activities have substantially less influence on decision-makers than direct engagements with decision-makers.

The main reason given by analyst firms for not conducting consulting is that it would diminish independence: making a recommendation in favour of one supplier would indicate bias. There is little logic for this. There is nothing unethical or biased about making a recommendation for a specific client. Just as a doctor prescribes a specific medicine for a specific ailment, so analysts should be able to do likewise. Two companies in the same sector with the same issue may need completely different solutions, based on their culture, organisation structure, current practices and infrastructure.

It is a complete cop-out to plead independence. It's more a lack of process to assess requirements and select the appropriate solution. And we feel it demonstrates a lack of conviction in the analysts' own opinion. At best it's an avoidance tactic, to deflect the wrath of vendors that are not shortlisted or selected. We think that most analyst firms miss out on maximising their influence by shying away from making strong recommendations.

It is no accident that Gartner, the biggest analyst firm, has built its reputation on advising its clients on which technology to buy. The third biggest technology analyst firm, IDC, punches with influence considerably below its weight precisely because it has almost no consulting contact with tech purchasing decision-makers.

Events

One of the big growth areas in marketing over the past 3 years has been events, including conferences, trade shows and seminars. The number of events in the technology industry has increased by 42 per cent between 2004 and 2007. As far as influencing decision-makers, most events are a waste of time. Remember the decision process – you need to influence decisions either at the beginning of the process or at the end, because that's when the ultimate decision-maker is involved.

An event is a single point in time, typically once each year. Decision processes are being initiated all year round. The chances that an event and a decision coincide are small, unless an event is so significant (and some are) that it sets the timeline for initiating the decision process itself. Therefore the chances that a decision-maker attends an event are equally small.

Decision-makers rarely go to events because they are senior people and extraordinarily busy. They'll seldom take a day out of their schedule to listen to product pitches. Decision-makers tell us that on average they get one hundred invitations and solicitations in a year. They are super-selective about which events, if any, they attend.

And have you noticed that all the events happen together? This is because of the 52 weeks in every year there are only about 28 weeks that are really available for events, due to seasonal, school and public holidays. And in every available week, it's rarely advisable to hold an event on a Monday or a Friday. So there's only three-fifths of 28 weeks, which is 30 per cent of the year. Meanwhile, the number of events is increasing, to be crammed into the same 30 per cent.

Most events are therefore information dissemination exercises, where sponsoring suppliers convey information on their products. This information may then be hoovered up by information gatherers and taken back to their organisation, where the chances of it reaching the desk of an imminent decision-maker are not good.

What events really are

So why are there so many events, and why are they commercially successful? The economics for events are pretty simple: sponsors pay to get in front of as many people as possible and the event organiser promises to deliver a bunch of delegates to the sponsors. It's a match-making exercise.

The primary argument for sponsoring an event is lead generation. Unfortunately most events are badly executed upon by sales forces. We have no hard data to back this up, but from our own experience and anecdotal evidence we reckon the average event attendee gets one follow-up, irrespective of how many times they drop a business card in the ever-present goldfish bowl.

The truth is that events make marketers look and feel good. It's tangible, action-packed, visible and expensive. What better way to attract the attention of management? And if management themselves are involved, by giving a keynote presentation, then they can feel good too. One hundred people listening to your every word – how gratifying is that?

Even if follow-ups are done, the quality of people attending events is low – they are information gatherers. The number of people attending is therefore *not* a measure of success, nor is the quality of the sponsor's keynote presentation or number of business cards collected.

Some events are influential, and they all follow a specific format. Decision-makers tell us there are two main reasons for attending an event:

- Decision-makers like to network with peers and influencers. This means that the event must be exclusive to high-level decision-makers. Smaller events work better as a rule, which is why the executive dinner approach is successful.
- Decision-makers like to hear information and insight. This means you should have an influencer to headline the event. This will attract the right sort of people, and guarantee that value is delivered on the day.

This second reason also means that decision-makers don't want to be pitched to. If there is a sponsoring supplier they have to be talked down from treating the event as a sales lead generation activity, and taught to regard it as a relationship- and credibility-building exercise. Decision-makers like to go to peer-level forums in particular, especially if there are influencers attending and they are supplier-free. Part of an influencer identification exercise will tell you which events are influential and therefore which you should attend.

Industry awards

The business model for awards is simple. Suppliers enter their products or case studies into the awards programme in whatever categories are available, and they pay a fee to the awards organiser. Sponsorship is available for individual categories, so the more categories there are, the more sponsorship opportunities there are. The entries are then judged by a panel, sometimes containing influencers plus representatives from the awards organiser firm and other industry insiders. The entries are discussed and winners selected. The organiser then hosts a posh dinner in a central hotel where the awards are handed out.

Awards decisions are usually conducted professionally, in secret and are rarely fixed in advance. Intellectually, it's a useful and fun exercise for the panel members to engage in, and since the results have little consequence they feel free to make the best decision. Awards are a commercial enterprise, and the cost of hosting the dinner is covered by the entry and sponsorship fees. The award winners get bragging rights for a year. Nobody remembers the losers so there's rarely any damage done aside from limited bruising to the ego's of those that didn't win on the night. All in all a system where we have winners and no losers. An ideal system, right?

Wrong. The only real winner is the awards organiser, of course. Awards are paid for out of marketing budget, so how effective are they in lead generation or closing sales? The answer is, not at all.

Let's look at the awards ceremony. The largest group of attendees at awards dinners, by far, are the suppliers. It's a night out to slap each other's backs and hopefully bag an award or two. The awards are badges that can be worn to prove to the boss that everyone is working hard. If you win an award then that shows that you're doing a good job, even if sales are a bit low. It's no coincidence that most industry awards feature a host of second-tier players, or new products, or innovative solutions. Awards are a proxy for profits.

Suppliers will also bring along to the dinner, as guests of honour, existing customers and prospects. Actually, prospects are rare because the host firm may not win, thus leaving them with egg on their face and the prospect talking to the competitor that did win. So the dinner descends to an expensive 'thank you' night out to existing customers.

What about after the show? – all the press activity listing who won what. If you have to win an award to have something to say, you don't have much to say that's interesting. If advertising is the price of being boring, then awards are a close second.

Let's be absolutely clear about industry awards – the Oscars they are not. Corporate customers care little about supplier awards. These don't feature on their radar of things remotely interesting or important when making strategic decisions. Awards are almost irrelevant to the most senior decision-makers, though are useful at the initial RFP (request for proposal) stages.

So industry awards are primarily self-congratulatory 'feel good' exercises, which have limited marketing value and all but zero influence on the top decision-makers. We don't mind if you use an industry award to soak up your marketing budget, but just be clear why you're doing it and what you expect to get out of it.

Key points in this chapter

1. Channel partners and competitors are the most under-rated influencers on your market. Though they need handling in completely different ways, both carry a message to the market about you, and are therefore players that you need to influence. In particular, don't ignore competitors just because they are hard to approach.
2. Analysts are an important category of influencer. But beware of generalisations in the category: not all analysts are influential, even within the top firms. Analyst influence is highly variable. The most influential analysts perform consulting engagements for end-user customer clients.
3. Events and awards are the most over-rated categories. They are driven primarily by the organisers' business motives – revenue and profit – and have little relevance to decision-makers.

Note and reference

1 The book to read on Technology Industry Analysts and Analyst Relations is Bill Hopkins's *Influencing the Influencers*, published by Knowledge Capital Group.

11

Marketing through influencers

How can you work with your influencers so that they convey what you'd like them to say?

'People are already talking. Your only option is to join the conversation.'
Andy Sernovitz, Word of Mouth Marketing

Marketing through influencers is where *influencer marketing* gets really interesting. *Marketing through* influencers is about enabling influencers to talk about you to prospects. Immediately, the affinity with *WOM* marketing should be apparent. WOM is all about getting people talking about you in a positive manner. Hopefully, they are already talking about you in some regard.

The ethics of *marketing through* influencers

The first thing to say is that we *not* talking about paying stooges to say what you tell them to say. Any idiot can do that, it carries no influence, and usually is counter-productive. *Influencer marketing* doesn't involve bribery, coercion or any other underhand means of getting influencers to advocate a position.

Advocacy is a legitimate exercise, as long as it's genuine and credible. There is a difference (subtle maybe, but important) between paying for the time of an influencer to speak *their* views, and paying to have an influencer speak *your* views. You should declare whether you're paying for a speaker. What do you have to hide by concealing this?

Paying an influencer risks undermining their independence and credibility, and hence their influence. It's no coincidence that analyst firms and magazines that operate on a pay-to-play basis have substantially less influence than those that do not. Commission an influencer to speak at an event or to write on a relevant subject. They're speaking as an authority on the subject area, and hence are demonstrating their influence. No true influencer will risk their reputation by saying something they don't believe.

You must never commission an influencer to endorse your product. Never place a paid-for by-lined article in a magazine. If an influencer wants to endorse your product, then great, but don't pay them to say so. If they really believe it, they'll say so anyway. How can prospects tell when an influencer is being genuine? Believe me, they can tell.

What does 'marketing through' really mean?

Marketing through influencers is all about embedding your messages in their marketing. If *marketing to* influencers is about increasing awareness and knowledge of your firm within the influencer community, then *marketing through* influencers is about increasing awareness and knowledge of your firm within the prospect community. In *marketing to* influencers you created messages about you for the influencers. In *marketing through* influencers, you create messages about what the influencers are saying, for their community. In other words, it's the influencers that will carry your message to your market, and because they are influencers they will be listened to and believed.

But why would influencers do such an altruistic thing? Wouldn't it compromise their reputations, or their status as independent, or incur legal or ethical inhibitors? We admit that this needs to be done carefully, and you can't go blundering in expecting influencers to carry blatant sales pitches or your slogans and advertising. Influencers will however use your message as long as they don't overtly sell your proposition and, importantly, that it adds value to the influencer's proposition. We said that influencers don't care about you. But they do care about themselves, and will use material from other sources to support their offer and positioning.

Importantly, you can become seen as a source of information and insight. A measure going forward would be how often influencers call you for your opinion.

Influencers love to influence, and you are giving them the tools of influence. If the message you create is valid, useful and pertinent to the influencers then the chances are that they will use it. They like to appear connected, and they like examples of how their influence is reaching to other firms. Importantly, influencers often have a degree of autonomy in the way they operate, even within large firms. Influencers are typically influential within their own organisations. So they can usually apply their discretion when incorporating into 'official' material any useful external collateral they encounter.

The tools of influence

Marketing through influencers focuses on providing your identified influencers with tools to be influential. While influencers gain their status through different ways, they have to then impart that influence to decision-makers, based on the type(s) of influencer role they play. If you determine the role played by an influencer you can see how they impact decisions, and offer to supply them with appropriate support. Your objective is to make your influencers more influential, and then ride the wave of increased influence.

Influencers will not carry your message if it distracts in any way from their message. Just as you can't make a sales pitch to influencers, you can't expect them to make a sales pitch on your behalf. So your message has to add value to their message.

There are three steps involved in this process:

■ Find out what messages your influencer takes to the market. Any message you ask them to carry must be 100 per cent aligned with what they want to say. How do you find out? You ask them, in the *Marketing to* phase.
■ Create one message that maps onto the influencers' messages. That is, you need something that *they* will want to pass on, not that *you* want communicated. Influencers don't care about you – they care about themselves. So make it easy for them. It may not come easy to you!
■ Create support material for influencers, based on that one message. This may just be a mapping of your existing collateral to their propositions or you may have to redraft your collateral. But realise that it's the influencers that have the influence, and for good reason. Listen to influencers – they want to influence you too.

Step one then is to find out what messages your influencers are carrying to their market.

For example, imagine you sell air conditioning units and you've identified that a heating services engineer is a key influencer. You have to find out what the engineer is saying to the market about his services. Is he competing on price or system reliability or ease of use? Note that he is unlikely to compete on the features of air conditioning products, as these would be your differentiators, not his.

The engineer tells you that he is currently regarded as a low cost supplier, a box shifter, but wants to add more value to his services. You determine that this engineer wants to compete on system reliability. This is critical information since, had you not asked, you'd be creating a 'We have cheap air conditioning units' message. You'd be amazed how often organisations change their core message and strategy. By engaging with the influencer you've discovered that the engineer is changing his marketing, and you have an inside track on your competing suppliers.

What you have to do now is to develop one message that supports his new market position. Easy. Your systems are the most reliable on the market. You can provide statistics that show that your systems have a mean time between failure of 10 000 h, so they need servicing only every 14 months. Most systems on the market recommend annual servicing. So by making the 14-month claim (which is well within your product's existing capability) you have given the engineer a competitive advantage. He can now differentiate on market-leading reliability, and attract more customers to offset any drop in service call-out revenues.

The support material for your message needs to be functional and brief. It must both communicate the key point (longer time between servicing) and yet not crowd the engineer's own marketing (friendly service, 24-h availability, or whatever).

Make an example of yourself

Marketing through influencers often happens where an early stage influencer is trying to make an impact. This might be a journalist conducting research, an analyst making a keynote speech, a regulator issuing a paper for consultation and so on. Influencers like examples to illustrate they are not just dreaming up wacky ideas. If they are defining a trend, then give them an example of how you support that trend.

Industry analysts form opinions by talking to other influencers at supplier and customer organisations. They look for new approaches and activities, then formulate these into models and frameworks. In 2004 the IT industry was awash with an emerging concept coined variously by analyst firms as real-time computing, dynamic IT and utility computing. The concept referred to computing resource that was available just as electricity is, something you can turn on only when you need it. The term that most people were comfortable with was IBM's phrase 'On Demand'.

It was simple and communicated the essence of the concept. IBM became the thought leader in the market, and even analyst firms qualified their own terminology by adding 'also known as On Demand'. Yet the analysts persisted with their own terminology, thus diluting understanding in the market. It also allowed other vendors to create their own terminology. Why did analysts feel the need to create terms where one existed already? Simply, because it wasn't their term, and it suggested favouritism towards IBM. It was IBM's message, not theirs.

There are many ways of creating simple messages and collateral that support influencers' own messages. The trick is to know what the influencers are saying. Once you understand that, and acknowledge that they won't carry a sales message, the rest is straightforward.

You could produce a single slide that illustrates a key point made by an influencer. Or create a graphic, a chart or picture, which captures a statement they've made. Or forward a statistic or data sheet that supports their market position. Or be a case study for them by being excellent at what you do.

What *marketing through* doesn't involve is sending branded memory sticks and mouse mats to influencers. Influencers already have too many mugs and t-shirts. And they won't use them in front of their clients.

Think exclusives

Influencer marketing is not for the lazy. If you identified the top 50 influencers in your target market, then you will have had to market to 50 individuals, with tailored messages. Similarly, you'll now have to create collateral to market through your influencers, and you can't use the same collateral for all of them. There are three good reasons for this:

- Influencers will come from different categories of influencer, and with different job titles. So a message that is suitable for a regulator will be different from that for a top-tier consultant.
- Even within the same category, influencers will have different positioning and strategic messages to take to market. Therefore any collateral you develop to support these messages will also differ.
- Influencers have big egos and don't want to use something from you that has already been used elsewhere. So you have to create an individual piece for each influencer.

Fortunately, there is a big upside to this extra effort. When you start seeing your embedded message in the market you'll know which influencer put it there. You'll also find that influencers share with (or steal from) other influencers, so you'll also see evidence of the interconnections within the influencer community. This can be fascinating, insightful and extremely gratifying.

Key points in this chapter

1. Getting influencers to carry your message is a legitimate exercise, as long as it's genuine and credible. There is an important difference between paying for the time of an influencer to speak *their* views, and paying to have an influencer speak *your* views. Don't confuse the two.
2. Influencers love to influence. So give them the tools of influence. Find out what they're saying, build a message that supports them, and build simple collateral around it. With collateral, less is more – don't crowd the influencer's own collateral.
3. Create different messages for each influencer. What you use in the extra effort required will be regained by higher traction from your influencer community.

Case Study G – IBM Information Management

Finding a new route to market

When Chris Livesey took over the responsibility for IBM's Information Management brand in the UK, Ireland and South Africa, the new incumbent knew the business strategy needed bringing in line with what he felt was potentially an untapped opportunity. Livesey decided that he needed to increase marketing's effectiveness, as there was little hard evidence of properly aligned marketing, sales and product development. The business strategy was put under review. But how to conduct that review?

Through a contact in the analyst relations team, Livesey examined the potential offered by identifying the market's influencers. The proposition was strong enough and the upside was compelling. But a new approach calls for caution, so a pilot project was conceived. IBM Information Management had previously prioritised on an IT audience but it was clear that the emerging customer for the new business was the business community in the retail banking sector, despite having strong technology awareness. Approaches to business prospects were met with referrals back to the IT department. If they identified the influencers on the business community, and then used these influencers to gain access to its target market, the business would have created a new route to this elusive audience.

A project was commissioned from Influencer50, a specialist *influencer marketing* firm operating in Europe and the US. The first step was to understand the penetration that the sales team had experienced, and to understand the marketing structure and existing activities. An in-depth research project was put together to examine the influencers in the business community. To increase the detail, and complexity, of the project, the business decided not only to target business people but to focus on specific job titles within business functions.

Influencer50 delivered its findings to a sceptical audience comprising senior marketing, sales, brand and AR leaders. IBM had operated in the business sector for more than fifty years, albeit predominantly in a technology-supplier capacity. How could they not know who the business influencers were?

Just before the influencers were revealed, each attendee in the meeting was asked to write down their best guess of the top five influencers. Of the 10 attendees, only two guessed even the correct organisations. No one guessed the names of the individual influencers. The highest analyst was ranked at number 15, and didn't appear on the firm's AR programme.

What the exercise revealed was that the business community IBM Information Management was targeting thought in a completely different way, using different reference points and vocabularies, attending different events, reading different magazines and newspaper, and did not read blogs. It revealed why and how IBM Information Management would have to radically rethink its strategy for reaching business people, and how to tackle business people that may have previously been reluctant to engage with the firm.

The audience was shocked. It caused a major rethink of its strategy to target the business community. But now it knew where to start. A programme was developed by Influencer50 to profile and then target the top influencers, approaching them with an invitation to participate in a business-focused influencer-only round table. Key influencers were targeted for special treatment to ensure they attended and were prepared to contribute. In turn, these key influencers were useful in attracting other influencers, and attendance then snowballed.

Critical to this process was the identification within the firm of nominated influencer-owners – senior managers given the responsibility to build relationships with two or three named influencers. This was to be done on a no sales pitch basis, but to be used as a two-way communication enabler. It also served to increase the awareness amongst senior managers of the *influencer marketing* approach being adopted.

Livesey is now executing well on a new business strategy, and a solid rationale that underpins it. If a journalist is called, if an event is scheduled, if a new partnership is signed, then it will all be traced back to the list of influencers. It will act as a unifying core between the various silos of marketing.

Importantly, the sales force will be happier. Access to business contacts will increase, and thanks to increased input from influencers the firm's proposition will be strong and more aligned to business needs.

'Services such as the ones Influencer50 offer are a precious insight into the way things really work', says Livesey. 'Understanding the value of your proposition – seen through the eyes of the people who genuinely influence buying behaviours in the market – is the difference between knowing what to do and pure guesswork.'

12

Marketing with influencers

Influencers can directly help in countering your most common sales objections. This chapter shows how.

Where *marketing through* influencers embeds your message in the collateral of influencers, *marketing with* influencers embeds their messages in your collateral. In fact, preferably the influencers' messages *are* your collateral.

The more astute among you will have noticed that *marketing with* influencers is the same as *marketing through* influencers, just in reverse. Instead of you embedding your messages and collateral in influencers' marketing (*marketing through*) it's the influencers embedding their collateral within yours (*marketing with*). The difference is that in both cases you are the driving force, and the initiative comes from your *influencer marketing* programme, not theirs. But of course there is nothing to stop an influencer's firm from using your organisation in the process, assuming it identifies your firm's executives as influencers. If this is the case, you may well find that you can support and reinforce each other's influence by embedding collateral in both directions. This is common today in formal commercial partnerships, but there's nothing to stop you doing this on a looser, more ad-hoc basis.

So why use influencers in your marketing messages? Think back to the reasons marketing is broken:

- There's too much of it
- It all sounds the same
- Nobody believes it anyway

Now, influencers (by definition) have influence over your target market. Influencer-led collateral therefore has a greater chance of reaching your market, of having it heard and of it being believed. So far, so good. There is, however, another issue with traditional marketing and that is its strained relationship with sales. The biggest gripe from sales is that marketing appears irrelevant in assisting the sales process, by creating high-quality leads or closing sales, or something in between.

Here's our idea to solve the ills amidst sales and marketing:

Align your influencer-led collateral with your sales process.

Whatever sales process your firm uses, it will probably look something like this:

Decision-makers take an interest in your product (initiate), they are educated in the benefits to them, they validate their opinions (thereby taking ownership of the process) and then they decide. Salespeople are skilled at taking decision-makers from one stage to the next. Ideally, this process happens smoothly and quickly, except it rarely does.

Eliciting sales objections

Sales should be pretty straightforward, identifying prospects and leading them down a logical path that results in a cheque. Why then is it so often hard to do? It's because prospects, awkward as they are, raise objections to block a sale. Despite your best efforts, the prospect has thought of a reason not to buy from you. If you haven't armed your salespeople with counter-arguments to these objections, then the sale cannot complete.

Sales objections differ for each firm and prospect. Examples include:

- 'I've never heard of your firm'.
- 'I don't know what your firm can do'.
- 'You don't know my business'.
- 'I don't believe your product works'.
- 'I don't believe your product will make/save me money'.

- 'Your proposal exceeds my budget'.
- 'Your solution is non-standard'.
- 'You can't provide the support service I need'.
- 'This is new technology and I'm not sure it will last'.

And so on.

Such sales objections are an integral part of the selling process: in fact, many have described sales as the process of overcoming objections. So, if objections are an everyday occurrence to salespeople, why do they hate them?

The reasons are twofold: objections are numerous and they are varied. This means that a prospect can declare any one of a dozen possible objections at multiple points in the deal discussions. The result is that salespeople must spend time addressing a prospect's concerns, which slows the sales cycle. The failure to successfully counter an objection ends in a loss, which reduces lead conversion rates. Inevitably the finger then points to marketing and its inability to deliver credible counter-arguments.

Firms across many industries tell us that they have three key issues surrounding sales objections:

1. 'We don't know what the sales objections are'.
2. 'We don't know how to counter those objections'.
3. 'Even if we can counter objections, the prospect wouldn't believe us'.

Let's examine these issues. Firstly, there are three proven ways to identify sales objections. They are, in declining order of effectiveness: conduct a win/loss analysis; hold a sales objection elicitation workshop; just ask your salespeople.

A win/loss analysis project involves someone *other than your firm* calling decision-makers that didn't buy from you. You can't do the calling because it's extremely unlikely that a decision-maker will tell you the real reason why you were not chosen. They're too polite, they don't really care and they feel rather awkward in telling you that your pitch leader had bad breath (or whatever the real reason was). (You *can* call the decision-maker that did choose you.) Win/loss is probably the most interesting project a third party agency can conduct, as they can get some great insight into the industry, as well as delivering juicy feedback to their clients. It is essential to gain the sales director's support for the process, as the results will affect his operation. You should also treat win/loss analysis as a learning exercise, not a blame game.

A 'sales objection elicitation workshop' is a fancy term for sitting your salespeople in a room and cajoling sales objections out of them. It's an effective way of determining what they perceive as the primary objections, and once the ice is broken (who's going to be first to talk about their failures?) they flood in. The health warning that accompanies such workshops is this: you'll only get the objections that salespeople perceive, or feel comfortable in admitting to.

Similarly, asking your salespeople on an individual basis elicits some good responses, but may not cover the real reasons why they don't close. How perceptive and realistic are your salespeople? Salespeople always know the typical objections that prospects raise, because they are at the sharp end of the process. They talk to prospects and prospects tell them why they can't or won't buy from them. Except sometimes prospects don't tell the truth.

It's not that prospects are deliberately deceitful: it's just that it can be easier to be less than completely honest. It can save the prospect from embarrassment, it can avoid the blushes of the salesperson or it can hide behind an 'official response'. Example: a prospect tells your salesperson that your product is too expensive. So you counter this with evidence of the ROI of the product. But did your prospect mean that your product isn't worth the money? Or that a competitor provides the same functionality for less? Or that insufficient budget has been allocated this quarter? Or that the prospect is happy to spend the money, but not with you because you're a new entrant to the market?

Occasionally, your firm may be only too painfully aware of its typical sales objections. You may have attracted negative press, or be in financial difficulties, or have a poor customer service record. But often these perceptions last longer than the actual events to which they relate. Are prospects just using these objections as a means of avoiding giving you the real objections?

Ideally, you'll get input from prospects themselves. The problem here is that, as before, prospects may not tell the truth. This is why firms engage with independent agencies to conduct win/loss analysis projects, because prospects and customers are more likely to give the real reasons for their decision to a third party.

Sales objections are enlightening, most notably for marketers. Often, objections will be revealed that are at odds with marketers' perceived wisdom. They challenge and confront. It can be a painful experience. The golden rule is that you must be truthful with yourself. If you are not a credible provider, if your customer service offends or if your product doesn't work, then you need to know this. There's no point in kidding yourself, because you can't kid your customers.

Decide which mechanism to use based on your firm's circumstances. But all three require engagement with salespeople. This is never a bad thing.

Why do prospects raise objections?

What causes a potential customer to voice an objection? The short answer is: Risk. Decision-making is a risky affair. Remember that decision-makers are risking their personal reputation, their company's money, competitive advantage, strategic success and a bunch of other important considerations. It's a wonder they raise so *few* objections.

Example objection	Example risk
'I've never heard of your firm'.	'I'm risking my personal reputation on a firm that no-one knows'.
'I don't know what your firm can do'.	'My company is risking its strategy on unproven technology'.
'You don't know my business'.	'There's a risk that you don't understand my requirements fully, so the implemented solution won't provide the stated benefits'.
'I don't believe your product works'.	'If the technology doesn't work I'll be fired'.
'I don't believe your product will make/save me money'.	'I'm risking budget on unproven RoI'.
'Your proposal exceeds my budget'.	'I have to take this proposal to my boss, which represents a personal credibility risk to me that I'd rather not take'.
'Your solution is non-standard'.	'The solution won't fit with my current infrastructure, and the procurement team won't authorise a purchase order'.
'You can't provide the support service I need'.	'This is a business critical process – I can't be left high and dry'.
'This is new technology and I'm not sure it will last'.	'I want to avoid a technology cul de sac'.

Objections are an opportunity to sell the strengths of your company. If you can counter an objection, you have removed a risk, and therefore stand in a great position to close a sale. However, you can only successfully and consistently deal with objections if you (a) know about them in advance and (b) can counter them effectively.

Countering sales objections

Once you understand your objections, you can start thinking about counter-arguments. Countering objections is hard because classic marketing doesn't normally operate at the granularity required. For reasons of scalability, marketing promotes the same message to all of its targets (in a segment). Conversely, you have to counter each sales objection one at a time, addressing each objection separately. It requires one message (counter-argument) per objection.

Countering sales objections requires specific arguments and supporting collateral for each objection. There is absolutely no point in using an ROI case study to counter an objection based on doubts over vendor capability. It just isn't relevant. You need a portfolio of collateral that addresses a specific objection and that supports the appropriate counter-argument.

What this situation demands is the creation of a new set of collateral, orientated around sales objections. This represents a substantial investment in effort from the marketing department, but it needn't require an equally sizeable budget. There are shortcuts. More later.

Example counter-arguments would include:

Example objection	Example risk	Example counter-arguments
'I've never heard of your firm'.	'I'm risking my personal reputation on a firm that no-one knows'.	'We are an innovative young firm with a powerful business model and strong financial backing'.
'I don't know what your firm can do'.	'My company is risking its strategy on unproven technology'.	'This new technology solves a long-standing business problem'.
'You don't know my business'.	'There's a risk that you don't understand my requirements fully, so the implemented solution won't provide the stated benefits'.	'Companies like yours are using our technology today'.
'I don't believe your product works'.	'If the technology doesn't work I'll be fired'.	'Our technology is leading edge, but robust'.
'I don't believe your product will make/save me money'.	'I'm risking budget on unproven RoI'.	'Our product makes you money'.
'Your proposal exceeds my budget'.	'I have to take this proposal to my boss, which represents a personal credibility risk to me that I'd rather not take'.	'This solution is innovative and can make you a hero in your organisation'.

(Continued)

Example objection	Example risk	Example counter-arguments
'Your solution is non-standard'	'The solution won't fit with my current infrastructure, and the procurement team won't authorise a purchase order'.	'Our solution meets industry infrastructure standards'.
'You can't provide the support service I need'.	'This is a business critical process – I can't be left high and dry'.	'We offer first class customer service'.
'This is new technology and I'm not sure it will last'.	'I want to avoid a technology cul de sac'.	'This technology represents the future for the industry, and early adopters will gain competitive advantage'.

Mapping influencers to counter-arguments

Influencers are only credible in a narrow field of expertise. It is vital that you match the message to the appropriate influential messenger. If the objection is technology-orientated, then use a techie. If it's a financial issue, then use a financially credible influencer. If it's proof points you need, use a customer influencer. And so on.

Influencer marketing offers real opportunities for creativity in marketing approaches, because it utilises a broad range of influencers. You may be targeting the top analyst in your industry, but your competitors are doubtless doing the same thing. Using a broad set of influencers allows you to use the right person for the appropriate message.

You'll find that you can map several influencers to each objection. That's fine. You now have multiple routes to countering that objection. Occasionally, you may discover that there are no obvious influencers that can match the objection. An example might be where you have no existing presence in a market – so you have no customer reference influencers. In such cases, think laterally. Is the new market so different from your existing customer base? Can you identify an industry expert to verify your capabilities? Can a partner influencer underwrite your technology with first line support?

Whatever influencer mapping you define, be aware of overusing your favourites. This is especially true for customer references, but it applies universally. That's why it's important to identify and utilise a long list of influencers. It keeps both the message and the messenger fresh, credible and pertinent.

Example objection	Example risk	Example message	Targeted influencer(s)
'I've never heard of your firm'.	'I'm risking my personal reputation on a firm that no-one knows'.	'We are an innovative young firm with a powerful business model and strong financial backing'.	FT journalist
'I don't know what your firm can do'.	'My company is risking its strategy on unproven technology'.	'This new technology solves a long-standing business problem'.	Management guru, *Harvard Business Review*
'You don't know my business'.	'There's a risk that you don't understand my requirements fully, so the implemented solution won't provide the stated benefits'.	'Companies like yours are using our technology today'.	Reference customer, top industry event.
'I don't believe your product works'.	'If the technology doesn't work I'll be fired'.	'Our technology is leading edge, but robust'.	Trade press journalist
'I don't believe your product will make/ save me money'.	'I'm risking budget on unproven RoI'.	'Our product makes you money'.	Professor at London School of Economics
'Your proposal exceeds my budget'.	'I have to take this proposal to my boss, which represents a personal credibility risk to me that I'd rather not take'.	'This solution is innovative and can make you a hero in your organisation'.	Customer in similar industry sector
'Your solution is non-standard'.	'The solution won't fit with my current infrastructure, and the procurement team won't authorise a purchase order'.	'Our solution meets industry infrastructure standards'.	Local purchasing authority

(Continued)

Example objection	Example risk	Example message	Targeted influencer(s)
'You can't provide the support service I need'.	'This is a business critical process - I can't be left high and dry'.	'We offer first class customer service'.	Systems integrator partner
'This is new technology and I'm not sure it will last'.	'I want to avoid a technology cul de sac'.	'This technology represents the future for the industry, and early adopters will gain competitive advantage'.	Industry-leading conference

Marketing with influencers

Countering sales objections is pointless if you deliver these counter-arguments yourself. Prospects don't believe you. Why? Because you're selling something. You have a vested interest. It's ironic that when you counter a sales objection the prospect raises the killer objection – disbelief. This means you need to generate specific pieces of collateral to support each counter-argument, using someone that the prospect will believe. These would be your influencers.

The key step is to map your sales objections to your influencer community. You'll have to create new collateral to address each objection – importantly, this needn't break the bank. Here comes the budget shortcut we mentioned earlier. Influencer-led collateral can include pre-existing material, so it can be cheap to gather. This can include articles, books, webcasts and so on. It does *not* have to have your brand on it.

So, if an influencer blogs positively on your product, link to it. If an influential journalist article advocates the benefits of your category of technology, order reprints. If an influential customer launches a new soft drink, and you supplied the supply chain management system behind it, send a case of the product to your prospects. As long as you attribute the source of influence appropriately, and you can map to a specific objection, then feel free to go ahead.

Addressing sales objections has one inevitable effect: sales will increase. It has immediate payback, by definition, as it directly results in sales. No problems there in associating marketing spend with ROI.

Example objection	Example risk	Example message	Targeted influencer(s)	Example influencer-led collateral
'I've never heard of your firm'.	'I'm risking my personal reputation on a firm that no-one knows'.	'We are an innovative young firm with a powerful business model and strong financial backing'.	FT journalist	FT article, citing technology trend and quoting your CEO
'I don't know what your firm can do'.	'My company is risking its strategy on unproven technology'.	'This new technology solves a long-standing business problem'.	Management guru, *Harvard Business Review* (HBR)	Guru writes HBR article citing business problem and emerging solutions
'You don't know my business'.	'There's a risk that you don't understand my requirements fully, so the implemented solution won't provide the stated benefits'.	'Companies like yours are using our technology today'.	Reference customer, top industry event	Customer advocates at industry event
'I don't believe your product works'.	'If the technology doesn't work I'll be fired'.	'Our technology is leading edge, but robust'.	Trade press journalist	Independent lab test results written by journalist
'I don't believe your product will make/ save me money'.	'I'm risking budget on unproven RoI'.	'Our product makes you money'.	Professor at London School of Economics	Academic prepares ROI analysis and case study

'Your proposal exceeds my budget'.	'I have to take this proposal to my boss, which represents a personal credibility risk to me that I'd rather not take'.	'This solution is innovative and can make you a hero in your organisation'.	Customer in similar industry sector	Customer's blog advocates this new technology, and how they won promotion through introducing it
'Your solution is non-standard'.	'The solution won't fit with my current infrastructure, and the procurement team won't authorise a purchase order'.	'Our solution meets industry infrastructure standards'.	Local purchasing authority	Approved supplier status with local purchasing authority
'You can't provide the support service I need'.	'This is a business critical process — I can't be left high and dry'.	'We offer first class customer service'.	Systems integrator partner	Gold Partner status with systems integrator, to provide after-sales support
'This is new technology and I'm not sure it will last'.	'I want to avoid a technology cul de sac'.	'This technology represents the future for the industry, and early adopters will gain competitive advantage'.	Industry-leading conference	Keynote speech at industry-leading conference

As a recap on *marketing with* influencers, the sequence of logic is this:

- Determine the reasons why prospects don't buy from you. These reasons are called sales objections.
- Define a counter-argument for each sales objection.
- Map each counter-argument to an influencer, such that the counter-argument is (or could be) advocated by that influencer.
- Create influencer-led collateral that specifically addresses each objection.

Hey presto – you've got an answer to each sales objection, and it's an answer that has substantial credibility (because it's from an influencer, not you).

The key points of this process are:

1. You need to know why people don't buy from you. The sales force is the custodian of this information, so you need to tap this resource. Sometimes it's easy – they just know. Other times they don't know, or they think it's price (hint: it's almost never price). In these cases, there are ways of eliciting the information, either from the sales force or directly from the market.
2. Arguments against sales objections are credible only if communicated by someone independent. A counter-argument conveyed by you doesn't work because 'you would say that, wouldn't you'. Influencers, by definition, are more credible.
3. Counter-arguments are specific to the objection. In other words, the counter argument 'Gartner says we're a top-right player in its Magic Quadrant' works only if applied to the objection 'We don't think you're a major player', but not if the objection is 'We don't perceive a need for your product'. This may seem obvious, but you'd be surprised how often an objection is countered by an irrelevant response.

The power of the approach is that it directly links influencers to sales objections, arming the sales force with specific collateral. If you get it right, the inevitable consequence is better leads, improved conversion rates and higher sales. Now, we can hear you ask, 'If it's that easy, why's it not done this way already?' Good question, two good answers:

Firstly, sales and marketing typically don't talk to each other. Read Philip Kotler's '*Ending the War Between Sales and Marketing*' for insight into why this situation exists. Secondly, it only works if you use influencers to counter sales objections. And most firms don't know who their influencers are.

Customer influencers and proxy references

We need to say something again. Customers (whether yours or not) are the most important influencers there are. If you identify your customers (or prospects) as also being influencers then treat with special care. And if you have existing customers willing to act as references then you'll understand the importance that other organisations attach to them.

Customers are the ultimate in authority and credibility. That's why a customer reference programme is vital. Reference customers, though, need to be managed carefully. Most industries suffer from reference fatigue, where the same clients are trotted out again and again to address every objection. There are suppliers who can't use the customer references they cite because of overuse. These customers are fed up being the marketing department for the supplier.

This points to a flaw in many customer reference programmes. Most customer case studies are too generic to be of any use in addressing objections. They cover too much scope, are overused in inappropriate situations and are difficult to maintain. Customer references are seen more as badges of success rather than useful sales tools.

Sometimes customer references are not suitable or just not available. Product launches, new market entry and new company start-ups are examples where customer references are, by definition, rarely possible. When you move into a new territory or segment or industry – you don't have any customers. So it makes sense to extend your client reference programme to a more rounded and balanced programme involving other people that your prospects listen to. Use influencers, or influencer-led collateral, as in-fill for your customer reference programme. Using influencers as proxies for customer reference is effective because:

- It avoids customer reference fatigue.
- Influencers are believed (because they are influencers).
- It allows tailored counter-arguments to be developed for each objection.
- Influencers have broader knowledge of the marketplace than customer organisations.
- Influencers are typically happier to share their experiences and provide deeper insight, because they have fewer commercial and competitive constraints.

Recruiting influencers

In our proprietary version of the *influencer marketing* model, we call the *marketing with* influencers step *Recruit*. The idea was that firms would enlist the services or input of influencers and embed them in marketing output. So we were using the term *Recruit* in its loosest form. It turns out that we were more prescient that we thought. Recruiting influencers onto your payroll is a pretty good way of embedding them in your markets, as well as your strategy and operations too.

Recruiting influencers happens all the time. In 2005 the top influencer in the Business Intelligence (BI) software market was Howard Dresner. Dresner was a Gartner vice-president and research fellow, meaning that he was extremely influential inside Gartner as well as outside. He was so influential that he is credited with coining the term BI that defined the market. As such, he was courted by the BI software vendors: as Dresner himself said at the time, 'I'm well acquainted with the strengths and weaknesses of every company in the field'. In October 2005, Dresner left Gartner to join Hyperion, a major player in the BI market.

Hyperion's competitors were livid. The other top players had invested considerable time and budget in briefing Dresner on their future plans and strategy, giving intimate details of their product's architecture and design. In a trice, this valuable competitive information was in the hands of their major competitor.

Now, issues of commercial confidentiality notwithstanding (and we've no reason to think that Mr Dresner betrayed any confidences), we think Hyperion (now part of Oracle) pulled off a coup. It hired the most influential person in the industry, continued to benefit from his wisdom and insight and removed the prospect of Dresner influencing the market in favour of a competitor. And while Dresner's influence in the market has undoubtedly diminished, because he now lacks independence and has a vested interest, he remains influential to some degree and 100 per cent in Hyperion's favour.

Another example of recruiting an influencer is Huawei's hiring of Mick Reeve as an advisor and public representative. Reeve had been group technology officer at BT until his retirement in 2006. He carried huge influence in the European telecoms market, sitting on the boards of important industry forums (including the International Telecommunication Union (ITU). On the other hand, Huawei is something of an upstart in the telecoms equipment market. It has grown quickly from its Chinese roots to be a substantial player in the global market, yet a low-cost tag still sticks. It needed to enhance its credibility with phone companies and large corporates. Hiring a senior specialist gives them the insight and profile they desire.

Key points in this chapter

1. Embed influencers' messages in your marketing collateral. It has a greater chance of reaching your market, of it being heard and of it being believed.
2. Align your influencer-led collateral with sales objections. Do this by eliciting your typical objections, creating counter-arguments, then mapping appropriate influencers to those counter-arguments. Try to use a broad spread of influencers, so as to keep them fresh.
3. Influencer-led collateral can include pre-existing material, so it can be cheap to gather. This can include articles, books, webcasts and so on. It does *not* have to have your brand on it. But pay attention to copyright and such like. If in doubt, ask.

Case Study H – a top three mobile handset manufacturer

De-risking a product launch

The mobile handset market is fiercely competitive, nowhere more so than in the business sector. Phenomenally successful in the consumer marketplace, a top three mobile handset manufacturer is fighting hard to displace a competitor as the enterprise market leader. The firm had developed an innovative device capable of defeating its rival in a features battle. But perception is everything, and the firm had relatively weak awareness amongst its target business customers.

Influencer50 was commissioned to identify those individuals most influencing the enterprise sector in Germany, in readiness for the firm's forthcoming new product line. Influencer50 worked together with the firm's global marketing agency, which was responsible for all aspects of the company's WOM go-to-market strategy.

The research uncovered the huge influence and buying power exerted by Germany's government-housed Ministry for Economy and Technology and the Fraunhofer Gesellschaft research facility. Corporates were shown to follow the buying advice of such groups to a far higher degree than in the UK or US. With the growing trend for large organisations to outsource their IT infrastructure, the systems integrators were seen to be increasingly influencing the bulk purchasing of smartphones and personal digital assistants (PDAs). And not just the major SIs, but many niche or 'boutique' firms. In contrast, infrastructure giants such as IBM and HP, trade magazines and industry analysts exerted less than expected influence.

Using this insight, the firm targeted the top 100 influencers on business-orientated handsets in Germany. It sent each influencer a pre-launch handset and supporting material. It also created an online forum to gather influencers' views on the product's feature-set, price-points, launch strategy and choice of resellers. Using the forum, influencers could contribute their own experiences and suggestions, and see the opinions and comments from other influencers.

The feedback was used to make last stage modifications to the device, to the user documentation and to the launch strategy. Importantly, high visibility of the handset was established within the influencer community. Influencers had trialled the product, fed back on its capabilities and each had read the inputs of the wider influencer group.

The firm was able to launch the new handset into a market whose influencers were already aware of it and its features. These influencers started influencing the market, and the handset sold quickly and in volume.

As the firm's spokesperson commented, 'The addition of influencer identification and marketing into our WOM rollout campaign for the new handset has been invaluable. We could already target our expected consumer-base through our ongoing marketing, but identifying and working with the top-tier of market influencers was beyond our reach – and we knew it'.

Importantly, identifying and targeting influencers had substantially lowered the risk in launching the handset. Mobile devices are expensive to develop and market launch is a critical point in the commercial success, or otherwise, of each product. Pre-influencing a market prior to launch minimised the risk to the firm and underpinned a successful product release.

13

Evaluating *influencer marketing*

How can you place a value on the benefits of *influencer marketing* to your company?

The trouble with picking apart traditional marketing as it is now, and pointing out its deficiencies, is that one has to suggest something else. That something else is *influencer marketing*, but how do you know it's any better than what we've got already?

We said in our introduction that there are three problems with marketing:

- It is misaligned with sales and doesn't result in increased revenues
- It's broken: it doesn't do what it's designed to do
- Marketing doesn't reflect the modern decision process

We don't position *influencer marketing* as a replacement for the portfolio of marketing activities that firms do currently. It's both unrealistic and unnecessary to throw all of marketing out. What *influencer marketing* can do is point towards where you should be focusing your attention.

There are three areas where *influencer marketing* provides tangible benefits measured in cash terms. They are:

- Quick win tuning of existing marketing programmes for optimal effect and budget utilisation.
- Establishing new routes to market.
- Proving ROI on marketing, by increasing sales.

Let's look at where you can get early payback for your efforts.

Quick wins from influencer marketing

Influencer marketing provides focus and direction for the allocation of your marketing budget and time that is otherwise arbitrary. In Chapter 2 we looked at how marketing budgets are divided up. The rationale that is used seems to be based more on how expensive particular activities are, rather than their effectiveness. This is spectacularly true in the case of advertising, which is pointless in all but a select few cases.

Identifying influencers, the first step in *influencer marketing*, gives you the telescopic lens with which to implement a rifle shot approach to marketing. By understanding the most influential journalists you can treat them with more care and attention, playing down your activities with the others. Once you know who the influential analysts are, you can focus your AR programme there, and reduce the time you spend on those less useful. You'll know the systems integrators and resellers that have greatest influence over your target market. You'll then be able to restructure your partner strategy and programmes around those that can deliver the greatest benefits. You'll understand the competitors that your target customers listen to most. You'll be able to choose which events to attend, and which to avoid.

Is this tangible and measurable? Clearly, some of the benefits depend on what you're doing right now. If you're measuring press relations by column inches expect this number to decrease through *influencer marketing*. Quantity will decline but quality, of the coverage and of the journalists, will increase. In terms of revenue impact, PR is not the most measurable of activities at the best of times. What you can do of course, is use your influential press contacts to carry your message, as per our *marketing through* influencers discussion in Chapter 11.

But you can certainly gain cash-measurable ROI by streamlining your events programme. We know firms that have saved the cost of identifying their influencers by cancelling two events in their programme that they'd presumed were influential. They had been attending these well-known trade shows and had suspected a dubious return. But they had persisted in attending because of the pressure from sales ('We need to be there, or we're conspicuous by our absence'.), and the fact that everybody else attends. One thing a list of influencers does is challenge perceived wisdom, and for the first time they had proof that their target decision-makers did not attend these events.

We also had a client that had been partnering with top-tier partners, the IBMs and Accentures and KPMGs. It turned out that none of these were influential in their target market, which comprised mid-size enterprises. We identified the real influencers in their market, and made an introduction to them at an influencer-only roundtable meeting. The result was a rethink in partnership strategy, two new commercial relationships and $700 000 in new business in 12 months.

One firm made contact with two key influencers in the public sector, a notoriously difficult industry to break into without good contacts and a track record. Within 2 months of identifying its top 50 influencers, the firm had commissioned two previously unknown individuals to advise on tendering for public sector contracts. Two months later, as a direct result of these relationships, it had been sent three RFPs worth an annual $2.9 million. This is work that the firm would never have been aware of beforehand.

Creating new routes to market

Influencer marketing provides new routes to market. Or it provides routes into new markets, whichever is most constraining your sales. A great example of this is Case Study H, in which the firm has begun to pre-launch its handsets with influencers before public release. If you are moving into a new geography or vertical market it makes sense to find out who the primary influencers are before spending too much time and effort in the wrong areas.

Influencer marketing also helps with repositioning your firm in your marketplace. Firms often start selling their products to middle managers and operational executives. Sooner or later they outgrow this market and want to gain access to C-level management. There they can sell a broader value proposition and increase sales per customer organisation. The trouble is that having spent time in the middle management layer, that's where the C-levels assume you should be. How do you get your new target audience out of this mindset?

Similarly, selling business solutions to business people rather than products to support staff is an oft-cited shift in strategy, yet in practice it is extraordinarily hard. This is because you have to shift perceptions. 'I'm a business person: why are you talking to me? My technical people are over there . . .'. An approach that works is to identify influencers in the new target audience, and then get them to carry your message. And you use influencer-led collateral to support your legitimacy in the market. The ROI from this activity is easy to measure: do you successfully penetrate the market or not?

Success is not always down to having a great plan though, so make sure you invest in the implementation and execution elements. *Influencer marketing* may tell you the most influential people in the market, but your salespeople may not be trained talking to C-level executives or business managers, or whatever your new target audience is. One of our early mistakes was to assume that client firms knew how to engage with their market, and just needed us to point them in the right direction. Not so, and we had to develop sales training courses to bridge the gap in skills.

Selling more

RoI in *influencer marketing* is measurable in cash terms. If you orientate your marketing programmes around influencers, then align those influencers with your sales objections, you can create a set of marketing messages that directly influence sales. The disclaimer that it's all in the execution still applies, but your salespeople will have fewer excuses and less cause to blame marketing! In fact, a predictor for RoI we often use it to measure the perception uplift of marketing's usefulness by the sales force.

Influencers increase the velocity of sales because sales objections can now be predicted and counter-arguments prepared. And because influencers are more likely to be believed you are more likely to get past these objections faster – certainly faster than your competitors! Sales cycles will reduce, close rates will increase and you can tangibly measure the impact on sales from your marketing programmes.

Lead generation

Our views on lead generation are very closely tied to those on marketing in general. Leads are difficult to generate when marketing doesn't work very well. Particularly if no one is listening to your message, all messages sound the same and prospects don't believe what you tell them.

It makes all the difference if you can get influencers to break down some of these barriers. For example, plenty of firms set up seminars or webinars in which their senior management just give a pitch. Why would a prospect turn up to listen to this? Instead, why not get an influencer to speak?

You could invite a customer or analyst or regulator or academic: someone to draw in a crowd, get people thinking and engage them in discussion.

Many firms use hospitality as a means of breaking the ice. So salespeople can call a prospect on Monday and ask whether they enjoyed the match on Saturday. Why not invite them to dinner with an influencer instead? The prospect might actually learn something, and the conversation is business-related so the prospect stays focused. It might not be so much fun, but let's stay in touch with the core purpose of marketing. The example we provide in Case Study A is illustrative. It constructed an innovative format for its seminar (a debate), hired an influential chairperson and two engaging and outspoken protagonists. In fact, the event *was* fun, as the debate wasn't too serious, and lots of interesting points were covered. Importantly, the issues raised by the audience reflected their reservations – objections, if you like – to homeworking, which proved useful in building successful sales campaigns to prospects.

You can use influencer-led collateral in your direct mail pieces, webcasts and podcasts, PR, research and (if you must) advertising. If you are using influencers appropriately you should get better returns from your lead generation activities.

We have noticed that, for some firms, the number of leads goes down over the course of an *influencer marketing* programme. This is because more time and effort is being taken on the type and quality of leads, rather than quantity. So returning from an event with the glass bowl filled with business cards (delegates only wanted to enter the prize draw) is replaced by a smaller number of engaged and informed prospects. It's not the number of leads you generate that's important, but the number you eventually close.

Price increases

It's easier to increase profits by raising prices than by cutting costs. In fact, according to McKinsey, a 1 per cent rise in price can lead to an 8 per cent profit increase. Nobody buys solely on price. If you need proof of this, take a look at the cars being driven on the road. They are all functionally the same, yet some people (or companies) pay five or ten times more than others, based on their perceptions of value.

Influencers increase the perception of value. Why? Because they are influencers! They are the most important, most respected, most listened to individuals in your market. Weaving them into your marketing strategy appropriately means that they implicitly are aligned with your firm. They confirm the value of what you are selling, and convey confidence in your solution. So you should be able to sell for more.

Influencer Promoter Score

There is one conclusive and persuasive strand of research that does provide tangible evidence of a link between marketing and sales. It is the Ultimate Question concept, defined originally by Fred Reichheld's paper *The One Number You Need To Grow* in the *Harvard Business Review* in 2003, and followed by the inevitable book *The Ultimate Question*. The basic concept is that you poll your customers on one key question – 'Would you refer us to a friend or colleague?' The result of positives minus negatives (excluding neutrals) gives you a Net Promoter Score (NPS). If you are interested in this idea, we also suggest reading Paul Marsden's work on *Advocacy Drives Growth*, which adds further proof points to Reichheld's work.

What is interesting is that NPS is very close in concept to the influencer opinion tracking concept we talked about in Chapter 9. The key difference is that you're asking influencers, not customers. What you are after, put simply, is whether your influencers would recommend you, or validate a decision in your favour, to your target market. You're asking the Ultimate Question: 'would you recommend us?'

This is valuable because influencer favourability should lead to customer favourability. And customer favourability leads to growth. Now as far as we know, there is yet no academic evidence to support our claim that influencer favourability precedes customer favourability. But it's a plausible proposition.

What to do with detractors

Inevitably, some people are more predisposed to your firm than others. It is this difference that allows us to detect an NPS amongst customers. Similarly, the idea of an Influencer Promoter Score depends on the spread of disposition across a market's influencers. It begs the question: if we have detractors how do we turn them into promoters for (or at least neutral towards) the firm?

Some firms we know label influencers as detractors or sceptics: influencers that are fixed in their hostility towards their firm. Nonsense. Influencers start out neutral. Always. They don't care whether you are better or worse than your rivals. This is because influencers don't buy from you. Even those influencers that have commercial relationships with you (e.g. systems integrators, resellers) only do so because it serves their self-interest. If you fail to deliver suitable margin they'll drop you without a second thought. It is further supported by the efficacy of the Delphi approach to forecasting. Delphi uses a panel of experts to reach a consensus forecast, proven to be a reliable indicator of future outcomes.[1]

The first step is to determine whether your perception of detractors is accurate. Some influencers appear sceptical in an interview situation, then actively promote you once they've digested your news and discussed it with others. For those influencers that publish their thoughts it's fairly easy to determine their favourability, but for other types of influencer it's much harder. You have to dig deeper into the DME to find out more.

So why would an influencer become a detractor? Are they naturally sceptical about any new initiative? Have you given them cause to doubt your sincerity? Have you offended (or, worse, ignored) them in the past? The biggest reason for an influencer becoming a detractor is that they haven't been marketed to appropriately. This means that they've probably been sent press releases (about you) rather than been consulted on relevant issues (about them).

Occasionally, an influencer will have an allegiance to, or be, a competitor. In fact, it's rare for a competitor to be an active and outspoken detractor these days, but it does happen. It's always worthwhile marketing to a competitor or a channel partner: if they have to insult someone let it not be your firm. And channel players are notoriously promiscuous, frequently changing their allegiances. With independent influencers you will sometime encounter an intellectual disagreement, where they just don't agree with your strategy or viewpoint. These can be the most difficult situations to deal with because influencers can be intransigent in their views. And then there are the petty reasons such as professional jealousy and envy.

There are three strategies for dealing with detractors. You can convert them, surround them with other influencers, thereby neutralising them, or you can ignore them.

Converting influencers is all about practising *influencer marketing*. If you follow the steps that we have outlined throughout this book we're confident that most detractors will come around. They want some TLC, and *influencer marketing* is an ideal way to deliver it. As we said, the most likely reason for them being detractors in the first place is that you were marketing to them badly or not at all. Change this, and you'll change the influencer.

You'll remember that influencers cluster together and that they get a lot of their influence from each other. Influencers love to influence, and they'll try to influence each other. Surrounding detractors with neutral and positive influencers means that some of the positive influence should rub off onto the detractors. So creating environments (forums, influencer meetings, even blogs) in which influencers can interact are very effective. This only works if you have more promoters than detractors, otherwise the opposite effect may occur. You also have to make sure that you follow up any group interaction with 1-to-1 marketing, to reinforce the positive messages relayed from the promoting influencers.

Ignoring influencers is a risky strategy, but it can be effective in some cases. What we're actually recommending is that you *pretend* to ignore the influencer, by excluding them from your overt attention. But you keep very close to the influencer to assess their actions and responses. Again, what you're trying to do is to create opportunities for influencers to meet each other, and if your detractor is excluded from these occasions it can soften their stance towards you. It could, of course, have the opposite effect, which is why we say it's a risky approach. This technique works best with influencers further down the order of priority – don't try it with your top 20 influencers. Once you detect some movement in their attitude, swiftly welcome them into the community again. Influencers hate to be isolated.

Key points in this chapter

1. You can use *influencer marketing* to tune existing marketing pro-grammes for optimal effect and budget utilisation. Your ranked list of influencers directs you to the most important journalists, analysts, trade shows, channel partners, forums, magazines and blogs.
2. By identifying the top influencers you also identify new routes to market. Use influencers to gain access to prospects, and pre-influence the market by involving influencers in product launches.
3. Use influencers in your lead generation activities. And use influencer-led collateral to counter sales objections and close leads. Your lead gen quality will increase, and sales cycles will decrease.

Case Study I – A mobile device management provider

ROI on influencer marketing in I week

This firm was one of the world's top three mobile device management software vendors with revenues of over $100 million and over 200 employees. Europe represented over 40 per cent of the global revenue. In addition to selling direct to enterprise clients, it also operated a reseller channel consisting of services companies, systems integrators, small-scale consultancies and VARs. The company wanted to better understand the sales process as it moved into new markets selling higher priced services.

Prior to the project, the company almost exclusively focused on a number of trade journalists and a small range of mid-tier technical consultancies. The traditional Big Four management consultancy firms were also invited to regular seminars. VARs were managed by channel representatives but had no involvement with the marketing team.

Using its new list of influencers, the firm now runs a 'buddy' system between senior management and the top influencers. it has reduced its emphasis on the Big Four consulting firms and increased its focus on the second-tier players, and has integrated its channel communications within its marketing activities to centralise messaging.

Importantly, it no longer measures just volume of media coverage but incentivises its PR agency to deliver only in the most influential titles.

Within a week of receiving the Report, the company had cancelled a proposed trade show booth, saving $16 000 (because our research showed its new target audience would not be likely to attend), had re-prioritised a planned print advertising campaign and secured $10 000 in additional funding from senior management, who had new-found enthusiasm for the marketing department's programmes.

'Our sales force have increasingly recognised the role of influencers in the majority of their major sales opportunities', says the Field Marketing Manager. 'We're now involving our senior management in acting on the Report's findings'.

Note and reference

1 Read 'The wisdom of (experts) crowds' by Robert Duboff, in Harvard Business Review, September 2007.

14

Influencer marketing and word of mouth

> Creating WOM is now widely accepted as an important goal of many marketing campaigns. How does *influencer marketing* relate to WOM?

We now want to take some time to explore a number of the newer developments in marketing, and how each relates to influencer marketing. Over the next few chapters we will cover movements like WOM, followed by social media like blogs, wikis and MySpace, YouTube and LinkedIn.

Why is influencer marketing different from WOM?

WOM is an extraordinary mechanism that communicates marketing messages throughout a community. To paraphrase a popular slogan from the 1970s, WOM reaches the parts other marketing tactics cannot reach.

There are few marketing approaches that can have had as much discussion in the twenty-first century as WOM. The ideas that underpin *word of mouth* are communicated best by WOM tactics, so that WOM is an instance of itself. This has been aided by numerous books on the subject. *The Tipping Point* features *connectors*, people that know a lot of other people and communicate ideas. Seth Godin's *Unleashing the Ideavirus* explores how and why ideas spread. *The Anatomy of Buzz* by Emanuel Rosen charted the mechanics of how to create and sustain WOM. Justin Kirby and

Paul Marsden edited *Connected Marketing*, a collection of solutions and approaches based on practitioner experience. And *Naked Conversations* by Robert Scoble and Shel Israel noted the migration of WOM from the real world to the internet through blogs. The definitive guide to implementing WOM is Andy Sernovitz's *Word of Mouth Marketing*.[1]

WOM is immensely powerful. Arguably it has created the most powerful brands of today, that of Google. Starbucks, Ikea, Nokia, Prada, Skype and Tamagotchi were all built predominantly or exclusively on WOM. In many ways it sits next door to, but is different from, *influencer marketing*.

Some problems with WOM

Much of the common perception of WOM is that it is spread evenly. The question that marketers usually ask is, how to get their ideas or messages to spread to their target market. Emphasis in the answer focuses on the substance of the message. The perceived wisdom is: create a viral message and watch it spread. The majority of activity, therefore, in WOM is in the creation of messages that are intentionally viral in nature. The big problem here is that it is difficult to predict which messages eventually do become viral. Who would have thought that Linerider would spread like wildfire? Or a yeti clubbing a penguin across a snowy landscape? (If you have to ask, you should be more connected . . . .)

There is another aspect to WOM that is regarded universally as a positive attribute – that it's good for messages to spread. Spread like what? Oil spreads on water until the layer of oil is a molecule thick (given enough space). WD40 spreads everywhere, into every nook and cranny, but that includes places you don't want it. Why do you want your message everywhere? This is traditional marketing mindset. Surely it's better to target your WOM efforts at an appropriate audience.

It strikes us that today's marketers want to use WOM in the next 50 years like traditional marketers used advertising in the previous 50. WOM, they think, hits the mass market and is the ideal replacement medium to combat the diminishing impact of TV and print ads. Those that think this way have missed the point of WOM.

Consider spam e-mail – you receive something irrelevant from someone you don't know. Whoosh – it's deleted without you even reading it. We even use automated tools to filter the spam out before we see it. Much of the generated WOM is the same as spam. It goes from the wrong people to the wrong people. Most marketers don't mind this, because WOM is free at the point of distribution, just like spam and advertising. So just keep sending it out and some of it will stick.

What most marketers actually want is a message that spreads like crunchy peanut butter – it spreads, just, but it stays within a defined boundary (the slice of bread). You don't want it running down your arm. Importantly, there are small areas with more impact (the crunchy bits) that influence the surrounding larger smooth parts. It's the crunchy bits that give the whole experience texture and flavour. Smooth peanut butter is bland, suitable only for the youngest of kids.

It matters whose mouth the words come from

This chapter is all about the inter-relationship between WOM and *influencer marketing*. It is influenced by a single idea that appeared in Seth Godin's *Purple Cow*. Seth's idea was that it is useless to advertise to anyone except interested *sneezers* (*connectors*) with influence. As we say in Chapter 2, advertising doesn't work anymore. Actually, that's not quite true: it does work on interested people, those that happen to be (a) interested in what you're selling, and (b) likely to spread your message to others in their WOM community. Unfortunately, the likelihood that you find someone with both of these attributes is tiny, which is why advertising on the whole doesn't work.

But imagine if you targeted only those people that were both listening and interested. More, that they would *sneeze* the message to tell other people, their friends or work colleagues or associates. This group doesn't listen to you, but they listen to the person that's initially interested.

Most marketing messages are blocked by a wall of indifference (Figure 14.1). They receive too many messages, they all sound the same,

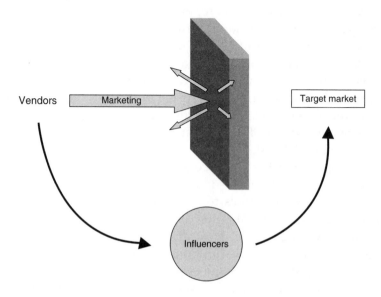

Figure 14.1   Influencers bypass the traditional 'wall of indifference'

and even if they were heard and different, they wouldn't be believed. People rarely buy just because they are marketed to. The marketing message is carried, corroborated, enhanced and personalised through influential WOM. WOM needs *sneezers* with influence. WOM carried by people other than influencers is just noise. People that try to carry WOM inappropriately, because they don't have sufficient influence, end up shouting at or boring their audience. In other words, it matters whose mouth the words come from.

Blogs are an archetype of this sort of WOM. Most blogs are just background noise. Others try to gain attention by shouting, making controversial, aggressive or offensive remarks just to get noticed. Only a few blogs carry influence in any market, and in some markets there are zero influential blogs.

Influencer marketing takes Seth Godin's idea of advertising to influential *sneezers*, and extends it to all forms of marketing. *Influencer marketing* is about changing a scatter-shot approach into a rifle-shot one. You target specific influencers, not generic prospect customers.

WOM, by its nature is difficult to control. Once the message is out there, there is no stopping it. It can die quickly, pervade the market or go where it shouldn't.

Dangers of WOM – the talker can get it wrong

Sometime WOM gets it wrong. Often these end up as harmless urban myths. But not always, with serious consequences. 3Com is a case in point. In 2000, suffering from fierce competition with Cisco, 3Com exited its high-end router business, leaving many of its larger corporate customers high and dry. Seven years later, 3Com is a different company. There are new people in charge, the product set is strong and focused, and few within the company remember the bad old days of 2000. Unfortunately, negative WOM still exists. 3Com's biggest sales objection today is: 'You screwed us in 2000 and we won't let you do it again!'

The problem with WOM is that the combination of it being wrong and out of control is explosive. You have a ton of clearing up to do, with the prospect that you'll never quite scrub the whole market clean. Unless you use influencers. Because influencers have the inside track to decision-makers they can carry a corrective message. 'It's okay to buy 3Com'.

If you are using WOM as a marketing tactic you must identify the relevant influencers. There are two main reasons for this:

■ Influencers optimise the message. Influencers talk to decision-makers – that's what our definition of influencers means. So, again by definition, influencers take messages to decision-makers. You therefore have an optimised route to your target market.

- Influencers amplify the message. A message carried by an influencer is reinforced just by the fact that it's an influencer doing the communicating. If the influencer says so, it must be true. So any WOM that traces its origins back to an influencer carries more weight and impact than one that can't be traced (or is traced to someone with little influence).

WOM is ideally suited to the world of influence. This is because WOM is a primary mechanism for exerting influence. Recommendations, experiences, gossip and stories from the field are all types of WOM, and all related by various influencer types. Some of this communication is formal and overt, published in books, analyst reports, journalistic articles and blogs. But much of it, up to 80 per cent we estimate, happens in closed circles. These can be private meetings, invitation-only events, on the golf course, in lifts, over lunch and so on. Much of the influence of consultants and third party advisors to decision-makers comes not in the form of specific strategic or project recommendations, but by WOM, whispered in the ear of the decision-maker. It is never published but sways the decision totally. The WOM mantra 'Nobody ever got fired for buying IBM' is the classic example of this, however out-of-date. It's informal, unprovable and possibly never even accurate. But it carried enormous weight in the 1970s and 1980s.

Why WOM doesn't work so well in B2B

We've discussed WOM as a powerful means of carrying a marketing message, and how influencers optimise and amplify the message. WOM messages are carried between peers and it works well in business-to-consumer (B2C) markets between consumer peers. This is because people like to talk to other people (peers) about common interests and whatever new stuff they've encountered.

But in a B2B context business people do not often talk to peers in other businesses. There are two main reasons for this:

- There are few opportunities to converse. Other than at trade conferences how often do business people get together? Not often enough.
- When business peers do get together they immediately encounter competitive pressures not to discuss what they are doing. Clearly this is less of an issue between non-competing firms. But these days the norm is for conferences to have an industry focus. This increases the value of the presentations and exhibitions, but decreases the likelihood that attendees will talk about their own businesses.

This is why reference customers are so valuable – they are a scarce resource. It is relatively rare that businesses are willing to discuss their procurement decisions with other firms, so customers have to be cajoled into being references. The incidence of what we call 'reference fatigue' is high, where the same customer firms are swamped with reference requests from their vendors.

Businesses do however talk to consultants and advisers. They read management books and trade publications. They attend conferences and join user groups. They listen to regulators and standards bodies. They seek out thought leaders, academics and other opinion formers. In other words, they use influencers as a proxy for genuine peer-generated WOM.

In a consumer context, most people use friends and colleagues as a reference point for purchase decisions. In a B2B context, most businesses use influencers.

What should you do?

Influencers are influencers because they have expertise, have access to decision-makers and *because they like to influence*. So they are more than willing to pass on messages that reinforce their influence. The crux of *influencer marketing* is to communicate your messages to influencers, and then see those messages being communicated by influencers to your customers and prospects.

Key points in this chapter

1. WOM is a powerful communications mechanism. But it matters whose mouth the words come from. Using influencers to communicate messages means that WOM is carried to the right people and with credibility and authority.
2. WOM doesn't work well in B2B markets. This is because of the lack of opportunities for business people to converse, and due to the commercial sensitivities that exist between firms.
3. WOM is prone to urban myth and just plain wrong messages. Influencers can optimise WOM by correcting erroneous messages and misunderstandings.

Case Study J – Adobe

Low-cost vertical industry marketing

Adobe, a developer, distributor and seller of software for business and creative use, hired California-based Rubicon Consulting to leverage a vertical market through an influencer marketing programme designed to select, recruit and develop an advisory group of influential users.

Adobe wanted to find low-cost ways to market one of its flagship products, photoshop, to vertical markets. The company knew there was a substantial revenue opportunity. Traditional vertical marketing is costly, requiring an in-house marketing team of three to four (frequently more) for each vertical. Influencer marketing leveraged enthusiastic customers and electronic communications to get the benefits at a fraction of the cost.

Influencers were defined as early adopters who make purchase recommendations and channel comments and ideas from a market to the vendor. The desired goal was interaction at decisive moments of trust. By making influencers into informal, extended members of the marketing team, the firm would reach its target consumers as those moments occurred.

There were four phases to the resulting project:

Target determination: Rubicon documented goals and expectations. An internal audit and data analysis were performed. The market segment to be pursued was determined. The deliverable was a written report recommending which vertical to pursue and success metrics with 90-day, 6-month and 1-year benchmarks.

Pilot plan creation: Rubicon determined programme steps and resources required. The programme was designed to educate influencers about Adobe's products and services, and to provide tools for ease of information sharing with influencers. The project would determine how, where and when opinions were being shared in the market, identify targeted key influencers and then create engagement programmes to leverage influencers.

Approaches included:

- Develop tools to make 'telling a friend' easier.
- Create forums, feedback tools and an influencer advisory group.
- Create blogs and other tools to share information.
- Participate openly on non-Adobe online blogs and discussions.
- Work with social networks. Host discussions/message boards about products.

- Support independent, grassroots groups that form around a product.
- Provide recognition and tools to active advocates.
- Track/respond to conversations by supporters, detractors and neutrals.
- Metrics and ROI measures.

Pilot plan execution: Rubicon deployed the pilot (using proprietary methods and tools), identified groups and individuals, then tested the tools, programmes and resources for 3 months. Influencers were recruited. A critical factor was selecting people likely to share their opinions and create a multiplier effect.

Recommendations for next steps and documentation of best practices: The firm received documentation on what worked, what didn't and recommendations for the future. A key employee was debriefed, after which they took on programme management in-house.

Rubicon concluded that influencer programmes must adapt to the unique needs of the market and that communication must be calibrated to methods preferred by the influencer group. Recruiting of influencers should be performed in two phases to ensure the proper mix of

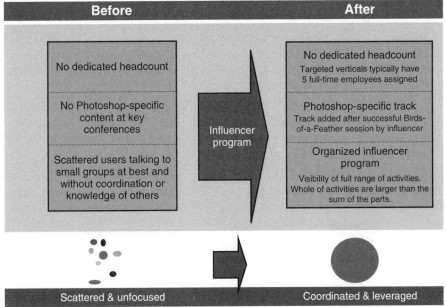

© 2007 Rubicon Consulting, Inc.

productive advisory group members. Insights gleaned from the first round of recruiting should be leveraged during the second round to achieve a mix of influencers that reflect all product subgroups. It is important to ensure that influencer group members are active, not silent.

It also found that influencers want companies to provide leadership in setting standards. Firms employing influencer marketing techniques must identify an in-house individual who will maintain relationships and momentum, and to measure responses and effectiveness to make sure that goals are achieved. (© Rubicon Consulting 2007)

Note and reference

1 Just for the record, we have no affiliations with these authors, nor do we get kickbacks for recommending their works. We simply acknowledge their influence on our thinking and we suggest that you let their insight influence yours too.

15

Social media – the new influence enablers

Everyone wants to know how influential blogs have become. Here we tell you.

Technology has changed the game of influence. The mechanisms through which individuals could exert influence used to be limited in number and in reach. To acquire global coverage you had to hold a position of status in government or an international corporation, or be widely published in respected media and journals. Nowadays, you need access to a PC and a phone line or wireless connection.

The web makes it easier to communicate in one direction and email facilitates mass targeted communication to people you know (or whose names you buy). But influence requires interaction, and the host of emerging social media enable influence to be exerted across a global audience.

Social media includes the online technologies and techniques that people use to share opinions, insights, experiences and perspectives. It takes many different forms, including text, images, audio and video. These sites typically use technologies such as blogs, message boards, podcasts, wikis and vlogs to allow users to interact.

It's no coincidence that WOM marketing is rising at the same time as social media technologies. They are part of the same phenomenon in which people prefer to communicate with other people on a personalised and (to some degree anyway) intimate basis. WOM formalises the process of tapping into everyday conversations, and maps out how to use those conversations as a marketing tactic. Similarly, social media technologies tap into the same conversations but enable them to be conducted online, in doing so reaching a new (and sometimes larger) audience.

Why influence *enablers*?

Social media by themselves do not influence decision-makers. It is the content, and more specifically the content creators, that carry influence. Social media *enables* the spread and reach of any message carried. It is the nature of the media to spread content widely – any piece of content can reach anyone on the web. But when social media are used by influencers the content is carried with authority, which makes its impact profound.

In only a few cases is influence gained through using social media. More commonly, it is a subset of pre-existing influencers that then migrate that influence on to social media. There, influence can certainly be enhanced, through the extraordinary reach of the web.

But social media is many years away from the enviable position of the likes of the BBC or the *Wall Street Journal*. These institutions can create influencers by giving them a forum in which to operate. Most journalists draw their influence in no small part from the title to which they are affiliated. Many of the claims on the influence of social media are based on the number of links, which are then compared favourably with more traditional influencers' web sites. The most that can be said today is that social media have influence amongst their constituent users. But influence, particularly in the field of decision-making, is a considerably broader community. That said, we are just at the beginning of this shift towards social media as influence *enablers*. This chapter is an attempt to hit a target that is moving quickly.

The influence of blogs

One of the most often asked questions on influence sources is: how influential are bloggers? And we can say that the answer is unequivocal – 'that depends!'. But it's currently less than you imagine.

Blogs are the most prevalent and fastest growing type of social media today. According to Technorati, there were over 70 million blogs in May 2007, growing from 50 million in September 2006. 125 000 new blogs are created every day – that's three new blogs every 2 s. The rate of growth is slowing, but at its current rate there will be 100 million blogs by early 2008.

As we have said throughout, context is everything. Influence depends on which market or segment you happen to be looking at. So it is with blogs – some consumer markets are influenced heavily by them, while others have yet to be influenced at all. What we can say for sure is that the majority of blogs have absolutely zero influence. The trick is to find the few bloggers that *are* influential.

The best place to start when examining blogger influence is the blogosphere itself. But finding influential bloggers is like finding needles in very large haystacks. Remember that influence is a product not just of awareness and frequency. So finding a blog that appears relevant is not the same as finding one that carries influence. Google, Technorati and others search on awareness (measured in the number of links) and currency of posts, which is a reasonable proxy for frequency. The more posts you make the higher the likelihood that you posted recently. But Google doesn't judge the quality of impact of a blog, nor on any other influence criteria. We're presented with a skewed view of the influence of blogs by those that measure the blogosphere.

This point was made to us back in September 2006, when we presented at a Social Media conference in London. We used our *Analyst influence is diminishing* slide, which compares the decline in share of influence of journalists and analysts, and the rise in influence of blogs (Figure 15.1).

Stowe Boyd, a blogging guru and evangelist, commented that in the US at least, the lines had already crossed – that is, blogs are now more influential than analysts and journalists combined.

The only way of making sense of this comment is to consider the influence of analysts and journalists on the blogosphere itself, in which case they probably are less influential than bloggers. But the blogosphere isn't (yet) the totality of real life. It certainly doesn't reflect the way that most consumers and businesses procure stuff. The influence of journalists is still huge in most markets. Even Technorati data bear this out – it shows that the majority of web sites are mainstream (traditional) media compared with blogs. In Q4 2006 blogs accounted for less than 25 per cent of the top 100 news sites (Figure 15.2).

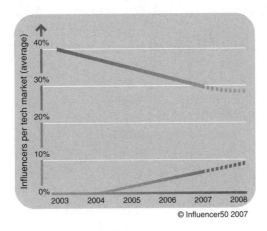

© Influencer50 2007

Figure 15.1   Influencer share is being distributed

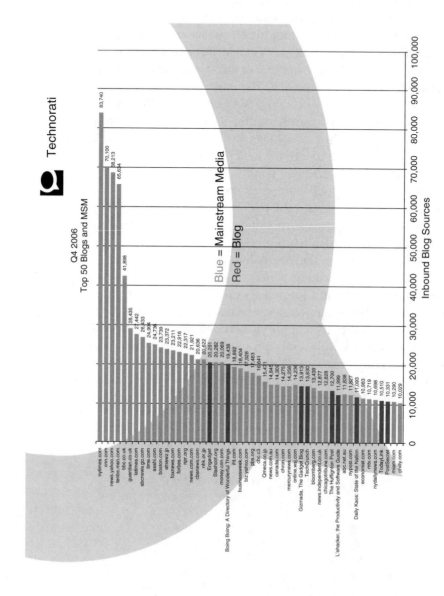

Figure 15.2 Blogs account for less than 25% of the top 100 news sites

Influencers blog rather than bloggers influence

An individual's influence is derived not from the fact that they blog, but from some other source, such as their job, or experience, or knowledge, or status. The fact that they blog is coincidental. The famed tech entrepreneur Guy Kawasaki defines a blogger as someone with nothing to say writing for someone with nothing to do. This does not sound like a definition of an influencer.

Bloggers tend to influence the blogosphere – other bloggers, plus those lurkers that just read (rather than contribute to) blogs. Few have made the transition from blogger to influencer, but plenty have gone in the other direction.

At Influencer50 we had a challenging introduction to the world of blogging. One of our clients, Marqui, posted on their blog a synopsis of the project that we'd done for them. The post was picked up by the Work Industries blog (http://www.iworkindustries.com/blog/) which commented thus:

> I don't think that the Influencer50 is a great way to tap into the collective and collected information on the web about your product/service and company. Inherently it's very limited – a standardized methodology with standardized outputs . . .

> . . . the darker side to outsourced reporting like Influencer50 is that it acts as a validator for companies who choose not to form relationships . . .

> . . . the existence of Influencer50 points to a deficit of engagement in technology companies and an engrained avoidance of risk.

Yikes! Standard procedure in command-and-control marketing strategy dictates a plan of damage limitation and immediate rebuttal. Unfortunately, that's what we did, posting a 500 word response. We shouldn't have bothered. Marqui also posted a response, more concise and more credible than our own, in defence of us. It said,

> These are pretty strong words about Influencer50's initial report. Have you commissioned one personally? The reason I ask is because Marqui was very involved in the process and the i50 team did quite a bit more than just 'standardized market research'.

Most effective was a subsequent post on Marqui's own blog which stated,

> I'm pleased to say that our initial report is now finished, and we are **delighted** with it.

This episode taught us a few things:

■ What is the influence of the detractor? In this case the answer was: none. The blogger has little influence over our target market (we checked). They'd never used our services and had no familiarity with our approach.

- Blogs appear to exaggerate the impact of detractors. Once something is posted on the web it's easy to assume that, since *anyone* can read it, *everyone* does read it. This is not true. The only people that commented on the negative post were the blogger, us and the client.
- The best strategy to correct a detractor is to use a promoter influencer, ideally a happy customer as in our case. In fact, we didn't even ask Marqui to post, they did it anyway. Blogs tend to self-correct.

It also taught us that the command-and-control mindset won't work on the Web. It's a lesson that has stuck with us.

The profile of an influential blogger

The most influential bloggers are different from 'normal' people. Normal people gain success through being charming and polite. They are statistically more likely to be tall and attractive. It's an advantage to be gregarious, even extrovert. They will be astute in the corporate political environment, possibly sycophantic, and certainly immersed in strategic, high-level issues. They are rarely *detail* people. With apologies for this gross stereotyping, it seems that influential bloggers may fit into the opposite end of the corporate spectrum.

Blogging offers an avenue for creativity and expression to those that may be uncomfortable in other social settings. It seems to help to be slightly quirky in personality. While this quirkiness may present as awkwardness in typical social situations, it often appears entertaining and thought-provoking in a blog. Influential bloggers are unlikely to fit into patterns expected by corporate employers.

Hugh MacLeod, who writes the controversial but undeniably funny *Gaping Void* blog and draws punchy cartoons, admits that he didn't fit in to the corporate mentality expected of a mainstream marketing agency. The technology analyst James Governor has gained substantial credibility through his Redmonk blog. Yet James acknowledges that a mainstream analyst career with Gartner or Forrester (in their current form) is unlikely given his antipathy towards corporate groupthink and fondness for expletives. Robert Scoble admits in his *Naked Conversations* book that he was a risk when hired by Microsoft. (He was right, and is no longer with Microsoft.) It may be that the best people to write, or contribute to, blogs are not the people you'd first imagine. It certainly won't be the corporate press officer or marketing copywriter – the end product becomes too polished to be authentic and too bland to be either noteworthy or comment-provoking.

You get influence through blogging by building a community. Blogging is very clique-driven. You can join a clique, but the initiation process is long, involving the building of credibility through insightful comments on your own blog and those of others. It pays to be persistent when it comes to blogging. It also pays to lurk around a few blogs to acclimatise to the tone and sophistication of the discussions.

What is most interesting about influential blogs is that the bloggers are not necessarily natural connectors. True connectors reach out to connect with people. Influential bloggers are sought out because they have influence in what they say. People connect to them.

The *Long Tail* is a type of statistical distribution that looks like this. (Figure 15.3)

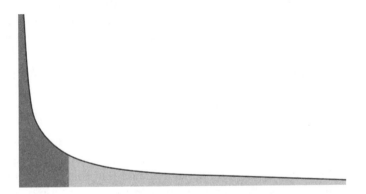

Figure 15.3   The Long tail

The idea is that *long tail* markets have a small number of instances (books, CDs, etc.) that have a high frequency (i.e. sell lots), and a high number of instances that have a low frequency (i.e. don't sell much). Markets are traditionally bound by physical and geographical constraints that force them to carry only high-frequency stock. So book shops only sell titles that will sell quickly and in high volumes. The web allows businesses to stock a huge number of items in warehouses. Although the demand for these items is low, it is not zero, and thus taps latent demand previously unserved.

The *long tail* is evident in the business models of Amazon, eBay, Google, iTunes and many others. It is also present in blogs and other social media technologies, where most of the content and traffic is concentrated at the *head* of the curve, but the tail still serves a tangible and reachable audience.

Chris Anderson, editor-in-chief at Wired magazine, first used the term in its current context, and it served as the title of his highly praised 2006 book.

Long tail influencers

Most blogs are written for *long tail* markets (see above box). This fact is simple to illustrate. Figure 15.4 below shows the 100 most popular blogs as rated by Technorati on a given day.[1] Note the *long tail* shape that is evident. And this is only for the top 100 blogs. There are over 100 million blogs, which equate to a very very *long tail*.

Long tail markets are, by definition, small and niche. Blogs are the diametric opposite to mainstream broadcast media, such as national TV, radio and newspapers. Blogs focus on specific areas of interest aimed at a (relatively) few people with that same interest. Broadcast media are aimed at the masses, using the law of averages.

In the last decade there has been an emergence of niche TV and radio channels aimed at specific demographics, whether based on music preference, religion, language, sporting affiliation or whatever. These are *long tail* markets too, but they have several disadvantages over social media:

- They are not predicated on interactivity (though some offer phone-in discussions)
- They are expensive to produce

In contrast, most social media engage the audience (if executed well) and are cheap to use. The cost of creating and maintaining a blog on your favourite subject is, largely, your time. The fact that this low cost of entry leads to multiple blog failures (due to apathy, lack of time, changing interests, etc.) is of little consequence. The availability of near-zero cost computing and network capacity means that serial blog creation is possible, and may indeed be the norm. Gartner estimates that 200 million

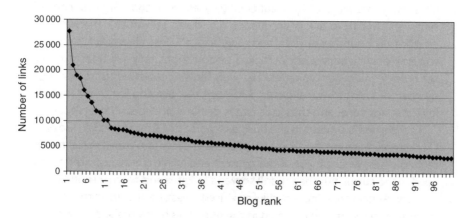

Figure 15.4　Blogs exhibit a long tail characteristic

bloggers have ceased posting. It may be that many of these have since created new blogs, though that's impossible to know.

So blogs proliferate. And they become more and more focused on increasingly narrow niches. There are 800 000 blogs about cheese, 17 000 blogs on platform shoes and 9000 blogs on pet hamsters. This is seriously *long tail* stuff! Because blogs and other social media are aimed at *long tail* markets there are two main implications for marketers:

- Blogger influence is restricted to that *long tail* niche, and irrelevant outside it.
- Blogger influence within that niche market may be substantial, out-weighing other real world influences.

Our case study of a large enterprise software vendor illustrates this (Case Study K). The vast majority of blogs on its product portfolio are written by techies for techies. It's the database systems and middleware technologies that attract bloggers. The business application software, for accountants and HR departments, don't have many blogs at all. In fact, bloggers are incredibility specific. It's not just 'technology issues', but security issues in the database management toolset, or an equally precise focus. Blogs are the domain of geeks.

What's relevant to *influencer marketing* is that you can create influencers from bloggers, Because bloggers are passionate about their subject they speak with credibility and, hopefully, authority. So they are ideal promoters. And they are authentic because they don't work for the firm. They typically work for the firm's customers or channel.

Why blog influence is overstated

The Technorati site has a quote on its homepage that reads: '100 million blogs . . . some of them *have* to be good'. The law of averages creates the expectation that, out there, some blogs are actually worthwhile reading.

In fact, the law of averages actually works against us. Average means that, by definition, most bloggers don't have authority or expertise, which would confer influence. And finding the ones that are influential is next to impossible.

When discussing influential blogs it is meaningless to talk percentages of 100 million. One per cent of 100 million is still 1 million, which is roughly 40 times greater than the highest linked (and probably therefore the most read) blog. So influential blogs, measured by links alone, are likely to be no more that 0.025 per cent of all blogs. The question is not what percentage of blogs are influential. The key question is, which blogs reach, and have influence over, *your* audience? Our best estimate is that, for any one market there is a maximum of seven blogs that have measurable influence. That's it – seven.

Maybe some markets have more than seven influential blogs. We pick seven as a likely average because that's the limit of most people's cognitive capacity. Once the number of blogs on a subject exceeds seven, people start to forget them. The seven influential blogs may change over time, but there will always be that limit, more or less.

We also set the maximum of seven influential blogs per market because that happens to be the average number of influencers in the top 50 of any category, real world or online, in a specific market. Some categories have more influencers, the media and consultants for instance, but these tend to be the more established categories with credibility and authority proven over time. In fact, from our own research, the number of influential blogs in the top 50 influencers in tech markets ranges from none to four. Even in these tech markets the number of influential blogs peaks at well below our theoretical average. Perhaps our average is too high.

Of course, there is an upward trend in influential blogs. 2005 was the first year we even detected an influential B2B blog. So it's early days yet. Today the influence of blogs in business is much lower than often presumed. Many markets have no blogging influence at all, and these markets aren't restricted to obscure fringes. The financial services industry in the UK has zero influential blogs (though there are influencers in the space that blog). It turns out that bankers in general don't read blogs. Neither do CIOs in the UK. We know, because we asked them.

So blogging influence is highly dependent on the target market. Demographics count. We'd expect markets dominated by the young, or technophiles, to have relatively heavy blog influence. If you are selling digital music then blogs are more likely to be influential. If you are selling hearing aids and zimmer frames, then blogs are probably not influential.

Content deficiency and a failure in the Cialdini test

As Hugh MacLeod observed dryly most blogs are not influential (Figure 15.5).

© Hugh

Figure 15.5 Blogging requires passion and authority. Which leaves out most people

The vast majority of blogs seem to be written for an audience of one – the author. They are, in every sense, online diaries. And while diaries of the famous may be interesting, the rest of us mortals lead pretty normal lives. Hardly worth recording for posterity.

Of course, most people also blog about market-relevant stuff, such products and services, suppliers, shops, prices and so on. But again, these are, in the huge majority, personal observations, anecdotes and rants. Few rise above the noise or ordinariness to emerge with authority. There is also a worrying trend amongst blogs to be either incorrect or offensive (or both).

To illustrate, Channel 4 aired a TV programme in March 2007 titled *The Great Global Warming Swindle*. The programme presented an alternative view to global warming and climate change, and proved extremely controversial. Inevitably, it quickly became a subject for blogging. However, and it's not clear how this happened, many bloggers reported the programme as a BBC production, when it was not. The BBC was subsequently dragged into a debate that it had nothing to do with, and suffered a tarnished reputation through mis-association with the Channel 4 programme.

Unfortunately, blogging is highly cross-referenced, and most bloggers didn't bother to fact-check their information. Once the message is out in the blogosphere, it is impossible to drag it back before damage is done.

In May 2007 Engadget, then the most widely read and linked to blog, posted a story claiming Apple's iPhone would be delayed 4 months and the Leopard operating system for 6 months. The news was picked up immediately by the stock market, and Apple's stock tumbled 3 per cent losing US$4 billion in value by the end of the trading day. But the source e-mail tip turned out to be a fake. It illustrates that blog links themselves don't equate to influence: expertise was absent, in this case the recognition of the requirement to check facts and foresight of potential consequences.

Such episodes undermine the influence of all blogs, especially those whose posts are based on the linked post of a third party (i.e. the majority of blogs). This criticism is not limited to blogs, but applies to all social media. Wikipedia is regularly criticised for the lack of accuracy in its entries. Social media may be inclusive and participatory, but these benefits come with a downside – the lack of editorial process and due diligence rank high among them.

Blogging has slid still further in reputation due to offensive remarks being posted to otherwise-moderate and well-written blogs.

Josh Bernoff, who co-writes the Groundswell blog, wrote a research note for his day job employer, Forrester Research. It suggested that Apple's iTunes music store sales were plummeting. Some people clearly think that proposing such an idea is tantamount to genocide, given the obscenities posted on the blog. Irrespective of the validity of the claim, which many questioned, there can be no excuse for profanity.

Worse still happened to Kathy Sierra, a prominent software development blogger. For some reason, Kathy found herself at the centre of vitriol of the most obscene kind, with threats of death being some of the more printable kind. Nasty stuff, to the point where police were contacted and Ms Sierra felt unable to leave her home.

What is it about blogs that people think they can use language that would get them arrested if they used it in the street? All bloggers need to be aware that the freedom of speech they enjoy has responsibilities attached. Otherwise, the freedom will be removed, by legislation or by consensus. Already there is talk of allowing only registered users on popular blogs.

Who's got time to write or read blogs?

The following was posted on http://www.hyperorg.com/blogger by D. Weinberger in June 2005:

> No, I'm not keeping up with your blog.
>
> I would like to. I really would. I like it and I like you.
>
> But we're now well past the point where any of us can keep up with all the blogs worth reading from the people worth keeping up with. Even with an aggregator.
>
> I just can't do it any more.

And that's when there were only 30 million blogs – there's more than double that number now.

This quote seems to reflect the confusion and bewilderment facing anyone trying to keep up with multiple blogs, even if using an aggregator like FeedBlitz or Bloglines. There are simply too many blogs to keep track of. If Web 2.0 is about 'joining the conversation', the problem is that there are too many conversations happening simultaneously. It's like trying to eavesdrop on all of the conversations going on at a party. You end up contributing (sensibly) to none, while upsetting the person you're supposed to be listening to.

And then someone invents Twitter. Twitter is blogging on speed. How anyone can maintain a proper job and use Twitter is beyond us.

Blogs need the oxygen of interaction

If you have time to read blogs you are exposed to a plethora of opinions, some of which may spark ideas, sympathy, outrage or some other emotion that compels you to blog in response. In return, others see your blog and

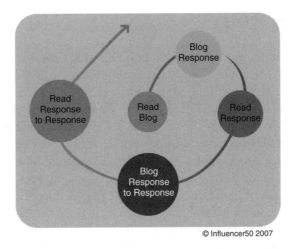

Figure 15.6   The virtuous cycle of blogging

respond in kind. There emerges a virtuous circle of read provocative post, write provocative post, read provocative responses, write another provocative post (Figure 15.6).

Without this positive feedback loop, people don't blog. That's why most blogs fail at less than 6 months, because they've stimulated insufficient provocative response. The blog, which thrives on comments, is deprived of its oxygen. The blogger gives up.

It's no surprise that few CEOs blog, and those that do seem to do so sporadically. Presumably, they're all busy running their companies. Quoted in *The Economist*, Seth Godin says, 'Blogs work when they are based on the values of candour, urgency, timeliness, pithiness and controversy. Does this sound like a CEO to you?' We'd ask, 'Does this sound like most people to you?'

We have the impression that people who blog either don't have regular (or full) jobs, or that blogging is their job. When Robert Scoble tells us that you've got to blog often and quickly (by which he means daily) it's no wonder that most succumb to normality, and their day job. This then limits the influence that blogs can have. It's the people who have 'proper' jobs – consultants, analysts, regulators, academics, etc. – that carry most influence. From Influencer50 research, we see that few bloggers have influence, and those that do come from other sources. Influencers blog, rather than bloggers influence.

If you are going to blog, in a business sense on company time, then it must be a planned activity, scheduled into the work day. This means that marketers must recruit influencers from within or beyond their firm and set to blogging, with allocated time and budget.

The tyranny of links

There is a limit to the number of connections a person can maintain effectively. It's about 150, and was established by Robert Dunbar, an anthropologist. The number is determined by the brain size of humans – there is a strong correlation between the size of the average brain and the optimal social grouping of those animals. Creatures with smaller brains socialise in smaller groups. Strange, but true. (Read Chapter 5 of *The Tipping Point* for more information on the Dunbar number.)

Why then do some people using social networking sites have hundreds or even thousands of connections? Do these people have huge brains? The attraction with connections is a complex situation, but there are several possible contributing factors.

Equating links with influence

As we said in our own Chapter 5, many people like to position themselves as connectors, because they equate links (and popularity) with influence. In fact, very few (3 per cent) in a community are genuine social connectors with influence – the rest are link gatherers. Link exchanging ('I'll link to you if you link to me') is common practice, but it doesn't have any relevance to influence.

People like to connect to connectors

People with large numbers of connections just seem to attract even more connections. Again it's the popularity equation, this time manifesting itself as popularity by association. 'I may not be very popular, but I'm connected to someone who is very popular, so that makes me feel good'.

Connections are a badge of belonging

In some popular social media sites, the number of connections is simply an acknowledgement of belonging to the social group. Every time someone connects they are saying, 'Hi, you're acknowledged as a participant'. This is a valid statement of membership, but it is not influence. This concept can be taken further, and some social networks regard a high number of connections as a measure of longevity or seniority in the network. It's the online equivalent of a chestful of medals.

Networks are not necessarily contiguous

Some social networks are often not contiguous of many hundreds or thousands, but several smaller networks connected by one individual. A connector might have a network for personal contacts, a network of customers, a network of professional colleagues and peers, a network of fellow hobbyists and so on.

Indiscriminate connection gathering

Name collectors often lack a selection system for inclusion. They basically add anyone and everyone that they encounter to their network. This misses the point of a social network, especially a business related network like LinkedIn, where at least you should know the person you're connecting to. Otherwise, if you recommend them you're exposing your reputation to risk.

Links don't differentiate influencers

A corollary of indiscriminate connection gathering is that links don't differentiate between a connection to an influencer and one to a regular user. Similarly, an influencer-generated link with a close colleague should be stronger than that with a casual acquaintance. There is no qualitative attribute attached to links. In social media, more is asserted to be better.

Key points in this chapter

1. Social media are enablers of influence: they are not by themselves influential. Today most influential social media users gain their influence through other means, and migrate it to blogs and other media. Influencers blog, more than bloggers influence.
2. The influence of bloggers is highly dependent on the subject matter. Blogger influence is higher in more technical subjects, and lower (sometimes zero) in more service-based and business-orientated markets.
3. Links are the best metric we have for measuring popularity of social media sites. But they can be faked or increased artificially. They also over-state influence in the general market, which in most cases extends far beyond the blogosphere.

Case Study K – a top three global software vendor

Determining the influence of blogging

In late 2006, Prompt Communications, a UK PR and marketing firm, was approached by the European corporate communications department of a large enterprise software vendor. The client wanted to know what was being said about it and its products in the blogosphere, and it was also keen to ascertain whether or not the emerging discipline of 'blogger relations' should fall into the remit of corporate communications.

The agency proposed a 3-month 'observation period' for the client, in order to establish what kind of people were blogging about the company, what sentiments they exhibited towards it, and what – if any – degree of influence the bloggers had on other key audiences like customers, employees, analysts and the media.

To conduct the observation period, the agency used its Blog Monitor, a customised portal site that scans the blogosphere and other online social networks for client-related content and aggregates relevant posts into one place for ease of viewing.

The portal quickly identified two types of particularly relevant blog. Firstly, there was a network of around 20 European-based English-language blogs that were entirely dedicated to discussing the client's products. Secondly, it noted a handful of UK-based blogs that regularly mentioned the client but were not exclusively dedicated to the client's company.

Blogs appended to mainstream media publications and written by those publications' journalists were viewable in the portal but not considered to be blogs for the purpose of the project. This is because the client's PR team were aware of these blogs already, and were already engaged with the journalists writing them.

A key finding was that the people who kept blogs dedicated to the client's company tended to be end-users of its more technical products. Their principal aims in blogging about the company were to promote and share their expertise in the company's products; to help other users with any problems, and to network with other users.

The second type of blog tended to be written by journalists and analysts, in a semi-professional capacity. This was an interesting finding, because it represents a blurring of boundaries between the mainstream media and the less regulated world of blogging. Despite their independence from established media and analyst firms, these 'hobby blogs' still carry a weight of influence, due to the already established reputations of the journalists and analysts writing for them.

The client was provided with weekly and monthly reports detailing activity and sentiment across all blogs monitored, and provided recommendations at the end of the 3-month period. Recommendations included making the marketing department aware of the end-user blogs, in order to make contact with popular bloggers and invite them to (for example) contribute articles and papers to the client's publications or to speak at events. Corporate Communications, meanwhile, were advised to continue monitoring the 'hobby' blogs of the journalists and analysts, and conduct outreach as appropriate to those writers as part of their existing media and AR activity.

The client continues to use the Prompt Blog Monitor to track what is being said about the company in the blogosphere. While there are still decisions to be made about whose remit it is to engage with bloggers, the trial has shown that there is a significant amount of discussion about the client in the blogosphere, and that many of the bloggers writing about the company wield a considerable amount of influence, either because they are already known journalists and analysts, or because they are super-users of the client's products, and therefore trusted experts in their field.

Note and reference

1 Sourced from Technorati popular blogs, as rated in the 6 months to May 2007, ranked by Technorati Authority (= distinct blogs linking to each blog).

16

Influencing through social media

Do MySpace, YouTube, LinkedIn and other social networking tools influence business decisions yet?

Which are the social networking sites with the most influence on consumer buying behaviour? It's not YouTube or MySpace or any of the other obvious candidates. The sites with the greatest influence on what people buy are Amazon and eBay.

In a survey by Jupiter Research,[1] 28 per cent of people said Amazon influenced their purchase decisions. No other site came close (Yahoo Answers was next with 4 per cent). eBay was not given as a response option, but given that eBay sales were $6 billion in 2006 we think it should be included as an influencer on consumer purchases.

Does this source of influence surprise anyone? Both Amazon and eBay sell stuff, and they each have an effective (though different) system of peer reviews. Amazon's peer reviews rate the products on offer, while eBay's feedback system rates buyers and sellers.

Both of these systems allow an important aspect of reviews, that of aggregation. The biggest inhibitor to online purchasing is the buyers' perception of risk, either of the product being unacceptable or the other party acting fraudulently. If one person says the camera they bought was great, it's just one person's view. But if fifty or a hundred reviewers say the same thing consumers detect a trend, and the purchase is derisked. Similarly, the eBayer ratings system shows how reliable buyers and sellers are – you'd trust someone with 99 per cent positive feedback rating with 1000 scores.

It's the aggregation of feedback and reviews that makes the system credible. Reviewers will almost never be known personally to the buyer, but there's safety in numbers. In effect, the feedback systems act as a proxy for a personal reference from a trusted friend.

How can social media influence purchase decisions?

Most marketers targeting social media have used traditional techniques, predominantly adverts. Eventually, sites need to make money, and the prevailing wisdom in marketing is that the most likely source of cash is adverts. Most personal blogs already carry ads, we're seeing short ads placed at the front of users' videos, video ads created specifically to spread virally and so on.

Slapping ads all over social media is anathema to social media. Ads don't work anymore in the real world because there are too many of them, and because they interrupt us inappropriately.[2] Consumers just filter them out. What makes marketers think that advertising on social media sites will be regarded as different? They're still ads, and consumers will still filter them out. This is what a YouGov survey found – 49% of respondents insisted that they didn't want ads appearing next to their social network profiles.[3]

The influence of social media is in the social connections inherent in the media. Although connections aren't everything as far as influence goes (as we saw in Chapter 15), they are important. They do convey a sense of security – safety in numbers – which, in the absence of other influential dimensions acts as a reasonable statement of trust. Connections can be faked, of course, but social media has a habit of detecting such bogus sites and hounding them out of existence.

So we expect social media to increase in influence at the expense of advertising. It is even possible that social media users will reject advertising as a legitimate exercise, and vote with their feet to dissuade sites from posting ads on personal pages.

What does this mean for marketers? It means that you have to get influencing, rather than placing ads. Persuade influencers to test out your products, to feedback via social media and to communicate their views and opinions to the network. This is what social media is all about – using influencers in a marketing context is appropriate and integral to the medium. Paid advertisements are for the boring. Instead place a comment or feedback to a user's blog. Attach a rating or a tag to a post. Encourage your customers to blog, create MySpace pages and talk about your product.

There is one mandatory clause in this social media influencing model. Influencers must declare where they are being asked (or paid) by a supplier to carry a message. In fact, whenever they have no vested interest and are acting freely, influencers should declare this is the case, for the avoidance of doubt. If you recruit influencers to carry your message make sure they issue a disclaimer, up front. It will enhance their credibility and your reputation.

If individual social media users elect to display ads then that's fine with us. Personally, we don't like having ads on our front lawns, but call us old-fashioned. We'd rather passers-by stop, admire our manicured turf and ask us to recommend a gardener. Marketers will be more successful by per-suading influencers to carry their message to the target audience. The best way to persuade an influencer is to have a great product. Then they will carry your message for free.

YouTube and MySpace have little influence on buyers – today

When thinking of social media, most people conjure images of teenagers doing strange things in front of video cameras, for the world to gawp at via YouTube or MySpace. Although such sites have created a huge impact on online advertising, due to the high volumes of traffic and the potential for adverts to be eyeballed, they have little direct influence over buying behaviour. It's possible that marketers may attempt to use social media as an influence enabler, carrying multimedia messages to an eager audi-ence. But the media themselves have little influence.

The primary reason for this is that the sites themselves are not orientated around purchases, in contrast to Amazon and eBay. Social media site users are not typically looking for product recommendations or referrals, and attempts to do this inappropriately results in a backlash from the com-munity. Pizza Hut and Wal-Mart are just two of the casualties of misplaced advertising on social media sites. Pizza Hut's fake delivery boy on MySpace has less than 400 'friends' (1000 would be barely respectable) and the video adverts are so contrived as to make a viewer flinch. Wal-Mart lasted just 10 weeks on MySpace, after posting reportedly fake user comments promoting its special offers.

The Jupiter study does reveal a fundamental truth about the way social media users assemble information. These online consumers trust social media sites. Do they trust them more than professional marketing content? We think so – the rate of abandoned online shopping carts has remained stable for 3 years at around 60 per cent in sites that don't offer peer reviews. Peer reviews add credibility, which helps de-risk purchases, and more people complete their purchases.

The implications of social media for marketers are therefore:

- You depend more on what consumers are saying about you than what you say about yourself. So you must engage with consumers, identify influencers and get them to influence the conversation.
- User-generated content – a core principle of Web 2.0 – uses language that is the antithesis of marketing-speak. Marketers need to learn a new language when using social media sites. Social media is a world without superlatives and assertions, foreign territory indeed for marketers.

The influence of LinkedIn

LinkedIn is a social networking service that allows individuals to establish connections between other people. It's a great way to stay in touch with former colleagues and friends. More importantly, it allows you to connect to people outside your network, by asking people inside your network to refer you. So your *reachable* network is the number of direct connections you have multiplied by the number of connections your connections have. The model scales very quickly. There are some 'connection gatherers' that boast hundreds of connections, but most people have between 30 and 100, which is a reasonable and manageable number of people you know.

But here's the clever part – each of your direct connections knows who you are, personally and by reputation. The likelihood is that they'd be happy to recommend you to their connections, or recommend their connections to you. The network is therefore ideal for recruitment and job hunting. If you could use a recruitment firm that only supplies candidates that come recommended by someone you know you'd be impressed, wouldn't you? That's what LinkedIn can do.

Your direct connections are, in fact, influencers on the job market that is centred on you or your firm. It so happens that LinkedIn is a network used primarily for business connections. But there are other networks that are purely social. How about a network for people you've met on holiday, or shop at the same trendy store. Influencers are market segment specific, and you are the defining characteristic of that segment. Now that's impressive.

Such *you-centric networks* are much more powerful than generic reviewer comments that appear on Amazon, eBay and other web sites. Much as we think reviewer comments are really useful and insightful, the fact that we don't personally know these reviewers means we have no idea if they see the world as we do. And that creates uncertainty when trusting their views. Or at least, it should.

Social networks like LinkedIn allow reviewer comments to be amplified and optimised because you either know the reviewer, or you know someone who does. You're only ever two degrees away from a *recommender*, which makes you more likely to trust what they say.

What's the relevance of all this to marketing? Simply, you can develop a connected network of customers that are (a) willing to talk about you and (b) willing to connect to other customers *that they know*. You now have a review and referral system that has built-in influence.

Influence and anonymity in social media networks

You can't be an influencer and be anonymous. Why? Because there is no way of telling who you are, what credentials you have and what (if any) vested interest you have in your comments.

It seems pretty obvious to us, but necessary to say, that it's important to know who's influencing your market. There are two primary benefits to this knowledge:

1. You can orientate a marketing programme around your known influencers.
2. Prospects can ignore the cacophony of noise from other people that are demanding their attention, and focus on people they know and trust.

Remember, we're talking about marketing here. It's possible to perceive situations where anonymous sources of information are useful, if not mandatory. Newspaper reporting of whistle-blowing is one. Witness protection is another. But these special cases aside, influencers must be identified if they really are to influence a market. And this means using real names too, not pseudonyms.

It's puzzling to see what benefits anonymity conveys to individuals in the context of marketing. Do they work for a company on which they are commenting? Self-identification is always the best strategy in marketing. Always. The alternative is to appear to have a vested interest, or to appear disingenuous, or just plain untruthful. Why would anyone give the benefit of the doubt to someone that's anonymous?

Doesn't anonymous confer privacy? Of course it does, but why is the person commenting on a public forum in that case? Anonymity always carries the perception that something is being hidden. This undermines any comment they may make. This has huge benefits to firms engaged in such activities, both in conveying transparency and in turn encouraging honest comment.

We suggest enforcing a requirement that all comments on the blogs, wikis and other social media owned or maintained by you to be identified as far as possible. We're not talking government regulation, ID cards and all that. Just that if you operate a forum for discussion on a market then let us all know who we're discussing the market with.

You want to be engaging with your influencers, wherever they come from. Should you let competitors contribute to your forum? – absolutely. The chances that a competitor, correctly identified, would trash you on your site are minimal. In fact it may help to validate you as a competitor, or contribute a challenge that is good for industry debate. Should you let negative comments appear? – sure. As long as you respond to such comments politely it can only be good for the site. There is plenty of research to show that negative comments actually enhance the credibility of a recommendation, and we believe the same is true in blog posts too. It illustrates both honesty and balance.

Do wikis influence decisions?

Wikis are forums for collaborative contributions from multiple people with a common goal. The best known wiki is Wikipedia, the online encyclopaedia, but there are estimated to be over 2500 wikis in existence that are edited by large communities.[4]

Wikis are a special case of social media, because it's arguable that they themselves are influencers rather than simply enablers of influence. In our earlier discussion of influencer types we noted that events (exhibitions, trade shows, etc.) can be influencers, because they are showcases for products and services. Presence at an influential event can exert important influence on decisions. Wikis may emerge as a similar phenomenon.

Wikis consolidate and extend the body of knowledge on a particular subject. There is little doubt that contributors to wikis include influencers in the real world. The whole point of wikis is that they gain their value from collaboration between individuals. Does this collaboration enhance or inhibit influence?

Well, it depends on who stands to gain or lose by the contribution of knowledge. In academia, for instance, there is a clear agenda of 'publish or perish', where the value of research is directly related to the rigorous review from esteemed peers and its subsequent wide release to the community. Since there is no commercial value ascribed to the knowledge there should be no financial inhibitions to collaboration. Indeed collaboration usually enhances the finished product.

This type of collaboration threatens one particular type of player – those that have a competing, and often dominant, product under traditional commercial and proprietary protection, such as licensing or patents. The same is true of influence. Those that stand to benefit from the sharing of knowledge through collaboration are those that stand to gain from the demise in influence from traditional influencers. Those that currently wield influence derived from knowledge will be reluctant to share it widely on wikis. If knowledge is available to everyone it ceases to be a scarce commodity, and its value plummets. Influence is then redistributed across those that can use the knowledge, or add value to it.

Those with influence through knowledge will seek to preserve their status as custodians of that knowledge, to retain their influence. Don't expect them to contribute to wikis. Such is the commercial world.

Wikis dissipate influence

As we said in Chapter 14, *influencer marketing* optimises WOM marketing by having the most influential people join the conversation. Behaviour is more likely to change as a result, because influencers love to influence others in the community. Social media technologies are the same thing, with the same benefits and deficiencies. Blogs, wikis and the rest are enhanced by the involvement of influencers. But the fact that anyone can, and does, contribute to a wiki can undermine the influence of the few true influencers. This is why Wikipedia has had problems. The average person can contribute to Wikipedia (benefit) but the average person is unlikely to be an authority (deficiency).

Now, the average person may be an authority on something, and if they blog or contribute to a wiki on that subject, then everybody wins. The reality is different of course. Thirty thousand people have made at least five edits to Wikipedia. There are roughly 100 000 contributors, which means that 70 000 have made less than five edits, or a maximum of 280 000 (70 000 × 4). There are 60 million edits in Wikipedia's archive, so the 30 000 are responsible for generating more than 59 million edits, averaging nearly 2000 edits each! In fact, fifty per cent of Wikipedia edits are made by less than 1 per cent of contributors – roughly 1000 people. Are these people really authorities on everything?

Clearly not: there are numerous stories of contributors claiming Harvard degrees and other qualifications that are fictitious. They fail the Cialdini test at the first hurdle (Does the person have verifiable expertise?).

The trouble is there is no way of really telling who wrote the entry, and no way of determining their credentials. So we won't know if we're reading something written by a janitor or a Harvard professor. Does this matter? It most certainly does if you are basing your decisions on information based on a wiki. Anonymity is a no–no if wikis are to be influential.

Influence and Second Life

And so we come to Second Life and other virtual world-based social media. In fact it's easy to dismiss Second Life as irrelevant nonsense, at least as far as substantial business decisions are concerned. It's hard to imagine Barclays Bank buying $10 million worth of hardware via Second Life, or tough contract negotiation being facilitated by avatars in a virtual world.

On reflection, though, there are ways of influencing that may lend themselves very well to virtual worlds. Business meetings are already being held there. There's no reason why you couldn't host an influential conference on Second Life, or have influential media and analysts release their research and reporting. Virtual demonstrations of product features are viable, and why not create virtual reference site visits and host customer testimonials?

We think marketers could be very productive using such a medium, but there are three reasons why they should hold back in the short term. The first (and you'll know this if you've tried Second Life) is that it's not very serious, from the silly names you're forced to adopt to the ridiculous clothing and 'body styles' of avatars. Business decision-makers are not going to take an approach by a horse-headed persona as a professional attempt at influence. It's fine for peddling fashion and music, but not for big business. Today.

The second inhibitor is the average audience in virtual worlds, which is unclear. Linden Labs, which operates Second Life, doesn't collect demographic information other than gender, age and geography, none of which is verified. So before leaping into Second Life it might pay to determine whether your target audience is a regular visitor, or even aware of it. The chances are, they are not. Today.

The third reason why firms should wait is that the normal rules of influence apply in virtual worlds just as much as in real ones. An environment where everyone is forced to adopt a pseudonym creates a culture of anonymity that undermines influence. Until this is resolved, businesses will be wary of who they interact with on Second Life. Always.

Influencing through social media

As a mini case study it might be appropriate to refer to a social media site using influence to gain mind- and market-share. MySpace is such an exemplar. When MySpace started in 2003 there were already several popular social media sites available including Friendster and Friends Reunited. Why did MySpace overtake these alternatives?

MySpace identified its key target audience, young people eager to connect and share their enthusiasm for particular music scenes. So MySpace recruited emerging bands and popular clubs as its first users. The founders, Tom Anderson and Chris DeWolfe, would drive around visiting music clubs and listening to new bands. The bands turned out to be MySpace's best marketing tool, becoming influencers by recruiting their fans to the site, and it snowballed from there. MySpace is now the premier music-led social media site, and it ranks as the second most popular site of all (only Yahoo has more visits, Google is third).

MySpace identified its target market, recruited influencers, and gave those influencers the tools of influence (the MySpace platform), prefiguring *influencer marketing*. The influencers and WOM did the rest, enabled by MySpace's philosophy of letting users have complete freedom over what was posted.

Identify influencers

Identifying influencers that operate within social media should be part of a larger exercise of influencer identification. Influencers rarely stay in one medium, and are most influential when they hop around, from blogs to newspapers to events, and so on. It is worthwhile though identifying specific social media sites that are hosts for clusters of influencers. MySpace is the preferred site for the music industry. LinkedIn may become the de facto standard for business contexts, (though it is under competition from Jobster, a recruitment-focused network) and Visible Path. But be aware of the tyranny of links – they don't necessarily indicate true influence.

There are some online services that claim to assist in finding people. One such site is Zoominfo, which trawls the Internet for references to people, then catalogues them by name, employers, job role and industry. While this type of index may be useful for hunting down names of people for lead generation or recruitment purposes, it has little relevance in the world of influence. Zoominfo rapidly gets out of date as people move jobs or roles. It also doesn't trawl the real world – obviously not, but it's a critical weakness. Don't be tempted to use business directories of contact names. These are sales prospecting lists and they don't reflect influence.

Marketing to influencers

You can use social media to engage with influencers. Find out if they have a blog or are connected into LinkedIn or another social network.

They may not have their own blog but contribute to a community blog or online forum.

The rules of engagement discussed in Chapter 9 apply – don't be tempted into shortcuts by using e-mail, or asking to swap blog links. Remember, influencers are a scarce resource, so don't risk alienating them.

A good example of marketing to influencers via social media is Case Study H, who identified and targeted the top influencers for the launch of its business handsets. It attracted influencers to a specially designed web site, where influencers could discuss and debate the various merits and drawbacks of the prototype devices. The firm tracked all comments, feeding these back into its ongoing development and marketing process. Importantly, the social media element is part of a rounded experience that includes sending the handsets and supporting materials in physical format. Influencers work across media, so a balance of real world and online contacts is essential.

Supply influencers with content and tools

Social media are excellent mechanisms for supplying influencers with tools. Bands promoting themselves on MySpace solicit influence by loading samples of their music. It seems obvious, but bands used to be restricted to sending out tapes or CDs to record companies and radio stations. Now they send them directly to consumers, and it's the consumers that decide which music is played on the radio or released on record labels.

Many businesses are turning to podcasts for a similar purpose. Podcasts are digital video or audio recordings which are hosted on a web site or blog. Typical they feature speeches, presentations or interviews, and are increasingly used as marketing collateral. We think that podcasts are great for getting your influencers a wider audience within your target market. Though they are less interactive than blogs, the medium makes the content very digestible. Podcasts downloaded to iPods and other portable devices mean that your prospects can view your influencer-led collateral at their convenience.

The most effective podcasts are those that feature influencers. HP Corporate TV features slick, case studies of firms such as Chevron, Dreamworks and DHL. But there's no real need to run to the expense of creating highly produced video and audio – short sound or video clips of customers or other influencers are equally effective.

Embed influencers in your messages

Embedding influencer messages in your marketing plans is considerably easier in these days of social media. Just link to the influencer and you're done. But sometimes you need to go a little further – customers just don't want to be taken to the water, occasionally you have to drink for them too. So embed quotes from blogs or podcasts in your social media output. You should still link to the originator, but basically you're saving your readers the trouble of that additional click.

Key points in this chapter

1. The social media that are influential on buying decisions today are those that contain user feedback. This means that user feedback will emerge as an important influencer in decision-making.
2. Anonymity undermines influence. There is no business reason for anonymous blogs or posts and it creates the impression you're hiding something.
3. Normal rules for *influencer marketing* apply to social media. You should treat social media as an extension to your normal marketing, so don't try to shoehorn traditional marketing approaches onto blogs and social networking sites. They work just as badly there as in real life.

Case Study L – Yahoo!

For *influencer marketing* at Yahoo!, blogging matters

Since the summer of 2004 when the Yahoo! Search Blog launched, blogosphere growth has exploded and Yahoo!'s participation and commitment to blogging have kept pace. The *influencer marketing* team emerged as part of an effort to raise awareness of Yahoo! Search technology among industry thought leaders and pundit bloggers. In 2005, *influencer marketing* expanded to extend the blogosphere conversation and give other Yahoo! businesses access to insights and innovators outside the company.

Over the last couple of years, *influencer marketing* has cultivated relationships with leading bloggers, some of whom have become as powerful and widely read as their mainstream media counterparts.

Yahoo! invites influential guests like Lawrence Lessig (http://www.ysearchblog.com/archives/000092.html) and Jimmy Wales (http://www.ysearchblog.com/archives/000100.html) to blog on the network. It sponsors events that foster dialog and collaboration between tech 'heroes' and influential bloggers inside and outside the company. It covers Yahoo! product launches and new programmes as well as its presence at technology conferences and events. It also provides tactical advice on every aspect of launching and managing a business blog – from content strategy and comment policy to community management and outreach on specific topics.

Last summer *influencer marketing* was asked to connect with youthful bloggers to help Yahoo! better understand how today's wired youth spend time online and identify trends among digital natives and young early adopters. This effort coincided with a corporate communications initiative to develop and launch a flagship corporate blog for Yahoo! – Yodel Anecdotal. The Influencer team brought two undergraduate interns on board—tech blogger Paul Stamatiou (now a senior at Georgia Tech) and Doreen Bloch (now a UC Berkeley sophomore)—as bloggers to help build Yodel Anecdotal (http://yodel.yahoo.com).

Yodel Anecdotal launched on 1 August 2006, with an inaugural post entitled 'Yet another self-serving corporate blog' and an engaging video tour of corporate headquarters that has been viewed more than 50 000 times. Under the stewardship of blog editor and senior PR director Nicki Dugan, Yodel has developed into a primary communication channel for Yahoo!

In less than a year, according to Technorati, Yodel Anecdotal climbed from being north of the 11 000th most popular blog (among the estimated 80 million blogs) to #839 (and climbing). More than 80 Yahoos have contributed to this multi-author blog, from summer interns to CEOs. Posts about everything from our management transition to the availability of unlimited storage in Yahoo! Mail routinely drive Yodel content to the top of Techmeme discussions.

The blog allows Yahoo! not only to communicate news, insights, culture and industry perspective, but also to solicit input from readers. More than 300 blog comments about a site redesign from Yahoo! TV loyalists helped the product team collect specific feedback on what users disliked and guide them to eventually improving the product. Readers from as far away as Brazil, Iran, India and Romania visit and comment, reminding Yahoo! of the breadth of its audience. In addition to video, the blog includes a Flickr photostream that has been viewed more than 90 000 times. Yodel Anecdotal puts a human face on the brand while engaging its users and industry influencers in important and meaningful discussions.

In 2006 *influencer marketing* produced a guide for company bloggers, developed in collaboration with a variety of internal stakeholders (representing marketing, corporate communications, legal, policy, editorial and others). It organizes quarterly lunch conversations and moderates an internal mailing list where dozens of Yahoo! bloggers answer each other's questions, share news and insights, exchange ideas, kvetch, cross-promote and try new things. Yahoo!'s influential and cross-disciplinary community of bloggers plays an essential role in connecting Yahoo! businesses with its most vocal and valuable customers.

Thanks to Havi Hoffman, *influencer marketing*, Yahoo!

Notes and references

1 iProspect Social Networking User Behavior Study (April 2007) conducted by Jupiter Research for iProspect.
2 Read *Permission Marketing* by Seth Godin to understand why.
3 Research carried out by YouGov for New Media Age and Brand Strategy, published May 2007.
4 Source: wikia.com.

17

Influencing consumers

The primary focus of our book has been on influencer marketing within the business environment. But influencers clearly exist in the consumer space too. In fact, most of the most innovative marketing campaigns to influencers have been within this sector over the past few years. The next two chapters look at the similarities, and differences, in how influence occurs in the B2B and B2C worlds.

This chapter examines whether consumers are influenced in the same way as businesses.

There is overwhelming evidence to support the claim that WOM marketing is a powerful force in today's commercial world. Each relevant study concludes, with a high degree of consistency, that:

■ The strongest group of influencers are friends and family, or at least people we trust.
■ We communicate with these people predominantly through WOM.

What the research doesn't show is any sense of how messages get into the community in the first place, who (if anyone) puts the messages there, and how marketing can tap into the potential of WOM. From a practical

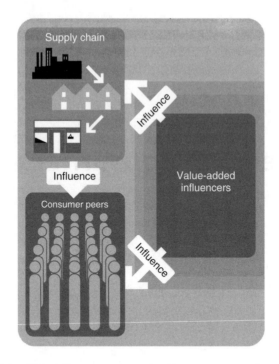

Figure 17.1   Main influencer categories in consumer markets
©Influencer50 2007

marketing point of view, before delving into the dynamics of WOM, it's helpful to identify three categories of influencer in operation in consumer markets. There are three main types (Figure 17.1):

- Consumer peers
- The supply chain
- Value-added influencers

The trick is to identify and market to those influencers that are easiest to reach and that will have a high and predictable degree of influence over the target market.

Who do consumers say they trust?

Who do you trust? We are all consumers, in addition to the other roles we play. We all buy stuff. So who do you listen to when you buy your stuff?

Why did you buy the most recent book you bought? You've read this author before? A friend recommended it? You saw it on a prominent shelf in the store? You were intrigued by the title? You read a review? Amazon suggested that you might like it based on your previous purchases? All of the above?

The number one influencer on you is: you! You buy what you've bought before, where you bought it before. Every salesperson has always known that the easiest sell is to people who've bought before.

But what if we have no prior experience? What then? According to research, we are more likely to follow what our friends and family tell us than any other source. And it doesn't seem to matter where we are or what we're buying.

■ Examining trustworthy sources of consumer information, a 2006 study by Globescan for AccountAbility and the UK's National Consumer Council asked 'What Assures Consumers?'[1] It found that family and friends ranked third out of 15 categories.

■ A study into online purchasing showed that satisfied customer endorsements positively influenced consumers' attitudes toward the store and their willingness to buy from the store.[2]

■ A GfK Roper Consulting survey[3] in 2006 identified the most important influences on what Americans buy are, their own past experience and personal recommendations (other than product-specific attributes).

■ A 2007 Corporate Culture research study for *Marketing* magazine shows that if a company earns consumer trust, 54 per cent will recommend the product to others. Importantly, customers tell 50 per cent more people about a bad experience than a good one.[4]

■ For the second year running 'A person like me' was ranked the highest credible source of information, outscoring CEOs, academics, governments, lawyers, PR, celebrities and (lowest of the low) bloggers.[5]

And there are numerous other studies that show the same thing. There are two interesting points to note on these remarkably similar findings. Firstly, they point to the primary sources of influence that we trust – people we know. More importantly, it's not people we'd like to know or people we've heard of. It's people that actually interact with us on some regular basis, whether at work, at home or on the golf course. As the Edelman Trust Barometer study says, 'people like me'.

Why is this the case? Why do we trust people to recommend products based on whether we know them, not because they are experts? There are several reasons:

■ We buy based on our own experience first. If we liked it we won't change. If we didn't like it we'll try something else. In which case, we'll rely on someone else's experience.

- That someone should be like us, because their experience is likely to be similar to ours. People we ask are like us, they have similar needs, wants, purchasing power, age, gender, health, children, aspirations. It's what Robert Cialdini calls social proof, or safety in numbers.
- Experience confers authority. If someone uses a product then that gives them credibility in providing an opinion. Few people are credible in recommending something they didn't like, or that they haven't used themselves.
- People talk about their stuff. Keller Fay Group released a survey of American consumers 'indicating that brands are a critical part of daily conversation'. According to the study, the average American discusses specific brands in ordinary discussion 56 times per week.

Examples of influencer marketing with consumer peers

Tremor

Tremor is a WOM marketing service implemented by P&G, the consumer products conglomerate. The premise is that the most effective way of marketing is advocacy from a trusted friend. This is interesting in itself, since P&G spends $3 billion each year on marketing. P&G wanted to target specific consumer segments (currently teenagers and mothers) that mapped onto product groups and ranges. It developed Tremor to stimulate WOM in its target segments – but how to do this accurately, ethically and measurably?

P&G begins by targeting highly networked consumers, *connectors* in Gladwell's terminology. These people would typically have a network of friends and acquaintances that are five to six times larger than average. The selection of a *connector* is tough: P&G declined 90 per cent of applicants for its trials.

P&G presumes (we think correctly) that its identified *connectors* want to connect, and it gives them the tools to do this. This might be product information, samples or coupons. Importantly, Tremor also provides the capability for *connectors* to feed back their experiences and insights to P&G. This closed loop ensures that the WOM activity is not unidirectional – from P&G to *connectors* to other consumers – but works in reverse too. Thus P&G knows what it's doing right or wrong – it can detect and respond to any negative comments and misunderstanding about their products.

Getting the message to be communicated right is vital. P&G has its traditional marketing messages worked out, but what it learned (through bitter experience) is that *connectors* don't care about the P&G message.

They care about a social message that facilitates connections – *connectors* like to connect, remember? So P&G developed product-related messages that de-emphasised its product features, and talked up the social reasons for product adoption. This is a great example of *marketing through* influencers – find out what the influencers' interests are, then give it to them.

Liquid Intelligence

Liquid Intelligence is an *influencer marketing* firm focusing on the beverages industry. Its proprietary methodology, 'Seal to Smile', encompasses the whole supply chain from manufacturers (who *seal* the product) to consumers (who *smile* as it is consumed). Its approach is to analyse the supply chain for influencers for its client, and then build a programme around these individuals. Because the focus extends beyond consumer WOM, programmes may focus on other key influencer such as bar owners and bartenders.

This is important to ensure that those selling the product not only take the money, but pour and serve the product correctly. (Guinness has made this aspect a piece of the folklore of its stout, with mystique bar staff instructed on how to pour the perfect pint, even decorating the head with a clover leaf motif. It gets Guinness talked about.)

Product ambassadors as pseudo-influencers

P&G demonstrates a sense for the right type of person to target – *connectors* with the appropriate social standing to (a) carry the message and (b) have the message listened to. *Sneezers* with influence, as Seth Godin would say. P&G spends considerable time and energy screening out people that would love to be part of the Tremor programme. Experience has shown P&G that time invested here pays dividends in the strength of message carried to the wider community.

P&G learned early on that, just because a consumer is a talker doesn't mean that they have influence. We all know talkers that carry little influence – they're called bores. A less sophisticated approach involves selecting consumers as 'ambassadors' and sending them a range of products in the hope that they'll talk about them. There are three immediate issues with this approach:

- Agencies pay their *ambassadors* to talk to their social networks about these products. Good WOM will carry because the message is right. Bad WOM is carried because the messenger is paid. Whose message would you believe?

- Even if *ambassadors* do have influence does it extend to all of the products being sent to them? Example: Rani Schlenoff is a BzzAgent *ambassador* in the US and has tried and tested over 18 products, including toothbrushes and candy bars.[6] Is Rani really a credible authority on these consumer products? Does she have dental qualifications or a particularly sweet tooth?
- There is insufficient attention paid to the social appropriateness of the communication. As Rani says, 'After the initial shock of me injecting myself into (strangers') lives, they are usually very happy to hear what I have to say'. Oh really? We can't imagine anything worse than being press-ganged into a product pitch when you were just expecting some polite social conversation.

This is traditional marketing mindset attempting to shoehorn itself into *influencer marketing*. It's 'interruption marketing', when we should be thinking 'permission marketing'.

Stealth marketing

The stealth approach is to place actors in a social context, such as in a bar, and engineer a conversation design to be overheard by 'real' people. The actors' aim is to engage the bar's customers in conversation, subtly extolling the virtue of the phone/shampoo/soft drink in today's script. At the end of the 'play' the actors declare their allegiance to the sponsoring brand, and everyone has a good laugh about the event. Or so the agencies promoting this sort of nonsense say.

This is WOM marketing at its worst. It is disingenuous, manipulative and contrived. Marketing today has a terrible reputation, based on its desired manipulation of target markets and use of inauthentic messengers, annoying prospects by interrupting them. The stealth approach carries this forward into *influencer marketing*. We'd prefer to position *influencer marketing* as a way of extracting marketing as a discipline from the tarnished reputation it has.

There's only one reason why you'd need to do this sort of thing, and that is if your product is not worth talking about. Otherwise, we have three pieces of advice to those thinking about this type of approach:

- Don't do it
- Please don't do it
- We'd rather you threw the whole influencer marketing approach away than engage in this sort of nonsense.

Why marketing to consumer peer influencers is not enough

Ultimately, there are two main drawbacks in targeting consumer peers directly in WOM. Of course, consumers are fundamental to the end result, which means them buying from you. It's just that consumers are a fickle and unpredictable bunch. The first main problem with WOM campaigns is that influencers are individual people, but there's no scalable way of identifying them amongst their consumer peers. There are two contributing factors here:

■ There are too many consumer influencers to identify them individually and accurately. There are millions of consumers to aim at, and even with sophisticated segmentation you still end up targeting tens of thousands of individuals. Your attempts at identifying influencers within this group is largely a hit and miss affair. It's expensive and it's imprecise. You don't really know whether or not the consumers you recruit are in fact influencers. You're playing the numbers game.
■ Who really has influence? One thing the various research studies show is that there is no way of identifying influencers through demographics, or social technographics or any other sociological classification. So most firms targeting consumers use the number of network contacts as a proxy for influence, which is a poor substitute. Influence is a much more complex concept than the number of people you know.

The other key problem is that, partly because there is a high number of consumer influencers and partly because you're never sure who really is an influencer, you cannot guarantee that what the consumer influencers are saying is what you want them to say. The fact that you've told the consumers something may mean that they don't believe you. Why? Because you're selling something. P&G's Tremor initially found this out the hard way, by trying to force a marketing message onto influencers, whereas influencers wanted a social message to spread. Most consumers feel uncomfortable talking in the way that marketing messages sound: it lacks authenticity because it appears scripted (which it is). So influencers change the message to something they feel more comfortable with, typically expressed in the vernacular. Of course, this may change completely the message that you want to convey.

This then creates a new problem with using consumer influencers: what happens if things go wrong and the message is being distorted?

Again, Tremor has a strong feedback element to it, but it's unlikely that Tremor can detect a miscommunication of its message in all cases, or where the message subtly changes.

To look at how to address this it's worth remembering why consumers listen to messages by WOM. People trust other people they know. They assume (usually correctly) that their neighbour or colleague wishes them well and has no interest in providing false, misleading or incomplete information. They're just passing on a good tip.

But where do these tips typically originate? If not planted by a WOM marketer, they come from positive experiences, either from using a product or service directly, or through after-sales care. And they come from other third party sources that are not necessarily known personally to us, but trusted because of some other attribute they possess. The first group of originators play primary roles in the supply chain of whatever is being talked about. The second group sits outside the supply chain but is focused on adding value through information, services and other characteristics that define and scope the boundaries in which consumers operate.

Influence red herrings

Brands

Above all else, brands convey trust. They validate perceived standards of manufacture and quality of components, design, robustness and utility. We all know the difference between an Audi, a Volkswagen and a Skoda and we ascribe appropriate attributes to each. They stand for different things. It doesn't matter to us that they are all made in the same factory and use the same engines. They are qualitatively different, and we know what to expect when we see a recognised brand.

Brands are enormously powerful indicators of influence that a business has over consumer behaviour. But brands are fickle. If brands convey trust, they also carry expectation that a given product quality will be delivered. If there's a mismatch then trouble ensues. Brand equity can evaporate quickly if messages appear that are inconsistent with the brand.

Brands are also heavily influenced by short-term trends. In Millward Brown Optimor's 2007 ranking of brand equity, it recorded:

- A 192 per cent year-on-year increase in the brand value of Marks & Spencer
- A 33 per cent year-on-year decrease in brand value for Home Depot

Other big winners in year-on-year brand equity shifts included Best Buy (+113%), Target (+88%), Google (+77%), ABN Amro (+72%), Apple (+55%) and Starbucks (+45%). Losers included T-Mobile (−32%), Dell (−24%), Intel (−21%), Budweiser (−15%) and Chevrolet (−10%).

Brands are part of the vocabulary of influence, but they don't themselves influence. There is no evidence whatsoever that supports a claim that brand awareness or 'equity' causes increase in sales. In fact we suggest that it's the other way around, that brand strength is a *consequence* of high sales, or of quality products and service.

We think brand equity is overstated, in its value and importance. There is scant academic evidence to show a link between brand and financial performance, and brand strength appears not to be an indicator of future performance, if the Millward Brown Optimor data is to be believed. Ironically, all of the 'loser' firms cited above actually increased their sales in 2006. Chevrolet set sales records in the Asia-Pacific, European and Latin America, Africa and Middle East regions.

One of the most powerful and instantly recognised consumer brands globally belongs to a business that doesn't sell anything to consumers. It doesn't have any direct relationship with consumers or retailers and is in fact exclusively a B2B firm. The Visa organisation is, in essence, a membership club for banks. It provides payment processing services between banks. Importantly, Visa acts as an acceptance market for all banks issuing credit and debit cards worldwide. It facilitates consumer transactions in the real world and online by confirming to purchasers and retailers that the tendered method of payment is going to be accepted (sufficient funds permitting). 1.5 billion Visa cards are accepted in over 170 countries. Yet Visa itself has no direct relationship with either the consumer or the retailer.

The Visa mark is tremendously effective at conveying an immediate impression of trust between retailer and consumer, even though they have never met before. In fact, it is the consumer's card-issuing bank that verifies the credentials of the cardholder, and it is the retailer's bank that authorises the seller to accept and process the card. Visa is simply the oil that keeps 1 billion transactions flowing each week. It's an example where the apparent influence is on consumers, whereas it is actually happening in the opposite direction. It is the consumers that are influencing banks, by demanding that their credit cards carry the Visa logo.

Why celebrities don't influence us

There's plenty of research now to destruct the assertion that celebrity endorsement influences consumer buying decisions. It may do so, in certain markets with particular attributes, but not in the majority of cases.

- In the 'What Assures Consumers?' survey, celebrities ranked on the trust scale at 14 out of 15, just above door-dropped leaflets and below government departments.
- The 'Dove' beauty products range has increased its brand acceptance by using real people in its adverts. A comparative study with 'Lux', which used a famous TV star as its 'face' showed a decline in brand acceptance over the study period.[7]
- Experts are more effective at influencing consumer buying behaviour than celebrities when it comes to purchasing technology products.[8]
- Consumers are not influenced by the attractiveness of the endorser when evaluating a technology product.[9]

Celebrity influence is constrained because we just don't believe what we're being told:

- Does actor Martin Kemp really shop at DFS?
- Does Tiger Woods outsource his IT to Accenture?
- Does Britney Spears just drink Pepsi? (Answer: No, and was dropped by Pepsi after being recently photographed drinking Coca-Cola.)

The appeal of celebrities is one of association – use this product and you could be as successful/beautiful/rich as the celebrity. In fact, today's consumers are too wise to this type of nonsense. Indeed, sometimes consumers complain that the ideals portrayed by celebrities are unattainable and such images are a bad influence. The research proves that it's better to use someone that's credible, because they are an expert or just because they are normal, than a so-called aspirational icon. Having someone who knows what they're talking about has more influence than someone who's just famous.

Of course, if you can get both then that's great. So use David Beckham to sell sports kit, but not DIY tools and assemble-yourself furniture. Similarly, using an attractive celebrity doesn't work for technology products, including mobile phones and music systems. It may not even work for beauty products, if Dove's 'Campaign for Real Beauty' is a benchmark.

Could it be that using celebrity endorsers is more about corporate schmoozing and hero worship than about influencing consumer behaviour?

Consumers and loyalty

'You want loyalty?' asks the ruthless bond trader in Michael Lewis's *Liar's Poker*. 'Then get a cocker spaniel'.

As marketers we sometimes start believing our own press. We think that consumers love our products, and are loyal to them. The truth is that only happy customers are loyal. Loyalty is a measure of customer retention, and you retain clients either by consistent good quality or bribery. Loyalty schemes are customer retention through bribery. Discounting to loyal customers is an oxymoron – you wouldn't have to discount if customers were truly loyal.

Customers buy from a repertoire. Think of petrol buying. Most drivers fill up at the nearest station, or one that's en route to their destination. Incentives, from Esso's 'Tiger Tokens' to Mobil's 'Speedpass' payment keyfob, are customer retention mechanisms.

So such marketing tactics are rarely influential. What they can do is prompt WOM, which is, of course, influential. What this means is that it is worth rewarding those customers that are influential as well as those that are profitable. This represents a shift from the Pareto 80:20 rule, where a minority of customers contribute the majority of the profit. While this may be true for your business, it ignores the influence of less-profitable but influential customers. It's easy to find out who your profitable customers are. Much harder to find out your most influential buyers.

> **Key points in this chapter**
>
> 1. People trust people like themselves. That's why WOM is powerful. But consumer influencers are hard to identify and to reach. WOM is therefore difficult to control and to direct towards your target audience.
> 2. There's only one reason why you'd need to do stealth marketing, and that is if your product is not worth talking about. Otherwise, don't do it.
> 3. People also trust third parties, whether based within the consumer supply chain or outside it. These parties are much easier to identify and to reach.

Notes and references

1 'What Assures Consumers?' survey cited by Jennifer Whitehead (2006), A-list celeb endorsements not trusted, survey finds. *Brand Republic* 19 July.
2 Kai H. Lim, Choon Ling Sia, Matthew K. O. Lee and Izak Benbasat (2006). Do I trust you online, and if so, will I buy? An empirical study of two trust-building strategies. *Journal of Management Information Systems*, **23** (2), 233.
3 Bradley Johnson (2006). Consumers cite past experience as the No.1 influencer when buying, *Advertising Age (Midwest region edition)*, **77** (47), 21.
4 Melanie Godsell (2007) Why should we trust you? *Marketing*, 10 January.
5 Edelman Trust Barometer 2007, published January 2007.
6 Quoted on *BBC News Magazine* March 2007.
7 VAR International study, cited in Celebrity Endorsements: The benefits of keeping it real. *Marketing Week*, 16 March 2006.
8 Dipayan Biswas, Abhijit Biswas and Neel Das (2006). The differential effects of celebrity and expert endorsements on consumer risk perceptions: the role of consumer knowledge, perceived congruency, and product technology orientation. *Journal of Advertising*, **35** (2), 17–31.
9 Barbara A. Lafferty and Ronald E. Goldsmith (2004). How influential are corporate credibility and endorser attractiveness when innovators react to advertisements for a new high-technology product? *Corporate Reputation Review*, **7** (1), 24–36.

18

Influencers in consumer markets

The nature of the supply chain bringing products and services from the manufacturer all the way to the consumer is a major factor in how buyers come to be influenced.

Most of the focus on influencers in the consumer world revolves around WOM marketing. This is understandable since WOM is controversial, challenging traditional marketing mechanisms. It also promises to be more effective than those old ways of marketing.

We've noticed, though, that WOM discussions centre on getting consumers to talk to each other, so-called C2C (consumer-to-consumer) conversations. But this narrows the view to one type of influencer – the consumers themselves. It ignores other influencers in the supply chain, plus a host of other opinion formers that provide input to decision-making. These influencers are important, but WOM techniques may not be appropriate or sufficient.

Consumers use non-consumer influencers for many reasons:

■ The product category involves high value or complex products that carry a degree of risk (e.g. financial, safety, legal risks). Expertise is required to advise on the product selection.

- There are personal issues involved that your average consumer prefers to discuss in private, possibly under protection of client confidentiality (financial, health, legal, etc.)
- Early adoption of a product category – no one you know has got the product you want to buy.

Consumers trust a host of other influencer types, many of which lie untapped and unexploited by marketing, but which are much easier to identify and target than consumers. You can break these influencers into two types: those in the supply chain and those outside it but that add value to the buying process. The placement of some influencer types in or outside the supply chain can be argued either way: it doesn't really matter. Using the supply chain is just a good way of starting to identify sources of influence. You must look inside *and* beyond the supply chain for influencers.

Supply chain influencers

A typical value chain for retailed products looks like Figure 18.1. Other consumer products may have quite different supply chains, but the principles of *influencer marketing* are the same.

There are no hard and fast rules about the degree of influence exerted by different types of influencer. It all depends on the market that you're looking at and the personalities involved. But generally, as far as the supply chain is concerned, the closer to the buyer an influencer is the greater the direct influence on the decision to buy. Influencers further up the supply chain tend to exert indirect influence through product quality, design, availability, prominence and so on.

Manufacturers

The role of manufacturers has changed radically in the last 10 years. Due to globalisation and outsourcing the manufacturer of goods is dissociated from the firm that designs and commissions the product. Dell became the archetype for this model, outsourcing manufacturing to trusted suppliers. Dell often never touched a product from manufacture to delivery, yet remained in control of design, branding and customer service.

Figure 18.1 A typical supply chain for consumer goods

But this model now pervades most manufacturing firms. Ford still assembles its cars but most of the components are manufactured by third parties. Coke is manufactured under licence by its bottlers and distributors around the world.

Manufacturers have influence over consumers in a number of ways. The manufacture of goods has become a social and political issue for many, so that manufacturers can impact sales according to attributes (some of which they have little control over). These include:

■ Health and safety standards
■ Location (local versus off-shore manufacture)
■ Source of raw materials (are they organic, sustainable, hazardous, natural or artificial, etc.)
■ Sourcing ethics (are factory workers exploited?, are they underpaid?, are ingredients tested on animals?, etc.)

The hypothetical 'ideal' product nowadays is organic, sourced locally or from sustainable and ethical suppliers abroad and safe to use/eat.

You can favourably position your product by emphasising the qualities and benefits of your manufacturing process. That is, if it's true. If it's not true, and your product is sourced (allegedly) from a sweatshop in the South Pacific then we suggest you need to think carefully about how to reassure customers when they find out (and they will find out). For example, you may need to engage value-added influencers (such as local trade bodies and charities) to confirm that $5 a day is a liveable wage in Manila. This is a serious issue, and one that major brands such as Nike and Apple have to deal with constantly.

Distributors and wholesalers

> As a merchant, you'd better have a friend in every town
> Middle Eastern Ancient Proverb

There are two major factors that have influenced availability of physical products: globalisation and the Internet.

Globalisation has meant that supply chains can be distributed geographically, with practically no limitations. The location of product manufacture is irrelevant to its ultimate point of consumption, thanks to integrated and low-cost communications and a global logistics infrastructure. This means that product firms can use manufacturers that provide the best quality, or the best price, or some combination of the two. The Internet enables stuff to be found, ordered and paid for, irrespective of the relative location of the buyer and seller. It's as cheap for a seller to reach a buyer in Paraguay as it is in Poole or Portland.

The Internet, of course, is more than a communications enabler; it's also a distribution mechanism. The supply of digital goods – music, video, photographs, books and so on – has changed the way such goods are sold and consumed. It also distributes product and company information, making it easier for prospective buyers to inform themselves. It's hard to consider the Internet as an influencer on modern decision-making, as it is so ubiquitous. Instead, the Internet has spread influence more evenly, and, arguably, diminished the influence of professional information gatherers and providers. Today the Internet is a hygiene factor: if you're on the web it's no big deal. But if you're not on the web, or your web site sucks, then this acts as a negative influence.

Retailers

Staff in the retail business may be some of the most important influencers in consumer products. These are the people that are in direct contact with consumers. They suggest products, make recommendations, and position favoured products in places of prominence. In many cases, it's the sales-people that are the primary influencers in a purchase decision, whether the person is called a sales executive, bank teller, bus driver or bartender. They are especially influential when they are recommending a product that is independent from the company they represent. You might be more suspicious of a cellphone salesman in a shop owned by a network provider – they are only going to try to sell you a handset that works on their network. But an independent reseller doesn't care which network or handset you choose, and so is likely to recommend something better matched to your needs (as opposed to theirs). Independent retailers are therefore more likely to influence a decision – what you need to do is influence these influencers, so they influence the decision in your favour.

The lowest potential for influence is where the product is tied to the retailer. Car dealership, telco-owned mobile phone shops, banks and tour operator travel agencies typically fall into this category. In these situations, consumers are never faced with an independent choice, and the sales staff can only promote their employers' products. Vested interest is total.

Salespeople sometimes have no vested interest in the specific sale and don't care whether you buy a Sony or a Panasonic TV – they just care that you buy something. Electronic stores typify this type. In these cases their advice can be trusted as far as the product comparisons go, which may be sufficient to influence a decision one way or another. Research shows that credibility is enhanced, and the chances of a sale increased, by conveying honest and occasionally unflattering information (remember this when updating your résumé . . .).

In supermarkets and other stores with large product ranges (including online stores) salespeople have no vested interest at all in what consumers buy. They are not on commission and have no financial incentive to promote one product over another. They are ideal influencers, because they can recommend products based on their own expertise or experience, or they have been trained in the benefits of a particular feature. Influencers like to influence, and by providing information to sales staff you are providing tools of influence that they can impart to consumers. For example, Samsung has over 30 people influencing retail sale staff. They merchandise, negotiate store positions and train over 85 000 retail staff a year. Samsung has doubled strategic displays in store as a result, increased recommend rates and net market share by over five points.

Is this unfair? Absolutely! Business is competition, and competition has winners and losers. Is it unethical? Not as long as the consumer knows they are in a sales situation (as indicated by the fact they are in a shop, for instance). You gain competitive advantage through providing tools of influence to salespeople on the shop floor.

A huge influence on buying food products is free samples. Costco does this to good effect, cooking samples of chicken satay on portable stoves, or serving Brie with a nice Merlot. It's an easy touch, customers ask questions of the staff ('Does it cook from frozen? What wine should I drink with this?') and there's often a discount on offer too. The technique aims at an impulse buy – the wafting aroma of oven-fresh muffins is often irresistible – and it works. Offering samples still works even though you don't sell what is being sampled. The word gets out that you give stuff away. You go to Costco because they give you samples of the latest dishwasher tablets. It gets you in the store.

Other retail executives, besides shop floor salespeople, are important too. Product placement in the retail location is hugely important. The manager at a supermarket branch can influence the sales of a particular wine just by locating it near to the entrance. Most consumers buying wine in a supermarket are not looking for a particular brand, region or grape – they just want wine. Making it easy to pick up a bottle of Chardonnay on the way in to the store is a great approach to selling.

Store placement is similar. That's why we have high streets and shopping malls. It clusters similar propositions together for the convenience of the customer. Have you noticed that there are always three or four coffee shops in a cluster when one would do? It's because that's where people go to drink coffee. The best place to open a shoe shop is next to an existing shoe shop. Your customers will go to the place where they can buy shoes.

These days the retail sector is dominated by big chains, and professional buyers for these firms are important influencers in the supply chain. These people determine the availability of a product on a national scale. For many manufacturers the buyers at Wal–Mart or Tesco or Carrefour are vital influencers.

Of course, supply chain influencers are well understood by businesses in consumer products. It's important to understand that no influencer works alone, and that they maintain and enhance their influence by connecting with other influencers. This is true in every sector, and it means that influence and opinions move across influencer types. What this means for the *influencer marketer* is that you can target influencers in one category with the knowledge that your message will spread to other influencers. Influencing supply chain influencers directly can be difficult as they have immense demands on their time and attention. But focusing on influencers outside but adjacent to the supply chain can offer a fast track to success. These influencers can add substantial value to decision-making consumers.

Value-added influencers

Some consumer products have a short supply chain and few value-added influencers. Heinz Baked Beans are manufactured, packed in cases and sent to a distribution centre, where they are then dispatched to retail outlets, to be bought by us. Not much to influence.

A bottle of distilled alcohol with some added colour and aromatic oils may sound a similar consumer proposition to Baked Beans. But call it fragrance, and a host of new influencers emerge, dwarfing the supply chain to insignificant levels.

The more complex a product becomes, or the higher the value ascribed to the product, the greater the opportunity for value-added influencers to make an impact. Conversely, the simpler or more commoditised a product is, the less scope there is for value-added influencers. Interestingly, instances of products within broad categories span across these dimensions. You can buy a cheap watch or a Rolex or a Breguet. They will sell to different market segments, and the role and type of influencers will vary for each.

Support and services

The major influencers in buying washing machines and central heating boilers are plumbers. We can't think of a group of tradesmen that are less adept at selling (they don't need to sell as demand for plumbers outstrips supply!), yet they massively influence the purchase of major domestic appliances. Give a plumber the briefest of requirements and you'll get a 'what you need is a . . .' recommendation that most of us would accept gratefully. Checking on the web for boilers just serves to confound consumers, which drives them back towards the initial advice.

Plumbers are part of a major category of influencers on consumer purchases, that of support and services staff. We take a very broad definition of this group. Importantly, it includes your own employees involved in support roles and those third parties that touch your customers. It is often here that organisations experience a 'moment of truth', the point at which your customer service is tested. Do you pass or fail?

Support staff may operate telephone call centres or provide after-sales service. Increasingly common is the outsourcing of support, so your partner organisations are just as critical in influencing. Customer support is what often differentiates successful companies from failures, and what determines whether you get positive WOM or public slanging. The UK's only cable TV and broadband provider has, we understand, great technology and a broad portfolio of programming and entertainment services. What we hear from influencers is that its customer service is terrible. A *Marketing Magazine* survey of customer service quality put NTL 58th out of 58. NTL says it has invested millions in customer service. The problem is that once you have a bad reputation it's extraordinarily difficult to shift it. To its customers and detractors the firm became known as NT 'hell'. It subsequently rebranded to Virgin Media, at a cost of £25m.

Consumer groups and lobby groups

One of the key elements of influence is trust, and individuals or groups that claim independence from sellers are often credible as influencers. Such organisations exist in most developed countries and include Which? in the UK, Consumer Union in the US, Union Fédérale des Consommateurs – Que Choisir in France and Stiftung Warentest in Germany. These organisations evaluate a host of consumer products and publish their independent views. Consumers use these reviews to inform their purchase decisions.

Consumer groups also have an important role to play in the lobbying of governments, retailers and manufacturers for improvements in products. For example, Which?, the UK consumer group, lobbies for food standards and health issues, and confronts governments and commercial firms on a variety of issues. It was the first to use the term 'Rip off Britain' to describe the UK's tax rules over new cars unfavourable in comparison with mainland Europe. The term stuck and has since been applied to many other tax and economic policy issues. Consumer Reports is well known for its product testing and was behind the introduction of the Flammable Fabrics Act, the Child Protection and Toy Safety Act in the US.

These organisations gain their influence through their not-for-profit status and independent stance on consumer-focused issues. The Roper study notes that Consumer Reports was cited by 15% of adults as a trusted source of information. CR was also voted the 'most trustworthy and objective' media outlet for information on consumer products in a 2005 American Demographics survey.

Some issue-specific organisations seem happy to align themselves with commercial firms if it suits their purpose. McDonalds has struck a deal with the Vegetarian Society to supply veggie burgers to its UK restaurants. McDonalds has had a veggie burger for years, but seeks the additional credibility and influence of the Vegetarian Society to attract health conscious consumers. This is sensitive and controversial territory, and previous attempts at aligning fast food with dietary organisations have caused clashes between vegetarian advocates and animal rights groups. The guidance here is to assess the strength and moderation of the influencer concerned. Engaging with an organisation at the extremes may promote a specific and strong stance on an issue, but may carry with it the risk of being dragged into zealous ideology.

Interestingly, McDonalds has found favour with Covalence, a Swiss-based firm that tracks ethical behaviour of multinationals. It found that McDonalds had made the most progress in the leisure and entertainment industry in 2007. Covalence is a good example of a lobbyist exerting global influence on large firms.

Professionals and experts

A true story. A lady visits her middle-aged professional parents and discovers they are clearing out their loft. The lady is intrigued to unearth the reason for the unseasonal spring clean. It turns out that her parents had been considering selling the house. This in turn had been prompted by a doctor's appointment attended by her father who, he believed, had been told he had two years to live. With the terrible news, the couple had decided to sell up and move to a bungalow, where the soon-to-be-widowed mother could live in comfort and security. Shocked by the revelation, the daughter enquires what's wrong with her father:

Oh, I didn't ask. He just said that I have two years to go. I guess I just accepted it.

What the doctor actually told the father was that he had two to go to his next check-up appointment. Why did this professional man, an expert in his own field, simply believe without question the advice from a doctor? Why didn't he question the prognosis, or ask for a second opinion?

The answer is that we tend to believe people with expertise and professional standing. Often, the choices or decisions or symptoms facing us are too complex. We need shortcuts. Sometimes it's easier if the expert makes the decision for us.

Consumers are influenced consistently and substantially by professionals of all types. Sometimes their advice is sought, other times it comes at us uninvited. Nevertheless, consumers listen. The professions that consumers listen to are varied, not restricted to the white collar professions. They include the following:

■ Doctors	■ Lawyers	■ Financial advisers
■ Builders	■ Teachers	■ Journalists
■ Academics	■ Taxi drivers	■ Hairdressers
■ Dentists	■ Gardeners	■ Architects
■ Council officials	■ Hotel concierges	■ Travel kiosk staff

As the developed world shifts from an industrial to a service-based economy we are awash with people who are professional advice givers.

Why are consumers influenced by professionals? There are three main reasons:

■ Professionals inject expertise and/or competence into the decision-making process. Clearly the expertise in question should be validated through stated qualifications, job role and position or some other means (such as a referral from another trusted source).
■ Professionals provide an independent view, with regard to the decision being made. The lack of vested interest is critical in such instances. Note that professional opinion and advice may be subject to bias despite lack of vested interest. This point is often misunderstood, but of primary importance in understanding the nature of influence. An 'expert' may not be a complete expert but have been coached, or otherwise briefed by a specific party. Your doctor may recommend a specific brand of headache relief, but they may have just had a visit from a pharmaceuticals sales rep., or the expert's information may just be incomplete, or may be subject to other biases emanating from the expert's background and personal experience. This explains why two professionals might conflict in their advice. There is nothing wrong with their advice, but each brings

their own personal prejudices to the table. There is rarely ever a completely independent view expressed.

■ Professionals can perform a useful service as information aggregators and consolidators. Often the number and variety of options available to consumers is bewildering, and navigating the choices is beyond many. Just think of the different types of mobile phone options on offer, or the number of mortgage variables. Professionals have the time and inclination to evaluate these options that most consumers would rather not expend.

Uniforms

It is a well-researched fact that people are influenced by those in uniform. They will comply with the oddest of requests if made by an official-looking person in a shirt with epaulettes and a peaked cap. Uniforms are marks of identification, but they also convey authority. Surprisingly, this authority is not necessarily situation-specific, and people are just as likely to obey an instruction to cross the road from an airline steward as they are from a policeman.

In a consumer purchasing situation, uniformed individuals are equally likely to have an influence. Most people are just as inclined to trust a policeman on which shampoo to buy, as they are on local neighbourhood issues and crime rates.

The uniformed community that has most influence on consumers and their purchases are shop floor sales staff. Here, uniforms are used to make staff stand out from consumers, but they also confer a degree of expertise. This expertise can quickly be tested ('Which aisle is the cheese in?', 'Is this lotion available in lavender?') and credentials are established. This is why many consumer-facing organisations make their employees wear a uniform.

Government agencies, regulators and legislators

Governments and lawmakers often seem distant from, and irrelevant to, consumer purchasing decisions. In some markets, however, their influence is substantial. There are some obvious and long-standing effects on consumer purchasing, such as tax. But since 1990 there has been steady increase in the regulation of telecommunications, food standards, pharmaceuticals, fuel emissions, exports, imports, recycling, road pricing and so on. Whether you agree with the policies or not, the impact on consumer behaviour is undeniable.

Such legislation tends to impact *whether* a consumer will make a buying decision, more than the decision itself. An interest rate increase may influence consumers into delaying a house purchase, or may hasten the transaction if the increase is announced before its enactment. But it won't affect *which* house they buy.

Similarly, standards on fuel emissions affect all cars. Taxes aimed at penalising gas-guzzling sport utility vehicles (SUVs) are aimed at all SUVs. The desired impact is (a) in the short term to divert consumers towards more fuel-efficient cars, and (b) longer term to persuade manufacturers to improve the efficiency of SUVs. At best the strategy encourages consumers away from one product category and towards another. But it rarely affects the decision on *which* car to buy.

How can you identify influencers on consumers?

When looking for influencers start with the supply chain, then ask two questions:

- Who within the supply chain has a direct or indirect influence on the consumer's buying decision?
- Who outside the supply chain influences parties within the supply chain?

It is vitally important to get the market segment correct, otherwise you will miss key influencers for sure. By example, let's look at the supply chain for coffee:

The supply chain for coffee is straightforward and the influencers are clear:

Inside supply chain	Outside supply chain
Grower	Intermediaries, including crop aggregators, traders and processors
Wholesaler	Government agencies – in some countries the government controls the coffee trade
Processor	Dealers/brokers/auctioneers – supply the coffee beans to the roasters in the right quantities, at the right time, at a price acceptable to buyer and seller
Exporter	
Roaster (usually the brand name firm)	
Packager	
Distributor	
Retailer	

If the segment is narrowed to ethically produced coffee, there are some supply chain differences. Co-operatives perform the wholesaling and processing functions. Alternative Trading Organisations (ATOs) buy the coffee at a fixed price rather than it being auctioned, as is normal practice.

Importantly, new value-added influencers have a substantial role. The Fairtrade organisation, for example, operates in 20 countries and manages the Fairtrade international labelling system. It influences retailers such as Costa and Starbucks, encouraging them to stock and promote ethical coffee. Note, though, that the influence from Fairtrade is neither unidirectional nor accepted blindly: although Fairtrade's motives are backed by Starbucks in principle, the retailer favours a different approach to ethical trade involving sustainable coffee farming. Starbucks is equally capable of influencing Fairtrade and other influencers, as well as consumers.

Other charity organisations may also influence the market. For example, Oxfam stocks Fairtrade coffee in its shops, as well as promoting the Fairtrade scheme in its own charity activities. Government agencies in consuming (as opposed to producing) countries can influence trade through their international development and aid programmes. And the media can convey the core messages to increasingly socially conscious consumers.

Value-added influencers can vary in their impact, both in amount of impact and its direction, for or against. The sales of bottled water now exceed $10 billion, influenced primarily by supply chain players and the social proof that bottled water is good for you. However, there is a small but growing group of detractor influencers that have an inhibiting effect on sales growth. For example, Tom Standage wrote a book called *The History of the World in Six Glasses*, in which he defines the progress of civilisation by the beverage of choice in six eras. In the book he berates the bottled water industry, claiming neither health nor economic grounds for its existence. The controversial UK consumer programme *Bulls**t Detective* made a point by bottling the distilled urine of the show's presenter and selling it as pure water (which, of course, it was). Regulators in food standards and water quality verification provided support for the claim, and in most developed countries the quality of water from the tap is at least as good as that sold in bottles. Will facts carry enough influence to challenge a huge industry? Only time will tell.

The more complex and high value the product, the greater the need for value-added influencers. Take the automotive industry. The supply chain for cars has become more and more complex, as manufacturers have acquired and divested various parts of the process. In parallel the market for cars has changed dramatically in the last decade:

- Overproduction has led to stagnant sales volumes and a reduction in margins to wafer-thin levels.
- The types of cars preferred by consumers changes frequently, from saloons to multi-purpose vehicles (MPVs) to SUVs to hybrids and so on.
- The environmental lobby has positioned fuel emissions as a major contributor to global warming, which heads the agenda of many local and national governments worldwide.

Value-added influencers can have a number of influences in the industry. Regulators and legislators not only set fuel emission standards for cars but can introduce penalties through the tax system for polluting vehicles. They can also introduce road pricing schemes such as tolls and congestion charges, all of which help to direct consumer choice towards smaller more fuel-efficient cars. They may take a further step and promote alternative transport mechanisms (such as trains, bikes and walking).

Consider the process of buying a house, something that most of us will be familiar with. The supply chain is short, typically involving a vendor, a buyer and an estate agent. Who would you seek out as an information provider? The primary property details come from the vendor via the agent. But they clearly have a vested interest in the transaction. They may make claim on the desirability of the house, its proximity to important amenities, crime rates and so on. Do you take their word for it?

If you're moving house within the same area you may know who to contact. You'll be able to check out whether a 'neighbourhood watch' system is in place. You may be able to knock on the doors of neighbours to ask about life in the area. Best of all, you may know someone personally who lives close by, and who will give the insider view.

Most people will also attempt to corroborate given details with independent sources. They will consult published crime figures, possibly even calling the local police station for advice. They will refer to school inspection reports and league tables. Local councils will be quizzed for pending planning applications.

As well as public information sources, there are influential people that will provide critical input into the decision. The local head teacher may be critically important if the main attraction for the property is its proximity to good schools. Before acceptance of a mortgage application a surveyor will assess the property condition and determine the value of the house. Builders and other tradesmen may then be asked for quotations for structural work deemed necessary.

The point is, if you're selling a house, these are the people whose views matter.

Surveys – your flexible friend

If you're moving into a new town from another area your information choices will be the same (using the power of the web) but your access to neighbours and local opinion formers may be limited. Instead you may use a proxy aggregator of information, such as a survey of good places to live. These surveys pop up frequently and exist for local areas as well as globally – Vancouver and Zurich are the best places globally to live, according to a 2007 study by Mercer.

Surveys are great at grabbing the public's attention, but they don't always create a consensus. According to a Channel 4 survey in 2006, Winchester is the best place to live in England. The criteria included crime levels, environment, lifestyle, education and employment. But six months later *Readers' Digest* published a survey on the best place to raise a family, in which Winchester came 47th. Both used public information sources. Why the big difference?

One major variance between the two studies was the weighting place on some criteria in the *Readers' Digest* list. The results were based on a survey of parents, who ranked each criteria on importance to family life. This raised the profile of education and crime, and downplayed the environment and employment. *Readers' Digest* also included a criterion for housing affordability – cheaper areas score better than more expensive towns. This measure was absent from the Channel 4 study.

What does this mean? Simply, that behind every headline and statistic there is subjectivity and opinion, even if this is just to set the context for the research. Just be sure that you understand the inevitable biases of research.

These examples show that research, official statistics and headlines can provide helpful direction, but they are but one source of input. They tend to average out any strengths or weaknesses that may exist, so may remove awareness of exceptional good or bad instances.

Key points in this chapter

1. Consumers trust a host of influencers other than people they know. These influencers are untapped and unexploited by marketing, but are much easier to identify and target than consumers.
2. Within the supply chain, the closer to the buyer an influencer is the greater the direct influence on the decision to buy. So retailers tend to exert more influence that manufacturers.
3. The more complex a product becomes, or the higher the value ascribed to the product, the greater the opportunity for value-added influencers to make an impact. Conversely, the simpler or more commoditised a product is, the less scope there is for value-added influencers.

19

How to structure
influencer marketing
in your organisation

So you've decided to adopt influencer marketing within your organisation. What should you first bear in mind?

We have now reviewed what problems traditional marketing faces, the changing nature of how buyers buy, and introduced the increasing role of influencers in this buying process. We have looked at how your company can work with influencers to your advantage, using both offline and online technologies, and we have compared how influencers influence in consumer markets with those in business (B2B) sectors. You should now have a good grasp of influencers in all their guises. And we hope this has left you with the confidence to adopt influencer marketing within your own organisation. On this assumption, there's some things you should know in advance.

Will targeting influencers soon be consumed within more traditional marketing disciplines?

Within 3 or 4 years, we openly expect that targeting influencers will be integrated within, rather than consumed by, several existing disciplines. The worry of course is that once integrated, those influencers identified will merely be treated like additional names to whom the direct mail team can abuse, with their brochures, discount offer promotions, gimmicks and trade show reminders. Not every communication issued by vendors will be relevant to both prospects and influencers, and though vendors currently don't need to make such a distinction, it's not too great a leap of faith to imagine that changing. If the marketing director has really understood why influencers are different from prospects, and the company's management team accepts the critical role that many influencers now play, then we don't think treating influencers as prospects will be allowed to happen.

Bringing influencers into the mainstream of marketing may even help raise the thought levels applied to all audiences. With desktop relationship management (CRM) technology now available to every member of the marketing department, and economically viable shorter print runs, there's no excuse for sending out every piece of collateral to every person on your database. Perhaps even environmental pressures will kick in here to help. Integrating *influencer marketing* may force marketing departments to better segment their audiences, treating each with renewed respect and placing more emphasis on two-way relationships rather than one-directional targeting.

Influencers don't influence to order

When salespeople work with prospects, they're categorised, warm, cold and hot, or short-, mid- and long-term or whatever, and this categorisation enables a company's progress with them to be mapped onto particular sales timescales, usually quarter by quarter. That way it can be decided who's worth persevering with and who are just 'tyre kickers' to use the jargon. Salespeople will get some kind of quick feel for this, though inevitably sometimes they're wrong.

But influencers don't work to such manageable timescales. For one, you may never know when they're active or dormant, for their influence won't be linear and measurable. Often they won't even know when they're 'influencing' and purchasing decision-makers may not know when they've been 'influenced', so no one even centrally involved in such discussions could note-take on how such influence had been enacted. When it's this esoteric, how could anyone ever claim to measure their success with influencers, and therefore cost justify their ongoing involvement with them? A good point, and one we've had to think about. A lot. So how should a new Marketing department be organised?

It has always bemused us when PR firms are showered with praise by their clients when a favourable product review appears in the trade media. Sure, the agency has to get that product in the hands of the right person at the right time, but beyond that, it has next to no control over how it fares compared to rival products. One reviewer may object to the flashing blue lights on the client's new product, while another praises its *Star Wars* look. Nor can PR sway its 'value-for-money' rating. Yet clients react as if they can, and do. It works both for and against PR.

Don't get us wrong, many PR firms do a great job, and they're completely necessary for client companies of a certain size. But for small companies we think firms should consider very carefully before employing one.

For many companies we would advocate disbanding the traditional 'PR' role and in its place hiring the 'VIP engagement' manager mentioned in Chapter 8. This role would manage relations with those that had been identified as the 50 top influencers to the success of the firm (the 'VIP'). This hire would be a knowledgeable, personable and market-literate person. Their task would be to establish unique working relationships with as many of the top 50 as were willing to be contacted, finding out how they wished to work with the company, and what information would most help them. This 'VIP engagement' manager would have the autonomy to arrange meetings with senior management, schedule their own working day around the needs of those influencers, and be measured on the increasing closeness of those working relationships. Some of the influencers would want steady news stories, some longer-term strategic steers, some technical details and others competitive positioning. None of this should be beyond the scope of an intelligent, experienced hire. There would be no advertising, no PR company fees, no generic trade show booths. Just intelligent conversation. Think of the cost-savings.

Securing an influencer budget

Imagine deciding to reallocate your combined PR and AR budget to influencer marketing. On average that would amount to 9–10% of your overall marketing budget. But influencer marketing typically costs only 50–80% of the cost of PR and AR. So at least 20 per cent of your existing PR/AR budget could be ploughed straight back into improving your existing customer's experience – whether that be telephone support, a smoother 'out of the box' experience or whatever. Your customers should notice that kind of investment. The rest you'd be spending on the top 50 influencers – they could have a pretty deep experience with your company for that amount. So long as you'd identified them in the first place correctly, those 50 would be seeding back into the regular decision-makers day-in day-out about what a great customer-focused company you are.

Introducing influencers into your mix

While the identification stage can be slipstreamed alongside a traditional marketing programme, the remaining stages cannot. The *marketing to*, *marketing through* and *marketing with* stages need to be integrated into a broader set of marketing activities, and this can only happen successfully if the marketing leadership in the company understands the implications of working with the influencers. It requires a mindshift in marketing, where the company is no longer just marketing *to* an anonymous demographic, but in parallel with that programme (targeting prospects), is establishing a set of 1-to-1 relationships *with* a small number of known individuals. For the majority of marketing departments, that's a far from easy transition to make.

So how should an organisation's *influencer marketing* progress be measured?

Give responsibility for influencers to a single experienced staff member. If an organisation's relationship with its key influencers is to be based on understanding and trust, then those influencers cannot be contacted by a different staff member each time. Continuity is important. The chosen 'VIP engagement manager' must not be incentivised according to crude numbers-based metrics such as 'frequency of contact'. These have no place in establishing the quality of such relationships. In time, say after 6 months have elapsed from first contact, those influencers may be willing to complete a short print or online questionnaire indicating their satisfaction level with the company's efforts and suggesting improvements.

Now these influencers may not knowingly be in the middle of any active 'influencing' on your behalf, in fact, the vast majority of their influencing may be without their knowledge, so there's really no point in asking them which deals they happen to be 'influencing' at any given time. If they are aware of a specific case, and they want you to know of it, you can be sure they'll tell you. You should never be seen to 'push' the relationship faster than the influencer wants to take it. This means that influencers themselves won't be helping you measure their usefulness to you. You'll have to look elsewhere. Perhaps to the prospect instead.

If each prospect you engaged with could list who they were being influenced by then you could measure each influencer's value that way. But of course they can't. Even after a deal has been signed, either for or against your company, the prospect is not about to outline every individual's role in that decision, and if you lost the deal, you probably won't be able to go in and meet with them again anyway. Rarely will the prospect be able or willing to clarify how their DME operated. They too won't be helping with your measurement.

Get your salespeople to help

Which leaves your salespeople as your most likely prime source for measuring your success with the influencers. We believe there are three stages during which your salespeople can help support your *influencer marketing* activities, especially when your senior management are leaning over your shoulder asking for progress reports.

- The first is throughout the first 6 months when there is likely to be no tangible signs of sales success due to the influencers. For much of this period you will have been focused on identifying them in the first place, and for the latter half you will have been establishing the best way to work with them. Your sales force now can best help you by verbally supporting your campaign internally, and by regularly feeding you supportive anecdotes and further insights into the decision-making process within their prospect customers. You should ensure that you have set internal expectations extremely low at this stage.
- During the 6- to 12-month period your relationship with the majority of your chosen influencers should be returning a 'feel good' factor, though not necessarily any return on sales. Your partner sales management should be applauding the effort you have been putting in to those influencers from partner companies and the sales channel, your PR and AR teams noticing the improved relationship with those from their categories. Your sales force should be beginning to pick up concrete examples where your activities are helping both with new sales leads and furthering the process with existing prospects. There may by now even be tangible examples of the sales process being smoothed by particular influencers. The sales force should now be feeding back such positive stories to your company's senior management.
- From 12 months onwards, your company's director of sales should be in no doubt as to the benefits that your influencer activities are now having on both lead generation and sales in progress. Some companies by now will have clear evidence of one or more identified influencers positively impacting a sales lead, and most others will have sufficient indirect evidence to remain firmly committed to the campaign. Amongst our own client experience, after 12 months there are more sales directors by now campaigning for a higher percentage of marketing resource to be placed on influencers, than there are those looking to scale back on

any spend. For most companies, a single case of an influencer-led purchase in a major customer is more than enough to financially justify an ongoing commitment to the programme.

Influencers can't be hurried

Take it off the quarterly 'deliverables' calendar. Some influencers may want to be contacted regularly, others no more often than every 6 months, still others only when significant company or industry events occur. There is no standard understanding, influencers need to be treated as individuals and should be allowed to dictate their own preferred 'terms of engagement'. These may then not fit neatly into your company's preferred reporting format.

Every 9 months or so your identification process for your company's influencers should be repeated, replacing any out-of-date players. While an individual may still hold the same role within their organisation, they may no longer hold sufficient influence to still justify a top 50 placement, whether due to political changes, company redirection, new and emerging players, etc. Your company needs to establish a process for handling those now relegated players, without simply choosing to ignore them. That won't win you any friends!

At the end of the day, there's one person's views which are most important to the continued funding of an influencer programme. Your CEO. And that's very good news for you. Arrange for your CEO to attend, and maybe even host, a twice-yearly dinner evening to which each of the top 50 influencers are invited. Not all will attend of course, not all will even be based in the same country, but a sufficient number will to reinforce the calibre, credibility, and let's face it, business potential of those influencers invited. Then get your CEO to sign-off on your ongoing influencer programme just days after one of these dinners while it's still fresh in their memory. There'll be no funding problem. We guarantee it.

What to expect when you commission influencer identification?

Almost without exception, our clients don't have much idea exactly what they'll be receiving. That's not to say we don't tell them, we try to tell them in considerable detail in fact, for delivering surprises is rarely a good idea with clients. You've no idea how they'll take to surprises. Most clients have only thought about influencers for just a few months by the time we deliver our initial identification report, and they're still getting to grips with what to do with this new knowledge. Almost without exception, their entire marketing experience has been based on marketing to prospects, whether that's an in-house database of current customers, a bought-in mailing list or the business cards of people who have stopped by their trade show booth over the past couple of years. Any training they've had, whether formal or on-the-job, has been with one audience – prospects – in mind. Marketing has traditionally a single purpose for all of these people – to encourage them to be customers – and preferably this quarter. Now what does the marketing department do when faced not with a cold list of hundreds or thousands of names, but the details of 50 individuals identified as being of extreme importance to your company? Well whatever you do do with them, you don't treat them as just another group of names for your database.

But the thought of this unnerves many marketers. They typically have no collateral to send such people, there are no staff in place to pick up the phone and initiate a respectful relationship with these new-found influencers, and there are no processes in place to document and track any discussions, let alone map their status on to existing objectives. It just doesn't neatly 'fit' into the rest of their marketing! And until it does, the adoption of *influencer marketing* will remain low.

And what do you actually get?

In the early days of our company, we'd routinely present to our clients more questions than answers. We didn't intend to, we'd even go out of our way not to, but however much we thought we'd prepared our clients we could almost see the puzzled look on their faces as they digested what on earth they should now do with their newly identified influencers. Throughout our research, right up to the minutes before our presentation, they had their thoughts on what to do with their soon-to-be acquired knowledge. In truth, many clients privately imagined that they'd be learning little new, that their years in their industry meant that they'd already be aware of the names of most of the influencers. They just hoped not so many as to render the identification research superfluous.

Then they see the names and we explain the reasons for including those that we have. It's easy now to picture the looks on many of their faces as they realise that despite all of their experience, all of their 'networking' seminars, all of the customer meetings they've attended, their relationships with their customers' top influencers are almost non-existent. It's like seeing years roll away from their experience as they take in just how much they have previously misunderstood about their sector. Yet they are no different from nearly every one of their competitors.

So what are the surprises?

Clients approach the identification stage expecting to be surprised. But only a little. They expect to recognise almost every organisation listed and perhaps half of the individual names. What they don't expect is more fundamental than this. Almost without exception we have found that our clients are unaware of up to one-third of the organisations themselves, and often two-thirds of the individuals' names. What becomes ever clearer is that while companies have made ongoing attempts to create relationships with several sections of their sector infrastructure (almost always predominantly journalists, analysts and channel partners), they have completely ignored whole other sections. And though some won't have ignored them, they will have totally misunderstood their significance and role. Even those clients that do have a structure in place to liaise with the top-tier management consultancies, the Accentures, KPMGs, PwCs and Deloittes of this world (and most companies do not), will have no knowledge of the fact that the second-tier consultancies may account for at least 40 per cent of the consultancy revenue marketplace. The result – too many vendors chasing the coat tails of the top-tier players while leaving the second-tier all but ignored. We are often surprised at how restricted a view our clients have of their industry – an extremely deep and detailed awareness of some players and almost complete unawareness of others.

In the tech sectors, we'd say that 90 per cent of the marketing directors within the top 100 vendors know their top-tier journalists and industry analysts pretty well, certainly to the level where they can name some individual names. We'd suggest that about 5 per cent could name a single individual within a major systems integrator or management consultant, even the CEO! And probably no more than 50 per cent could name more than two integrator firms that their company even does business with. Yet integrators and consultants should be a core audience for the marketing director. You see what we mean about blinkered knowledge.

Key points in this chapter

1. Rather than PR, hire a 'VIP engagement' manager, to manage relations with the top 'VIP' in your market.
2. The ultimate measurement for *influencer marketing* is an improvement in sales, so your sales staff should be asked for their feedback on its implementation.
3. Once you have a ranked list of your top influencers what do you do with it? Don't mail it, or treat it as another prospect list. How about starting by getting your CEO to host a dinner for your top 50 influencers.

20

Making *influencer marketing* work for your company

There are bound to be obstacles in your way as you adopt *influencer marketing*. How can you prepare for these?

How can I take this book and act on it tomorrow?

We don't want this to be a textbook. We want it to be a practical 'how to' book explaining why identifying the major influencers in your company's marketplace makes such undoubted marketing and business sense, and to inspire you to start without delay. To achieve this, we need to explain how you can migrate your existing, already approved, part-underway traditional marketing plan into an influencer campaign. The good news is that while it will undoubtedly be a revolution in the longer-term, it can start life for you as an evolution. There, that's one fear over.

Barriers affecting the broader adoption of influencer marketing

We've thought about this many times over the past few years. Will it take a single event to finally convince marketing directors that their traditional marketing mix is just fundamentally broken, or will something happen that convinces them of *influencer marketing's* sense? Inertia tells us that it will be the former. People rarely voluntarily move to better things. They wait until they just can't continue with the old ways anymore. If this wasn't true, we'd have all changed our lifestyles on account of global warming long before now. Even when we see the danger signals, we shut our eyes for as long as possible.

At least in recessions people reconsider marketing

Clearly *influencer marketing* will have to continue to build up its fan base inside large organisations, and start boasting very measurable benefits, but even this won't be enough on its own. No, instead the acceptance of *influencer marketing* will be tied to the discrediting of traditional marketing. We've already mentioned a few global organisations who have gone public this year with their admission that they can't even measure any significant uptick in product sales as a result of their billion dollar marketing campaigns. You'd have thought this would be enough to cause a crisis of confidence in marketing circles, but it hasn't. Another economic recession, a deep one, would force many firms to dramatically downscale their marketing activities, even bringing them to a complete halt in some cases. Two years of no activity and *influencer marketing* would sweep in to fill the vacuum, almost guaranteed. But none of us would welcome going through that pain barrier. The market 'adjustment' from 2000 to 2004 was bad enough. So we think the best we can hope for is a groundswell of chief executive opinion that marketing is no longer contributing enough, along with further admissions from brand-name vendors that they can't equate marketing spend with any boost in sales. And it may be enough. It certainly has a right to be.

Emergence of new study data

But more likely is that a number of supporting studies will start to gain credence. In recent years, there has been a small number of research studies designed to analyse the measurable effect of traditional marketing on the sales effectiveness of commercial companies in multiple industry sectors, and of various sizes. Two in particular we have read of only began in late-2006 and will not be delivered until 2008. Imagine if they show negligible, or at least insufficient, return on the bottom line. Imagine if such findings reach the majority of management boards. Imagine them still signing off budgets on the scale that they have done to date. Imagine the marketing executives telling the board that they intend to spend this year in much the same way as they did the previous year. No, we don't think so either. Marketing will have to change in order to secure a budget in future.

Why's it hard today to secure a budget for influencer marketing?

This seems a more straightforward answer. *Influencer marketing* pro-grammes are new and they have to deliver tangible ROI over two or more years before they are considered 'reliably beneficial'. A good return from the first year of adoption can easily be attributed to being a novelty, the kind of short-term boost that any change could enjoy. And in the short-term, tangible ROI may prove difficult for some companies. We have no doubt that there'll be a 'gut feel' ROI, that those companies will inherently feel that it makes sense to be doing this, and that the sales force will agree, but in terms of mapping such returns onto some kind of quarterly spread-sheet, well, that's less clear. The issue is the time lag involved, nothing more. So it won't be for the faint-hearted. Considering the need for ROI, you too will be bemused at how broadbrush advertising, with no ROI to speak of, will have no such fight on its hands to retain a place in the budget, and a very significant place at that!

Marketing conservatism

We're also in an era of great conservatism in marketing. The emphasis on accountability inevitably has resulted in increased cost justification of traditional processes and attempts to improve their efficiency. It is a natural first step to remove areas of wastage within existing activities before evaluating the benefits of new ones. And marketing directors need to be aware of what new thinking in marketing there is. An IT director for example receives weekly and perhaps daily magazines, bulletins and papers on the latest trends, products and technologies. Comparative product reviews enable the reader to compare and contrast various options and read customer testimonials before deciding on which solution to choose. Many competitors can even be 'googled' to find which technology they are using. In this sense, IT directors find it easy to keep abreast of their options.

Marketing directors have no such luxury. Sure, websites and online forums exist – sites such as MarketingSherpa and ClickZ are extremely useful, if almost entirely US-centric – but there are relatively few reference points to aid marketing directors. How does one uncover their rival's breakdown in marketing spend or change in audience targeting? Outside of personal networking, today's marketing director has very few signposts, so how are they to know when their thinking has become outdated? We see this as the most significant single reason for outdated marketing continuing to exist – the lack of awareness as to what new thinking exists. And *influencer marketing* is very much new thinking.

Introducing influencer marketing into your company

As we've said earlier, the role of influencers is something that few within a marketing department will have ever thought about before. Introducing an initiative to start marketing to influencers is therefore likely to lead to a lot of blank faces. Your first objective is to get those in your team to better understand influencers. There are only upsides to commissioning one or two key influencers to come to your company and explain to your team their role, their typical view of vendors like yourselves and how they would like, and not like, to be approached going forward. Not all will make themselves available for commissioning – industry leaders, those within end-user companies and market regulators will almost certainly not appreciate being approached – but there will typically be a majority among your top 50 who will make themselves available, for a fee of course. This is an ideal opportunity for your staff to understand what it's like on the other side of the fence, what it's like to be on the receiving end of vendor marketing and to be advised on what marketing approaches may actually strike a chord with that individual. Of course, there's the rub. Such a meeting will help you understand the viewpoint of a single individual, not a whole influencer category and certainly not the full range of influencers. But it's a start, an important and significant start, and well worth the investment.

In the same vein of helping your marketing team better understand the sales environment, how often, and thoroughly, do members of your sales force explain the buying process to those in marketing? Explaining what may have caused the initial lead, how that lead is followed up, what catalysts, pressures, objectives and the like are typically mentioned by prospects, how competitors tend to respond, what aspects are ripe for negotiation, what reassurances are often needed, what tick boxes need to be ticked before a sale can be closed. Certainly in the marketing departments that we have been a part of, none of this was ever formally explained. Yet experienced salespeople are highly sought after, they know the ropes, the tricks, when to push and when to let go of a prospect. The kind of knowledge you can't get from a book. And marketing teams are the poorer for not knowing it.

What the sales force could do to help the cause of influencer marketing

Sales forces can certainly help in the introduction of *influencer marketing*. Those responsible for sales management are instinctively very supportive of *influencer marketing*. It hits the right buttons for them. It is 'serious' marketing, as opposed to the frivolous spending that so frustrates them. They can see what *influencer marketing* is trying to do, and they know it's a job that needs to be done. But they often let themselves down by not documenting their honest assessment when losing sales, or at least, when losing track of the customer's decision-making process. This misses an opportunity to emphasise how the sale failed and the importance of the ever-present background influencers. If this were more routinely documented, the role of those influencers would have risen to prominence more quickly.

Too often salespeople log the reason for lost sales as 'specification changed', 'decided to stay with incumbent supplier', 'personnel changed within decision team', or 'initial scope of purchase scaled back', without any further explanation. It assumes that nothing could be done. This is typically not true, and in those cases reaching the influencers in the early stages may have made all the difference. For behind those bland, four or five word sign-offs, lie untold stories of how decision or progress committees had decided to expand, scale back, change focus, lean to and from certain suppliers, delay implementation timescales, avoid particular technologies, invite new advisors to join, etc. Any one of these ideas would have been brought to the table by just one of the team's influencers, an individual most likely unknown to any of the prospective vendors. You can see how a pre-existing positive relationship with that individual could well have facilitated a different outcome.

Were salespeople more incentivised to really dig down to better understand the specific reasons for prospect opportunities being derailed or lost, then we believe there would be greater appreciation for the role that influencers can have, and therefore greater urgency applied to the act of addressing them. We think this is a major factor in gaining boardroom backing for this initiative.

Correct influencer identification is crucial

Implementing *influencer marketing* begins with influencer selection and targeting. It is crucial that this activity is done right because, in theory, plenty could go wrong. Identifying influencers is not an easy task – it's taken our experience, our determination and a fair few mistakes to evolve a methodology that we're pretty happy with, and it can't just be replicated by anyone who tries. Coming up with a list of people in your market sector who have little or no real influence is easy, and you possibly won't know that this is the case for several months, by which time you may have wasted more time, money and effort on them. So correct identification in the first place is key.

How you approach first time the influencers will have a massive effect on your chances of establishing a working relationship with them. Too many times we've seen vendors approach their selected influencers as if they were sales prospects. Remember they'll probably never buy anything from you. Ever. And certainly not if you treat them like prospects. Explain that your research has told you that they're important to your marketplace and you're looking for a way to work with them. How would they like that relationship to take shape and how could you help them do their job better? Most will welcome that approach. Inevitably some wont. But then, some won't agree to any form of relationship with you, and you just need to respect that. At least them turning you down will almost certainly mean they'll turn down any subsequent advance from your rivals too.

Of course, there's always a chance that a significant number will turn down the opportunity to have any kind of relationship with you. We suggest this may be more due to how you communicated your intentions than just a run of bad luck. But any influencer taking their role responsibly knows that much of that power comes from the knowledge they already have, and that they need to keep updated. It's very much in their interests to understand emerging market trends. Emphasise how you can help them here.

Don't expect too much too soon

You can also expect too much too soon in return for your new influencer focus. Watching out for a sea change in your sales success 3 months after commencing your influencer campaign is almost certainly going to disappoint. During this time you need your conviction to hold strong. Within the year your sales force will begin to feed back anecdotes and ad hoc conversations that will encourage you, and the sales force will likely acknowledge that this approach is necessarily a slow burner. You'll need strong management to see this period through, since there will be quarterly pressures on every line of expense. But we've never heard of one of our client companies abandon their commitment to influencers once we have got them involved. It makes too much sense to just disregard. And you'll find that your senior management know it too.

If you have read this book this far, you're probably taking the concept of *influencer marketing* pretty seriously. You want to adopt it and you want to adopt it properly. Setting realistic expectations and measuring its success sensibly. But there'll always be some marketing executives, and perhaps more likely their commissioned agencies, who will push the parameters too far. Their tactics will include 'leaning' on those identified influencers, perhaps commissioning them for legitimate work but with the implied assumption that that influencer will later 'look after' the commissioning company in business deals. This isn't *influencer marketing*, it is influencer buying, and nothing to do with this book. We want to raise the ethics and transparency of marketing, not further discredit it.

Any objections?

Since the concept of *influencer marketing*, with its focus on targeting the few people that really make a difference to the majority of sales decisions, makes such blinding sense, you might well be asking how anyone can raise an objection to it. Well they can, as frustrating as this is to us. The six most common objections to adopting *influencer marketing* are:

1. 'We don't have a budget allocated for this'.

Influencer marketing will save you budget, dramatically, by identifying where the decision-makers go to get information. Wouldn't you like to know specifically which events to attend, which media to engage with, which partners to partner with? The fact is that if a marketing director becomes sufficiently persuaded of the benefits of *influencer marketing* mid-way through his or her budget year, they are still likely to be able to access small areas of budget that have been left uncommitted, which when added together, can at least begin to piece together the initial research/identification stages. Though we've all heard the 'all budgets are committed' response throughout our careers, this is rarely such a black and white issue and most experienced executives will know the value of withholding some for contingencies.

2. Adopting *influencer marketing* represents personal risk.

Possibly, but as Seth Godin says, 'Being safe is now too risky'. Marketing is under board-level scrutiny. The sales director is blaming marketing for poor lead generation and weak collateral. *Influencer marketing* helps align marketing with sales and create influencer-led collateral that contributes to increased sales. Nevertheless, some marketing executives prefer not to take personal gambles, opting instead to fall back on traditional activities or those prompted by senior management. Without that encouragement taking on new initiatives is out-of-character. With many, we'll focus on how personally unrisky this is, how it's only common sense, how it has the support of the sales team, how it's an evolution from their current position. But it's undoubtedly different. And to some, different will always be too risky. Circumnavigating that person, while politically questionable, may be the only realistic route.

3. 'I don't want to be the first. Tell me who else is already doing this?'

Everyone wants to feel that they're not the only ones sold on the concept, that they're not pioneering into new territory, that they can learn from the earlier mistakes of others. They also want to know that when questioned by senior colleagues in their own company, they can refer to other familiar companies as support for their decision. For an initial period of perhaps 6 months, there will be little tangible progress to speak of and in that time the company must hold faith and rebuff those questioning their judgement. Client references can be key to this.

4. 'We're kind of doing this already thanks'.

The words 'kind of' always tells us that the company isn't doing any-thing like it. But the marketing director suffers from the 'not invented here' syndrome. Can they identify the top 50 influencers in your market by name? (Most can guess 5–10, those always being journalists and analysts, and rarely if ever are they all in the top 50.) And does the company have a coherent and integrated programme to reach and influence them? Our own firm even guarantees that, if a company commissions us and is able to guess more than 20 of the top 50 influencers we will give them 50 per cent of their money back. Not surprisingly, to date we've never had to.

5. 'My PR agency already does this for me'.

This response springs from the same attitude as No. 4. We always feel deflated when we hear this. It means we haven't differentiated ourselves enough, or even at all. We can virtually guarantee the PR company isn't doing this already, or anything like it. But in the marketing director's mind it can be rationalised as simply an extra list of names to which the agency can send their press releases. We could always ask what the agency is now doing with those people, having identified them as influencers. But we already know the answer. You can see why we leave deflated.

We're also worried about the emergence of Influencer Relations. While some firms understand that the influencer community is now much broader than previously recognised, others are just tacking the *influencer* term in front of their PR and AR operations, and carrying on as before. *Influencer marketing* goes further than forging relations with Influencers and should be regarded as an integrated component in marketing.

6. 'I can't see how it would integrate into my existing marketing activity plan'.

Simple. We don't expect anyone to just throw out their activity plan the minute we meet them. Especially since *influencer marketing* is not an immediate impact activity. To start with, it even takes us 3 months to identify a client's influencers, and it would take a company new to this far far longer. So we advocate slipstreaming *influencer marketing* into this year's activity by funding the identification of those influencers as soon as possible and segregating a budget to work with them within two or three quarters' time. But we like this question, because those we're talking to expect it to be more problematical than it is. It's a short step to reassure them.

How does the influencer model differ from one industry sector to another?

The model itself doesn't differ at all, though the way the model is applied clearly does. Different industry sectors exhibit very different infrastructures. In the consumer space, especially for products costing less than $100, purchasers exhibit impulse decision-making, where any research they may have done can be overturned at the last minute by point-of-sale offers, sales staff attitudes, peer group advice, etc. The ramifications of choosing one product over another are usually minor.

Within B2B markets, in whichever industry sector, the level of research is relatively similar to each other, though the nature of that research can differ markedly. In certain sectors, such as pharmaceutical, the make-up of those within the influencer groups may be oriented towards regulatory, legislative and corporate policy. In the creative industries sector for instance, with less regulation and greater emphasis on differentiation and competitive advantage, the influencer groups are likely to be more experienced in market trends, competitor knowledge and client management. But once their membership is in place, influence itself is applied in identical ways.

While our own research has majored on technology markets both in Europe and the US, our clients have come from numerous sectors and the span of identified influencers is always diverse. We have yet to research a sector where a single influencer category comprises more than 25 per cent of any top 50. Our measurement criteria (see Chapter 8) is designed to span multiple industries, whatever their infrastructure. Should you believe that your industry sector has particularly unique characteristics, then you may wish to add an additional criteria reflecting this, skewing the eventual results accordingly. The methodology, though, should remain intact.

Steps 1–5
Rolling out an Influencer Marketing Program

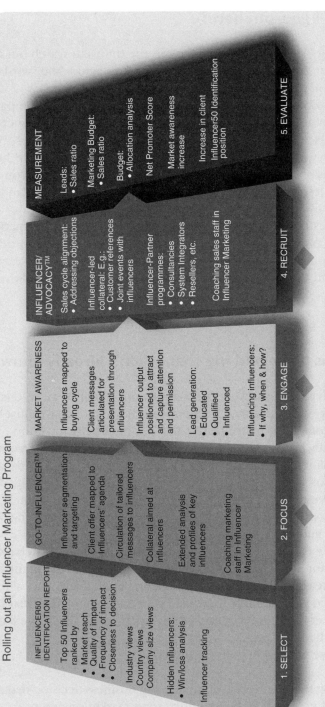

INFLUENCER50 IDENTIFICATION REPORT	GO-TO-INFLUENCER™	MARKET AWARENESS	INFLUENCER/ADVOCACY™	MEASUREMENT
Top 50 Influencers ranked by • Market reach • Quality of impact • Frequency of impact • Closeness to decision	Influencer segmentation and targeting	Influencers mapped to buying cycle	Sales cycle alignment: • Addressing objections	Leads: • Sales ratio
Industry views Country views Company size views	Client offer mapped to Influencers' agenda	Client messages articulated for presentation through influencers	Influencer-led collateral: E.g.: • Customer references • Joint events with influencers	Marketing Budget: • Sales ratio
Hidden influencers: • Win/loss analysis	Circulation of tailored messages to influencers	Influencer output positioned to attract and capture attention and permission	Influencer-Partner programmes: • Consultancies • System Integrators • Resellers, etc.	Budget: • Allocation analysis
Influencer tracking	Collateral aimed at influencers	Lead generation: • Educated • Qualified • Influenced	Coaching sales staff in Influencer Marketing	Net Promoter Score
	Extended analysis and profiles of key influencers	Influencing influencers: • If why, when & how?		Market awareness increase
	Coaching marketing staff in Influencer Marketing			Increase in client Influencer50 Identification position
1. SELECT	2. FOCUS	3. ENGAGE	4. RECRUIT	5. EVALUATE

PR/AR Direct Mail Internet Marketing Advertising
Email Marketing Strategic Alliances Direct Sales
Referral Systems Telephone Marketing UP-selling

Figure 20.1 Rolling out Influencer Marketing: Influencer50's SFERE process

So where do I go from here?

There you have it. The things to prepare for, the things to watch out for, the obstacles that are bound to be put in your way, and some words of advice to help you navigate them. We wish you luck.

Influencer marketing can't be a prescriptive formula. Every company, every market sector, every size of organisation has its own infrastructure and requirements when it comes to working with its influencers. And since luck alone won't get you very far, throughout this book we have given you a series of common steps, objectives and advice on overcoming the likely obstacles. Knowing these, you should now be able to plan and implement your own campaigns, allowing you to start this very day.

Figure 20.1 illustrates the progression of a concerted influencer marketing campaign as practiced by our own company. This tracks the process from identification through influencer engagement, through advocacy to measurement and evaluation. We suggest your own company follows a similar process.

What has this book told me that I didn't already know?

Sometimes we all read business books, happily nod along as we read each chapter, agreeing with the author's general assertions, then as we close the final pages, wonder what we've learn't that we didn't already know. We wonder if it's really been worth the past few weeks of late nights, frequent tea-making breaks and shutting ourselves away from our friends and family. Most of us like to feel that our viewpoint has been changed in some way, that we can see further than we could before picking that book in particular, at least now have a few extra interesting snippets to discuss with our friends and colleagues.

Just as we have closed each chapter with a 'Key points in this chapter' reminder, we wanted to close this book with a reminder of the points we intended you to leave with. The reasons we wrote the book to start with. If we haven't altered your opinion, increased your understanding or clarified the current market for *influencer marketing*, write to us. Maybe we'll give you the cost of the book back.

This is what we wanted to convey to you.

1. The increasing role of external influencers in business decision-making.
2. That these influencers can be identified for a market segment.
3. That they come from all walks of life, they are no longer just journalists or industry analysts.

4. That there are ways of establishing relationships with many of them that will help both parties.
5. That sales benefits will unquestionably result for you.
6. That redirecting part of your marketing budget towards influencers will yield significant cost-savings for you.
7. Your company's sales force will be enthusiastic supporters of your new marketing approach. Think how that will help your career!

Key points in this chapter

1. We are in an era of marketing conservatism caused by the lack of awareness of new thinking in marketing.
2. Salespeople, more than anyone else, can best bring the importance of influencers to the attention of the management team. But make sure they are reporting real reasons for winning and losing sales.
3. There are always objections to any change. It is your job to be prepared with answers. Try adopting an *influencer marketing* approach to these internal barriers.

21

The future of influencer marketing

You now understand the 'here and now' of *influencer marketing*. You're sure it can help you. But what of its future?

Where is our research leading us? We've been spending quite a bit of time thinking about this. Wondering where our research is helping lead our industry. We've come to the following conclusions.

Customers will market to themselves

Marketing will migrate from one founded on a series of discrete activities, as it has been for 20 or 30 years, towards one based on end-user effects. Traditionally those in charge of the marketing function within companies look at the skillsets and budgets available to them, decide what they want to communicate and estimate how best to reach their target audience. End-users have negligible say in this. That will change.

Whole campaigns will be designed by customers, mirroring their own experiences when buying. Vendors will reward them with heavy discounts. We see it currently with testimonial-based adverts, customers speaking at vendor conferences and sales call references. That will become just the tip. Customers will commonly take a special place on the vendor's management board. What better way to understand your customer than to report to one? All this means that customers themselves will significantly increase their influence, across every industry sector. Our measurement will need to take this trend into account.

Listening not talking

The emphasis for marketers will be on listening not talking. Far greater investment will be made by vendors in understanding their prospects – new products will not be launched until they have been thoroughly soft-launched to early adopters, top influencers, etc. Vendors will no longer be able to afford to launch products until they are guaranteed market success. The stakes will simply be too high. Vendor representatives will to all intent 'live' with their prospect base, in a bid to understand their aspirations, pressures, motivations and undocumented requirements. You only have to see supermarket giant Tesco, one of the most efficient and aggressive companies in the world, and how it is approaching its expansion into the US. To out-compete Wal-Mart, the runaway US leader, Tesco has placed numerous executives, as well as hundreds of consumer researchers, actually into the houses of potential shoppers, living with them for weeks at a time, in order to more thoroughly understand the mindset of their intended customers. No wonder they say 'retail is detail'.

Everything will be pre-launched

Marketing offers and campaigns will be pre-tested by their audience, dramatically reducing the perceived culture gap between what sellers are trying to sell and what buyers are wanting to buy. We met with a brand-name equipment company recently who told us that the budget for the smallest of the eight new product launches this year was $34 million and increasing fast. Such companies cannot afford to launch a 'dud'. They need the market to react favourably from day one. They now have a policy to 'pre-launch' every product before the public sees it, enabling them to gain feedback from their major market influencers – early adopters, retailers, industry commentators, etc., ensuring that all product shortcomings have been ironed out in advance. This makes good business sense.

Formalised 'influencer' metrics

An acknowledged set of cross-industry 'influence' metrics will be established. This won't stop individual firms trying to improve on them independently, but just as there are widespread, if still contentious, metrics for measuring the effectiveness of online ads, print ads, media coverage, WOM 'buzz' and the like, so there will be an agreed yardstick for 'degree of influence'. No vendor will keep pouring money into creating influencer relationships, year in year out, unless the benefits can be tracked. Often this cannot be as simple as recording their role in particular sales deals. Their influence may not be overt enough to enable that. But vendors will demand some flesh for their pound. Influencer relations professionals will have little choice but to work together and agree some benchmarking.

Influencer networks will emerge

As awareness for business influencers increases, it is logical to assume that many of the currently disparate group of influencers within particular market sectors will create more formal networks of their own. Currently, when we host evening dinners or social meetings that bring together say, twenty of the top influencers in the mobile phone ringtones marketplace, the majority have never met before. Number one may be a regulator, number two the purchasing director of a major retailer and number three a commercial musician. They won't even have mixed in the same circles. They have influenced their sector from completely different directions. Yet by combining their skills, contacts and experiences, they could offer the complete 'soup to nuts' understanding of the buying process. Now how valuable would that be to a commercial operator looking to exploit that market? This will undoubtedly become a new niche within the professional services marketplace.

'Influence trees' will be automated

Inevitably as with any new study of customer/consumer behaviour, what starts out as individual expertise and insight will eventually become commoditised. At this moment those who understand and analyse the purchasing process are few and far between. As our research increases and we can begin to predict behaviours, activities and outcomes, so we will create automated modelling tools, refining their accuracy with each iteration. How long before we type a particular phrase or company name into our search engine and within a single second see a 'family tree-style' graphic showing the first recorded mention of those words, no matter how regional, with it branching out into each chronological mention after that. In this way you could see the earliest adopters of that phrase and who snowballed your message. Which sources particular journalists used to initiate their own stories, which documents first brought your company to the attention of a particular management consultant, which financial analysts' advisory note first caused a prospective client to question its acceptance of your bid. Overlay one phrase on another a few times and you'll soon be creating your own trend analysis.

Taking the short cut

Why market your company or product to separate groups of journalists, analysts, resellers, buyers clubs, retailers or the like, with the considerable time and expense of this, when you can identify the same early adopters time after time after time. Take the short cut. Take extra care in selling your message to just that top handful of people and let their own efforts and activities inform the remainder of the chain. Think of the resource you would save.

Imagine the software required not just to track the spread of such phrases within publicly available publications, online sites and blogs, but in commercial conference speeches and public forums. Developers are working on it already, taking their lead from the security forces who have for many years pioneered the tracking, or eavesdropping, of various words considered to be of potential threat to the public. Then imagine a commercially tailored version of this being adopted inside a particularly large organisation, whether private or public sector, enabling a graphical illustration of how certain words, phrases or thoughts have been disseminated, communicated and travelled throughout it. While many will shiver at the thought, it would provide a quantum leap in our understanding of how influence is applied, though its application clearly needs to be harnessed. We should all hope that privacy laws will be successful in limiting the extent to which such 'word travel' can be mapped.

More information necessary

The need for more information, both opinion and data, on current marketing has struck both of us recently. In researching this book we have been surprised at the lack of relevant market data on marketing spend levels, activity breakdowns, ROI proof points and evidence of activity trends. Data outlining how much will be spent on online advertising compared to the previous year, the number of editorial pages compared to 5 years ago, or the cost of customer acquisition at a top bank may be fairly simple to find, but try and identify the preferred marketing staff deployment, average trade show spend or what new initiatives have succeeded or failed for your top three rivals and there is little if any information available. Such information is exchanged only through peer and agency member gossip, with the movement of staff recruited from one company to the other, and very occasionally from attending marketing-oriented speeches at industry forums. There seems to be little culture of continual improvement. Marketing publications, if read at all, are read only for their news and recruitment sections. Perhaps it has been left to book publishers, much like our own, to promote new ideas. No wonder the pace of marketing thought leadership is slow.

Well before this book was started we knew how most marketing departments operate in a knowledge vacuum, unaware of how they have kept up-to-date, or been left behind, with modern thinking. It has allowed some departments to become astonishingly ineffective yet without their senior management ever realising this. We have never heard of a management board benchmarking its marketing director's performance against industry-leading cost per customer lead, programme vs. employee cost or other such metrics. Performance is routinely measured against that of the previous year, only highlighting relative gains or losses. Unfortunately, this places the emphasis on squeezing more out of last year's thinking rather than implementing any bold new initiative.

Not that our firm intends to enter it, but we can't help thinking there are significant market opportunities for those with end-user or commercial 'buyer' experience to form niche management and/or training consultancies focused on educating and advising vendors' marketing teams, across every market sector, as to how buyers in their sectors are making their purchasing decisions, and how marketing departments can best be realigned to reflect this. Of all the strategic marketing, sales lead generation, operational management and tactical fulfilment agencies and consultancies that we have come across, we know of none that focus and promote themselves on this. Yet we believe its proposition to be compelling. And the sales force could do worse than listen too.

Influencer evaluation

In 5 years time the role of influencers will be taken as read, no one questioning their importance. Measuring their respective influence will be both qualitative and quantitative. Our own measurement criteria for individuals will be based to a greater degree on public deliverables and less on subjective opinion. What's more, we can see influencers fighting harder for their influence level to be recognised. A high ranking within an influencer league will be worn like an armband, touted prominently in that person's résumé, and rewarded by their company managers. We saw proof of this a few years back when the short-lived US print title *High Technology Marketing* ran an annual 'Most Influential' chart, predominately featuring industry journalists, publishers, analysts, consultancy heads and vendor executives. In its final year of publication, 2003, every one of the journalists, analysts and publishers in the top 10 issued a press release announcing their ranking, or included details of it in their online biography. It clearly meant something to them and they saw the advantage of promoting this. For whatever reasons, people want their credibility to be recognised, and if this is helped by being seen as an influencer, then so be it. People will increasingly want to be included in influencer lists. It's human nature. They will ensure more information is known about them, enabling those evaluating them to then base that evaluation on more complete data. A self-completing circle. And another reason why influencer leagues will thrive.

Internal influencers

We also saw a glimpse of a possible future when a telecoms leader, one of the world's largest, recently asked us to scope a project to identify the hundred most influential employees within its own global organisation. Now this company employs well over 100 000 staff and it is fortunately well aware that the 100 most influential are not necessarily the 100 most senior. Now we've all read books and articles about engendering passion at work, about creating motivated teams, about enthusing a giant, distributed workforce with the same, single vision and commitment. And how the charismatic, driving leadership of its CEO is typically the required catalyst for this to happen. Well we'd suggest that identifying the most influential employees within your organisation is a pretty unbeatable route to achieve this too. Now these wouldn't be influential in terms of purchase decision-making necessarily, but in terms of carrying ideas forward, making initiatives happen, delivering on objectives, leading teams, communicating action plans and the like. The measurement criteria would clearly need to some extent change.

We can see enormous potential for such research, not only in the sense of deciding who should be in the company's 'inner circle' when communicating central directives, but at the macro level too. Once senior management understands exactly who the most influential 100 employees are, doesn't that bring into question why they're not among the 100 most senior?

At minimum, if the most influential were to hear of their inclusion, you would imagine this significantly affecting their leverage during performance appraisals. For an organisation's management, this could easily prove a double-edged sword, but one many would be willing to risk. It will surely not be long before such analysis of one's own employees is more commonplace.

The future for journalists and PRs

In some marketplaces, the traditional beat of the specialist journalist will all but disappear. Much as we're believers in Chris Anderson's '*Long Tail*' principle, we just can't see how the niche print and online publications, which will proliferate in number, will require or be able to financially justify employing niche contributors. News, and increasingly features, will be aggregated globally, and buyers won't care about buying publications from their local region. The number of journalists will continue to decline, with those remaining having to become 'jack of all trades'. Original thought pieces will increasingly be delivered by industry analysts, who we see more and more encroaching on the traditional journalists' turf. Publications will prove a ready and willing vehicle for the analysts' already written content. Repurposing will be crucial to deliver the cost reductions so necessary for the publishers. With less niche journalists there will be less niche PR consultancies. There simply won't be enough journalists' requirements to satisfy, and the commissioning vendors will soon take this into account when deploying their forthcoming budgets.

Blanket marketing

'Blanket' marketing, the kind epitomised by AOL's never-ending distribution of net-access CDs in the late 1990s, IBM's e-business TV advertising in 2000–2001 and HP's multiple-spread print advertising in 2002–2003 will become frowned upon and counter-productive to the companies behind them. Prospective customers will despise the wasteful resources required for such campaigns, shareholders will demand cost-justification and market commentators will question why the vendor cannot separate out its prospects more efficiently. We see marketing departments reorganising along end-user/prospect marketing and *influencer marketing* lines. Occasionally the campaigns will merge, most often they won't. End-user marketing will be solution-specific, content-specific and price-specific. *Influencer marketing* will take over the current field of branding. Instead of activity-specific marketing, as is the case today, tomorrow we will see audience-specific marketing. It is the only way in which the cost of marketing can be justified.

Full circle to education

And so, finally, we come back to education, a subject we've tried largely to avoid here as it's beyond the core scope of this book. As we complete our research, a final short Google search for graduate-level CIM educational courses in the UK reveals over 30 companies actively engaged in providing training for those new to marketing. There is no shortage of subject matter – advertising, PR, message communication, sales liaison, market segmentation, routes to market and many more. We can forgive the fact that there's no apparent course on *influencer marketing* – it's a new subject – but out of over 400 individual topics we couldn't find one, not one, on what buyers want to buy or how buyers approach the buying process. You could argue that this would be the remit of a sales course, not a marketing one, but if the marketers of tomorrow aren't versed in what it's like to be a buyer, how can we expect them to know what marketing output will ever help the seller?

Geographic and cultural dependencies

Back in 2006 we had a meeting with Mark Stouse, the VP of Corporate Communications at BMC. We had explained to Mark the concept of *influencer marketing* and he got it immediately. Towards the end of the meeting, he asked us what impact different cultures would have on our scoring model and on the process we use to identify influencers. We had to admit that we just didn't know. But it raised some important issues.

For example, Millward Brown Optimor tells us around 85 per cent of commercials use a celebrity in Japan, the world's highest number. So are celebrities more influential in Japan than in other countries? In India, the dominant culture is to buy from people you know and like whether or not you need what's on offer. Conversely, you don't buy from someone you don't like, even if what they're selling is what you need. In the US, Americans buy what they need, from people they don't necessarily like. So do social influences count for more in India than in the US?

Our rule to date has been that influencers influence on a local level. The set of influencers for B2B markets in UK has low overlap with those in France and Germany, and the same is true in consumer markets. But overlaps do exist, such as between countries sharing a language. So German influencers have an impact in Austria and Switzerland. Where language commonality exists cultural similarities are frequent. But if your target market is in China then you'd better determine the influence dimensions carefully, accounting for differences in the way that influence happens.

Some global industries transcend culture and therefore probably share their influencers. Corporate and wholesale banking is a global and real-time business where influencers across countries and cultures will exhibit more similarities than usual. But political and regulatory difference will still apply, so it's important never to assume.

Arguably, segments with few, big firms share influencers across countries. The big banks probably share influencers within Europe, possibly globally.

What happens when influencers know they are influencers?

Most of what we've written about in this book is based upon a premise that your influencers don't know that you know they are influencers. In fact, our experience shows that most influencers don't regard themselves as any more or less influential than other people in the industry. There are some exceptions to this, like analysts and journalists, but generally influencers are unaware of their impact. So it makes us wonder what will happen to the dynamics of influence when everyone knows who the influencers are.

We expect the whole nature of influence to change as influencers become aware (through the rise in influencer marketing) that they have influence. Influencers will want to maintain or increase their influence. Those that don't have influence will want to obtain it. Those under influence will want to understand its intentions and potential outcomes. True influencers may leave their employers, hoping that their influence follows them. Influencers may club together to form co-operatives to wield even more clout.

Importantly, knowledge of one's influence may impact the effect of *influencer marketing* itself. We think this could go two ways: it may prepare the influencer for your approaches, which they reject because you're trying to influence them. Or they may come to expect the special attention that firms give them because of their influence. On balance we think the latter scenario will play out. Influencers would rather be talked to than not, and the fact that they are prepared for your approaches should enhance the whole concept of *influencer marketing*. Let's hope so.

Index